MORE UNIX ® FOR DUMMIES ®

MORE UNIX® FOR DUMMIES®

by John R. Levine
and
Margaret Levine Young

IDG Books Worldwide, Inc.
An International Data Group Company

Foster City, CA ♦ Chicago, IL ♦ Indianapolis, IN ♦ Braintree, MA ♦ Dallas, TX

MORE UNIX® For Dummies®

Published by
IDG Books Worldwide, Inc.
An International Data Group Company
919 E. Hillsdale Blvd.
Suite 400
Foster City, CA 94404

Library of Congress Catalog Card No.: 95-77049

ISBN: 1-56884-361-5

Printed in the United States of America

10 9 8 7 6 5 4 3 2 1

1B/SS/QV/ZV

Distributed in the United States by IDG Books Worldwide, Inc.

Distributed by Macmillan Canada for Canada; by Computer and Technical Books for the Caribbean Basin; by Contemporanea de Ediciones for Venezuela; by Distribuidora Cuspide for Argentina; by CITEC for Brazil; by Ediciones ZETA S.C.R. Ltda. for Peru; by Editorial Limusa SA for Mexico; by Transworld Publishers Limited in the United Kingdom and Europe; by Al-Maiman Publishers & Distributors for Saudi Arabia; by Simron Pty. Ltd. for South Africa; by IDG Communications (HK) Ltd. for Hong Kong; by Toppan Company Ltd. for Japan; by Addison Wesley Publishing Company for Korea; by Longman Singapore Publishers Ltd. for Singapore, Malaysia, Thailand, and Indonesia; by Unalis Corporation for Taiwan; by WS Computer Publishing Company, Inc. for the Philippines; by WoodsLane Pty. Ltd. for Australia; by WoodsLane Enterprises Ltd. for New Zealand.

For general information about IDG Books in the U.S., including information about discounts and premiums, contact IDG Books at 800-434-3422 or 415-655-3000.

For information about where to purchase IDG Books outside the U.S., contact IDG Books International at 415-655-3021 or fax 415-655-3295.

For information about translations, contact Marc Jeffrey Mikulich, Director, Foreign and Subsidiary Rights, at IDG Books Worldwide, 415-655-3018 or fax 415-655-3295.

For sales inquiries and special prices for bulk quantities, write to the address above or call IDG Books Worldwide at 415-655-3000.

For information about using IDG Books in the classroom, or ordering examination copies, contact Jim Kelly at 800-434-2086.

For authorization to photocopy items for corporate, personal, or educational use, please contact Copyright Clearance Center, 222 Rosewood Drive, Danvers, MA 01923, fax 508-750-4470.

About the Authors

Margaret Levine Young and **John R. Levine** were members of a computer club in high school — before high-school students, or even high schools, *had* computers. They came in contact with Theodor H. Nelson, the author of *Computer Lib* and the inventor of hypertext, who fostered the idea that computers should not be taken seriously and that everyone can and should understand and use computers.

Margy has been using small computers since the 1970s. She graduated from UNIX on a PDP/11 to Apple DOS on an Apple][to MS-DOS and UNIX on a variety of machines. She has done all kinds of jobs that involve explaining to people that computers aren't as mysterious as they might think, including managing the use of PCs at Columbia Pictures, teaching scientists and engineers what computers are good for, and writing and cowriting computer manuals and books, including *Understanding Javelin PLUS, The Complete Guide to PC-File, UNIX For Dummies, MORE Internet For Dummies, WordPerfect For Windows For Dummies* (with David C. Kay), and *The Internet For Windows For Dummies Starter Kit.* She has a degree in computer science from Yale University and has recently started keeping chickens.

John wrote his first program in 1967 on an IBM 1130 (a computer roughly as powerful as your typical modern digital wristwatch, only more difficult to use). His first exposure to UNIX was while hanging out with friends in Princeton in 1974. He became an official system administrator of a networked computer at Yale in 1975. He began working part-time for Interactive Systems, the first commercial UNIX company, in 1977 and has been in and out of the computer and network biz ever since. He got his company put on Usenet early enough that it appears in a 1982 *Byte* magazine article, which included a map of Usenet sites. He used to spend most of his time writing software, but now he mostly writes and cowrites books (including *UNIX For Dummies, The Internet For Dummies, MORE Internet For Dummies, Internet Secrets,* and *The Internet For Windows For Dummies Starter Kit,* all published by IDG Books) because it's more fun. He also teaches some computer courses, publishes and edits an incredibly technoid magazine called *The Journal of C Language Translation,* moderates a Usenet newsgroup, and occasionally shows up on TV (which turns out not to be as much fun as it looks like). He holds a B.A. and a Ph.D. in computer science from Yale University, but please don't hold that against him.

ABOUT IDG BOOKS WORLDWIDE

Welcome to the world of IDG Books Worldwide.

IDG Books Worldwide, Inc., is a subsidiary of International Data Group, the world's largest publisher of computer-related information and the leading global provider of information services on information technology. IDG was founded more than 25 years ago and now employs more than 7,500 people worldwide. IDG publishes more than 235 computer publications in 67 countries (see listing below). More than 60 million people read one or more IDG publications each month.

Launched in 1990, IDG Books Worldwide is today the #1 publisher of best-selling computer books in the United States. We are proud to have received 3 awards from the Computer Press Association in recognition of editorial excellence, and our best-selling ...For Dummies™ series has more than 17 million copies in print with translations in 25 languages. IDG Books Worldwide, through a recent joint venture with IDG's Hi-Tech Beijing, became the first U.S. publisher to publish a computer book in the People's Republic of China. In record time, IDG Books Worldwide has become the first choice for millions of readers around the world who want to learn how to better manage their businesses.

Our mission is simple: Every one of our books is designed to bring extra value and skill-building instructions to the reader. Our books are written by experts who understand and care about our readers. The knowledge base of our editorial staff comes from years of experience in publishing, education, and journalism — experience which we use to produce books for the '90s. In short, we care about books, so we attract the best people. We devote special attention to details such as audience, interior design, use of icons, and illustrations. And because we use an efficient process of authoring, editing, and desktop publishing our books electronically, we can spend more time ensuring superior content and spend less time on the technicalities of making books.

You can count on our commitment to deliver high-quality books at competitive prices on topics consumers want to read about. At IDG Books Worldwide, we value quality, and we have been delivering quality for more than 25 years. You'll find no better book on a subject than an IDG book.

John Kilcullen
President and CEO
IDG Books Worldwide, Inc.

WINNER
Eighth Annual
Computer Press
Awards ≥ 1992

WINNER
Ninth Annual
Computer Press
Awards ≥ 1993

IDG BOOKS

IDG Books Worldwide, Inc., is a subsidiary of International Data Group, the world's largest publisher of computer-related information and the leading global provider of information services on information technology. International Data Group publishes over 235 computer publications in 67 countries. More than sixty million people read one or more International Data Group publications each month. The officers are Patrick J. McGovern, Founder and Board Chairman; Kelly Conlin, President; Jim Casella, Chief Operating Officer. International Data Group's publications include: **ARGENTINA'S** Computerworld Argentina, Infoworld Argentina; **AUSTRALIA'S** Computerworld Australia, Computer Living, Australian PC World, Australian Macworld, Network World, Mobile Business Australia, Publish!, Reseller, IDG Sources; **AUSTRIA'S** Computerwelt Oesterreich, PC Test; **BELGIUM'S** Data News (CW); **BOLIVIA'S** Computerworld; **BRAZIL'S** Computerworld, Connections, Game Power, Mundo Unix, PC World, Publish, Super Game; **BULGARIA'S** Computerworld Bulgaria, PC & Mac World Bulgaria, Network World Bulgaria; **CANADA'S** CIO Canada, Computerworld Canada, InfoCanada, Network World Canada, Reseller; **CHILE'S** Computerworld Chile, Informatica; **COLOMBIA'S** Computerworld Colombia, PC World; **COSTA RICA'S** PC World; **CZECH REPUBLIC'S** Computerworld, Elektronika, PC World; **DENMARK'S** Communications World, Computerworld Danmark, Computerworld Focus, Macintosh Produktkatalog, Macworld Danmark, PC World Danmark, PC Produktguide, Tech World, Windows World; **ECUADOR'S** PC World Ecuador; **EGYPT'S** Computerworld (CW) Middle East, PC World Middle East; **FINLAND'S** MikroPC, Tietoviikko, Tietoverkko; **FRANCE'S** Distributique, GOLDEN MAC, InfoPC, Le Guide du Monde Informatique, Le Monde Informatique, Telecoms & Reseaux; **GERMANY'S** Computerwoche, Computerwoche Focus, Computerwoche Extra, Electronic Entertainment, Gamepro, Information Management, Macwelt, Netzwelt, PC Welt, Publish, Publish; **GREECE'S** Publish & Macworld; **HONG KONG'S** Computerworld Hong Kong, PC World Hong Kong; **HUNGARY'S** Computerworld SZT, PC World; **INDIA'S** Computers & Communications; **INDONESIA'S** Info Komputer; **IRELAND'S** ComputerScope; **ISRAEL'S** Beyond Windows, Computerworld Israel, Multimedia, PC World Israel; **ITALY'S** Computerworld Italia, Lotus Magazine, Macworld Italia, Networking Italia, PC Shopping Italy, PC World Italia; **JAPAN'S** Computerworld Today, Information Systems World, Macworld Japan, Nikkei Personal Computing, SunWorld Japan, Windows World; **KENYA'S** East African Computer News; **KOREA'S** Computerworld Korea, Macworld Korea, PC World Korea; **LATIN AMERICA'S** GamePro; **MALAYSIA'S** Computerworld Malaysia, PC World Malaysia; **MEXICO'S** Compu Edicion, Compu Manufactura, Computacion/Punto de Venta, Computerworld Mexico, MacWorld, Mundo Unix, PC World, Windows; **THE NETHERLANDS'** Computer! Totaal, Computable (CW), LAN Magazine, Lotus Magazine, MacWorld; **NEW ZEALAND'S** Computer Buyer, Computerworld New Zealand, Network World, New Zealand PC World; **NIGERIA'S** PC World Africa; **NORWAY'S** Computerworld Norge, Lotusworld Norge, Macworld Norge, Maxi Data, Networld, PC World Ekspress, PC World Nettverk, PC World Norge, PC World's Produktguide, Publish& Multimedia World, Student Data, Unix World, Windowsworld; **PAKISTAN'S** PC World Pakistan; **PANAMA'S** PC World Panama; **PERU'S** Computerworld Peru, PC World; **PEOPLE'S REPUBLIC OF CHINA'S** China Computerworld, China Infoworld, China PC Info Magazine, Computer Fan, PC World China, Electronics International, Electronics Today/Multimedia World, Electronic Product World, China Network World, Software World Magazine, Telecom Product World; **PHILIPPINES'** Computerworld Philippines, PC Digest (PCW); **POLAND'S** Computerworld Poland, Computerworld Special Report, Networld, PC World/Komputer, Sunworld; **PORTUGAL'S** Cerebro/PC World, Correio Informatico/Computerworld, MacIn; **ROMANIA'S** Computerworld, PC World, Telecom Romania; **RUSSIA'S** Computerworld-Moscow, Mir - PK (PCW), Sety (Networks); **SINGAPORE'S** Computerworld Southeast Asia, PC World Singapore; **SLOVENIA'S** Monitor Magazine; **SOUTH AFRICA'S** Computer Mail (CIO),Computing S.A.,Network World S.A., Software World; **SPAIN'S** Advanced Systems, Amiga World, Computerworld Espana, Communicaciones World, Macworld Espana, NeXTWORLD, Super Juegos Magazine (GamePro), PC World Espana, Publish; **SWEDEN'S** Attack, ComputerSweden, Corporate Computing, Macworld, Mikrodatorn, Natverk & Kommunikation, PC World, CAP & Design, Datalngenjoren, Maxi Data,Windows World; **SWITZERLAND'S** Computerworld Schweiz, Macworld Schweiz, PC Tip; **TAIWAN'S** Computerworld Taiwan, PC World Taiwan; **THAILAND'S** Thai Computerworld; **TURKEY'S** Computerworld Monitor, Macworld Turkiye, PC World Turkiye; **UKRAINE'S** Computerworld, Computers+Software Magazine; **UNITED KINGDOM'S** Computing /Computerworld, Connexion/Network World, Lotus Magazine, Macworld, Open Computing/Sunworld; **UNITED STATES'** Advanced Systems, AmigaWorld, Cable in the Classroom, CD Review, CIO, Computerworld, Computerworld Client/Server Journal, Digital Video, DOS World, Electronic Entertainment Magazine (E2), Federal Computer Week, Game Hits, GamePro, IDG Books Worldwide, Infoworld, Laser Event, Macworld, Maximize, Multimedia World, Network World, PC Letter, PC World, Publish, SWATPro, Video Event; **URUGUAY'S** PC World Uruguay; **VENEZUELA'S** Computerworld Venezuela, PC World; **VIETNAM'S** PC World Vietnam.
04/27/95

Acknowledgments

Margy thanks Jordan (for being an all-around great husband), Barbara Begonis (for watching little Zac while I wrote), Bill Gladstone and Matt Wagner (for getting us in the *Dummies* biz in the first place), and all the terrific folks at IDG's Dummies Press (Diane, Megg, Milissa, and Becky, you know who you are).

John thanks all those same people (he is, after all, related to Jordan and Zac, albeit not quite as closely as Margy is); Steve Dyer, for providing a home away from home for the Internet For Dummies Central computer; and the many organizations that have provided Internet access, including TIAC (Bedford, Massachusetts), ClarkNet (Baltimore, Maryland), the World (Brookline, Massachusetts), Cornell University (Ithaca, New York), and Northwest Nexus (Seattle, Washington). But mostly he thanks Tonia, for putting up with him with love and good cheer, even in the depths of manuscript-deadline panic.

(The publisher would like to give special thanks to Patrick J. McGovern, without whom this book would not have been possible.)

Credits

Executive Vice President, Strategic Product Planning and Research
David Solomon

Senior Vice President and Publisher
Milissa L. Koloski

Editorial Director
Diane Graves Steele

Acquisitions Editor
Megg Bonar

Brand Manager
Judith A. Taylor

Editorial Manager
Kristin A. Cocks

Editorial Assistants
Stacey Holden Prince
Kevin Spencer

Acquisitions Assistant
Suki Gear

Production Director
Beth Jenkins

Supervisor of Project Coordination
Cindy L. Phipps

Pre-Press Coordinator
Steve Peake

Associate Pre-Press Coordinator
Tony Augsburger

Media/Archive Coordinator
Paul Belcastro

Project Editor
Rebecca Whitney

Technical Reviewer
Larry Barr

Project Coordinator
J. Tyler Connor

Production Staff
Gina Scott
Carla C. Radzikinas
Patricia R. Reynolds
Dwight Ramsey
Theresa Sánchez-Baker
Chris Collins
Laura Puranen

Proofreader
Kathleen Prata

Indexer
David Heiret

Book Design
University Graphics

Cover Design
Kavish + Kavish

Contents at a Glance

Cartoons at a Glance

By Rich Tennant

Page 74

Page 5

Page 22

Page 228

Page 109

Page 258

Page 177

Page 150

Page 23

Page 201

Table of Contents

Introduction

- -

*W*elcome to *MORE UNIX For Dummies*! Our first book, *UNIX For Dummies,* barely skimmed the surface of the vast pool of sludge that is UNIX. And since we wrote it, thousands of people got UNIX accounts to access the Internet and are sinking deeper into that morass daily.

Hence, this book. In it, we bring you up to date on new developments in the world of UNIX (if you care), initiate you into the mysteries of writing shell scripts, introduce you to ways to surf the Internet from UNIX, and other nifty topics. If you like surfing swamps, you're in the right place!

How to Use This Book

You don't have to read the book straight through. We'd like to think that our writing is so compelling, our ideas so dynamic, and UNIX so fascinating that you won't be able to put it down. We can imagine you carrying the book with you everywhere as you stumble blindly through your daily routine, unable to stop reading even while brushing your teeth or saying hi to the boss.

Well, we can dream. We realize, however, that although our writing *is* compelling and our ideas *are* dynamic, UNIX falls a little short, and you may have trouble staying awake even to the end of this introduction. So you may want to peruse the table of contents and just read what looks good. For example, if you are interested primarily in writing shell scripts and using neat-o UNIX utilities, jump straight to Part II, "UNIX Scripts." If your contact with UNIX is entirely so that you can wander the Internet, Part V, "UNIX and the Internet," is for you.

Who Are You?

As we wrote this book, we assumed these things about you:

- ✔ You are a normal person trying to get something done using a UNIX system — not a rocket scientist looking to become the next great UNIX genius and not someone whose idea of a fun afternoon is reading the pages of the UNIX on-line manual.

- ✔ You have a copy of *UNIX For Dummies* lying around somewhere. *MORE UNIX For Dummies* builds on our first book, and we occasionally suggest that you refer to it.

- ✔ You are ready to find out more cool ways to use UNIX!

How This Book Is Organized

This book is split into five parts, each with its own theme. Each part of this book stands on its own (assuming that it stands at all — or that you can stand it). Here's what each part of the book is about:

Part I: Welcome Back!

Part I includes recent news in UNIX Land, including new versions of UNIX and a new UNIX shell. We also review how to tell which version of UNIX you have and which shell you are running.

Part II: UNIX Scripts

If you want to speed up repetitive tasks, you can learn in this part how to write whiz-bang UNIX scripts. We describe two useful programs that no UNIX nerd can live without: awk and sed. Sed is great for mechanical editing tasks, including fancy ones, and awk is useful for doing things to text — you can even use these programs to balance your checkbook (eat your heart out, Quicken).

Part III: Editors and Mail Programs

Most UNIX folks spend an enormous amount of their time running their favorite text editor and most of the rest of their time checking their e-mail. (Some people use their text editor to check their e-mail, of course, but we explain that in Chapter 12, "Have a Big Emacs!" Others use programs that accomplish useful work, but that's inexplicable in the context of UNIX.)

The most widely used editors in UNIX Land are vi and emacs, and we have devoted a chapter to each. We also wrote chapters about our two favorite mail programs, elm and pine, because they are so much better than the old-fashioned UNIX mail program.

Yes, editors and mail programs are the plodding workhorses of the software world, but if you can make them gallop, you can get an incredible amount of work done!

Part IV: Pointing and Clicking with Motif

OK, all you Windows and Mac users! We've heard just about enough gloating about how easy it is to point and click with a mouse rather than type confusing commands. Motif has become the standard UNIX graphical user interface, and we can now point and click with the best of them! The chapters in this part tell you how. (Windows bigots may note that Motif *already* looks the way Windows 95 will look in — well, whenever. Welcome to the future.)

Part V: UNIX and the Internet

Everybody has to be on the information superhighway these days, even when it seems to be turning into the information supersoaker, the information super-market, or just plain information soup. If you use a UNIX shell account to get at the Internet, this part of the book is for you. We describe how to use UNIX programs to fool around with Gopher, FTP, Usenet newsgroups, and even the World Wide Web.

Icons Used in This Book

This icon warns you away from particularly nerdy, technical information. You can usually ignore stuff marked with this icon, thank goodness.

When you see this symbol, we're explaining some nifty timesaving technique.

Timber-r-r-r-r! Watch out below!

You can find out more about this topic in *UNIX For Dummies*. (If this seems to you like a shameless way to be sure that you buy the other book, we can't argue with your logic.)

This icon alerts you to particularly juicy information related to locating something or someone on the Internet.

What Now?

Before you dive in to this book, you have to know which UNIX shell you use. If you don't already know this little fact, skip directly to Chapter 3, "Far Too Many Versions of UNIX and a Few Too Many Shells," to find out how you can tell. Occasionally you have to know which version of UNIX you are running — Chapter 3 talks about this subject too.

And now, skim the Table of Contents, choose a juicy-looking topic, and dive in!

Write to Us

We authors love to get e-mail from our readers. If you liked this book (or even if you didn't), drop us a line at `moreunix@dummies.com`. You get an automated response confirming your e-mail address, and, if you ask a question or make a comment, you might eventually get an answer from an actual author.

Note that this e-mail address contacts only us authors (and only the authors of *...For Dummies* books about UNIX, the Internet, and WordPerfect for Windows). To contact IDG Books to ask for a catalog, inquire about bulk or educational orders, or for other reasons, see the addresses and phone numbers on the copyright page of this book. You can also try mailing a message to `info@idgbooks.com`, the publisher's swell new e-mail address.

Part I

Welcome Back!

In this part...

Welcome back to the world of *UNIX For Dummies*! This part of the book brings you up to speed on what's been happening in UNIX Land and reviews which version of UNIX you have and which shell you are using. It's a good place to begin reading if you want to dip your toes in a bit before diving in to chapters full of commands and procedures.

Chapter 1
We're Ba-a-a-ck!

*W*elcome to *More UNIX For Dummies,* the long-dreaded sequel to *UNIX For Dummies,* the book that made UNIX easy and fun to, uh, well, the book that, uh, made UNIX sort of tolerable. Here in *MORE UNIX,* we have lots more tips, tricks, hints, and other swell stuff that lets you turn UNIX from a blunderbuss into a slightly more tractable blunderbuss. In particular, you learn about these subjects:

✔ Lots more about the UNIX programs you have to use the most, particularly editors such as emacs and vi, and mail programs such as elm and pine.

✔ An introduction to shell scripts, which are canned collections of commands that let you automate simple and even not-so-simple tasks.

✔ Sed and awk, two text-processing programs that make it easier to handle files containing text and that are also useful when you have to glue the output of one program into the input of another, not quite compatible, program.

✔ An in-depth look at the UNIX networking tools and how they work on the Internet; these chapters are particularly useful to Internet users whose providers saddled them with a UNIX shell account.

This chapter brings you up to date on developments in The World of UNIX, including versions of UNIX. If you couldn't care less (and who could blame you?), skip right to Chapter 2, "A Short Refresher Course."

What's Old, What's New

UNIX is now 25 years old, giving it the rare distinction of being one of the few pieces of computer software that is older than many of its users. (It's far from the oldest, though. Some mainframe systems from IBM and UNISYS date back to the early 1960s. Somehow, with all the great advances in computers over the decades, we're still running the same, old software on our flashy, new computers.) The overall structure of UNIX, therefore, doesn't change much. For those few readers who haven't already memorized *UNIX For Dummies,* Chapter 2 contains a short review of UNIX basics, with some notes about new stuff thrown in to entice those of you who *have* memorized it to read on anyway.

Let a Hundred Versions Blossom

One of the things that makes UNIX a constant source of surprise and excitement is that there's no single UNIX system. Instead, there are dozens.

Some prehistory

Back at the dawn of UNIX time (shortly after 1970), there was indeed a single version of UNIX, running on a few PDP-11 minicomputers at AT&T Bell Labs in New Jersey. In about 1973, however, they gave a copy of it to some student friends at Harvard, and of course the Harvard people began making improvements of their own. Hundreds of copies of early UNIX went out to colleges and universities all over the world, all of whom began making changes and improvements of their own, and, to the consternation of AT&T, they started swapping their improvements around. (John is not entirely blameless here: In 1976 he sent out both a modified UNIX shell and control software for some then popular disks that were the size of washing machines and held a princely 20 megabytes.)

In the late 1970s, some Bell Labs guys tried as an experiment to take a copy of UNIX, which at that point ran on only a PDP-11, and modified it to run on a different kind of minicomputer. Somewhat to people's surprise, it worked, and within a few years UNIX had spread to lots of minicomputers and later to pretty much every kind of workstation. (Its popularity on workstations is easily explained by noting that if you were a workstation vendor, the cost of buying a copy of UNIX and modifying it for your particular workstation was about a tenth of the cost of coming up with new system software from scratch.)

A great deal of UNIX work happened at the University of California at Berkeley, and around 1980 so-called Berkeley UNIX, also known as BSD (for Berkeley Software Distributions), became the standard software on minicomputers and workstations. (An amazing amount of the work was done by a guy named Bill, about whom we said many not altogether complimentary things in *UNIX For Dummies*. But because he's now an extremely rich vice president of a large UNIX system maker and is still 6'4" and in excellent physical shape, we don't mention him here. Except that we just did. Oops.) There have been lots of versions of BSD UNIX, of which the last is called 4.4BSD (a cutesy way of writing BSD UNIX version 4.4). Berkeley now says that it's out of the UNIX development business and has disbanded what remained of the BSD development group, so 4.4 is it.

Meanwhile, back in New Jersey, AT&T continued to develop UNIX on its own, coming up with UNIX System III and then (mysteriously skipping System IV) System V, now up through System V, release 4. (Oddly, the amount of change from version to version has little to do with the amount of change in number.) The change from System III to System V release 1 was nowhere near as great as that from System V release 3 to release 4.

SVR4, as UNIX aficionados call it, combined all of System V with most of BSD and a great deal of Sun Microsystems' SunOS and was intended to be an all-purpose, all-singing, all-dancing version of UNIX. It wasn't really bad, even though it was much bigger than any of its predecessors, causing a miniboom for makers of computer disks.

Through about 1990, all significant versions of UNIX still required a license from AT&T because they contained code from Bell Labs. But Berkeley then decided that BSD had mutated so far from its AT&T origins that pretty much all of the BSD code was not derived from the AT&T originals, and it began giving away all but a few AT&T-derived parts for free. A few lawsuits immediately followed, all of which have been settled, leaving 4.4BSD UNIX available for free and its source code available to anyone who chooses to download it from the Internet.

As you might imagine, a frenzy of downloading then happened, along with a great deal of fiddling and improvement. A group of volunteers filled in the few gaps in BSD that remained when Berkeley deleted the remaining AT&T code and then ported BSD to 386 and 486 PCs, and the results spread rapidly throughout the academic world. The primary strains of BSD are now NetBSD and FreeBSD, two similar continuing-development projects (which would be one project except that the two groups of people involved can't stand each other) and BSD/OS, a commercially supported version of BSD.

In the meantime, AT&T decided that what with all the changes in the phone and computer businesses, it would get out of the UNIX software business, so it initially spun some of it out to an organization called UNIX International and eventually sold it, along with the UNIX trademark, to Novell, which retitled it Unixware. Much acrimony followed that decision because of disagreements about who got access to which parts of newly developed UNIX and when, with the final result that the UNIX name now belongs to X/Open, a standardization group.

A few other developments are worth mentioning. One is that, around the time SVR4 came out, many competing computer vendors (notably DEC and IBM) thought that AT&T and Sun were getting a wee bit too big for their britches and formed the Open Software Foundation to produce a competing allegedly standard version of UNIX called OSF/1. But OSF/1 turned out to combine the MACH system kernel from Carnegie-Mellon University, a great deal of BSD, some disk-management software from IBM, and a bunch of other eyes of newts and spleens of toads into a not altogether pleasing whole. These days the only large vendor using OSF/1 is DEC. IBM has its own mutant version of UNIX, called AIX, which is sort of, but not very, similar to BSD. (John must admit some guilt for this as well, having had a fair amount to do with the design of version 1 of AIX. But he promises not to do that again.) OSF's other notable product is the much more successful Motif, which we discuss later in this book, in Part IV, "Motif."

Meanwhile, somewhere in northern Europe, a guy named Linus Torwalds thought that it would be fun to start from scratch and write his own version of System V. Amazingly, he did, it worked, and he began giving away the code for free. (This is a task on the order of building a working automobile in your garage, starting with nothing but some sheet steel, a welding set, and an old engine and transmission from the junkyard). Linux has been picked up by the on-line community even more enthusiastically than any of the BSD versions, and you can buy CD-ROMs that contain Linux for $50 or so. (The $50 is for the CD. Linux is free.)

You can't tell the players without a scorecard

To summarize, this list shows the current major living versions of UNIX as of 1995:

- ✔ Commercial versions based on SVR4, such as Sun's Solaris and Novell's Unixware, running on computers from desktop PCs to giant supercomputers

- ✔ Commercial versions descended from various BSD releases, primarily HP's HP-UX and IBM's AIX

- ✔ Free and commercial versions based on 4.4BSD, primarily FreeBSD, NetBSD, and BSD/OS, running mostly on PCs and the occasional workstation

- ✔ Free Linux, for PCs

- ✔ OSF/1, mostly on DEC workstations

The biggest change from past years is that there are now free versions of UNIX that really work, particularly Linux, which has made UNIX much more popular among PC users.

An actual standard!

Adding a modest amount of coherence to the wild and wooly mutations of UNIX is the POSIX standards effort of the Institute of Electrical and Electronic Engineers (IEEE). Unlike many of the putative standards declared by the various competing UNIX camps, POSIX is defining an actual standard, trying to come up with the largest possible common set of UNIX features that *all* UNIX systems either already support or could easily be modified to support. The POSIX effort is producing what will eventually be a huge set of standards for everything from shell commands to printer management to real-time instrument control and will doubtless take until the end of time to complete. Fortunately, the first two parts of POSIX that are completed are probably the most useful. POSIX 1003.1 (the 1003 presumably means that the IEEE already had 1002 standards before

POSIX came along) defines which facilities programmers writing C language programs on POSIX must have available, and 1003.2 defines the set of common user commands. Most systems now support 1003.2 ("dot two" to UNIX aficionados), so you can count on seeing most if not all of the POSIX commands on any modern UNIX system you want. This has also somewhat lessened the divergence among UNIX systems, as some vendors throw away their quirky versions of commands in favor of standard POSIX-compatible ones. (There's still enough wiggle room in POSIX that it hasn't lessened the divergence as much as you might hope.)

Incidentally, POSIX stands for *p*ortable *o*perating *s*ystem *i*nterface, with an *X* thrown in to make it sound cooler.

Good GNUs and bad GNUs

We complete our tour of unlikely software developments at the Free Software Foundation in Cambridge, Massachusetts. The FSF was founded by a brilliant but quirky programmer named Richard Stallman, who had come from M.I.T., where people wrote lots and lots of software and gave it all away. He firmly, some would say fanatically, believes that all software should be free, and he set up the FSF to produce lots of high-quality, free software, culminating in a complete free version of UNIX. (By "free," the FSF means freely available, not necessarily given away for free. The FSF has an elaborate "copyleft" and license for its software which says, basically, that you can charge as much as you want for FSF software, but the people to whom you sell it must be able to give it away. It's therefore perfectly OK to charge for support for FSF software, and at least one company, Cygnus Support, makes a pretty good business that way.)

Despite a great deal of initial skepticism, the FSF has raised enough money and been given and lent enough equipment to do just that. The FSF's project GNU (for *G*NU's *n*ot *U*NIX) has produced versions of most of the UNIX user-level software. The best-known and most widely used pieces are GNU Emacs, which we discuss in Chapter 12, "Have a Big Emacs!," and the GNU C compiler (GCC), which is now used on all the free versions of UNIX and quite a few commercial ones. They've also done versions of most of the common utilities, such as sed and awk, which we discuss in chapters 8 through 10.

The GNU crowd continues to work on new stuff, including its *pièce de résistance,* the GNU Hurd, a complete working version of the guts of the UNIX system with lots of swell extra features and options. Early on, fans of free software awaited the GNU Hurd with much eagerness, but now that Linux and the freely available BSD versions have arrived, the eagerness has abated somewhat. But Hurd or no Hurd, GNU Emacs, GCC, and the GNU utilities are here to stay.

Who — Us? Leave Well Enough Alone?

Along with the profusion of versions of UNIX comes a profusion of programs and versions of programs. Although the old standard programs such as cat (the program you use to copy a file to your terminal) are pretty much holding still, the new and interesting programs are under furious development. All the popular newer programs, such as GNU Emacs, mail programs including elm and pine, news programs including trn and nn, and particularly Internet programs including Mosaic and Netscape, have new releases every few months. The most extreme case is Linux, where you can find a new version on the Internet every few *days.* (Enthusiastic software developers never sleep. We can attest to this from personal experience.)

The results of this situation are twofold:

- ✔ Wonderful new software is constantly available, with swell, useful, new features and options.
- ✔ The way that programs work changes all the time, and you can't count on things being the same from one day to the next.

Unfortunately, you can't have one without the other. Therefore, despite our best efforts to tell you how all these programs work today, the versions you find on the UNIX system you personally use may be older or newer than the ones we describe, so they may work slightly differently. Sorry about that.

Chapter 2
A Short Refresher Course

• •

In This Chapter

▶ A few words of review

▶ Typing commands

▶ Files and directories, again

• •

*B*efore we dive in to the wonders of *MORE UNIX,* here's a crash course in UNIX basics. If you find this chapter a little too concise for your tastes, you might want to flip through the first few chapters of *UNIX For Dummies* before proceeding deeper into this book.

Typing Practice

All UNIX systems, even the ones with mice and stuff, are driven mostly or entirely from the keyboard, so a certain amount of typing (who are we kidding? — a *lot* of typing) is unavoidable. Except when you're running a full-screen program such as a text editor, UNIX considers your input a line at a time. When you're typing, you can backspace over your mistakes and tell it to ignore the entire line you've been typing so that you can begin again. Which keys do you press to accomplish these tasks? We were afraid you'd ask that. UNIX makes it easy to customize these "line editing" keys, so by golly everybody does. Here are some likely candidates:

For backspacing, try pressing Backspace, Del or Delete, or Ctrl-H. If none of those keystrokes works, try the bizarre traditional backspacing key # (it's on top of the 3 key on your keyboard).

For ignoring the entire line ("line kill" in UNIX-ese), try pressing Ctrl-U or Ctrl-X. If neither of those works, the bizarre traditional key for that is @ (usually found as Shift-2 on your keyboard).

If you're trying to type someone's Internet mail address that contains an @ sign and UNIX jumps to a new line whenever you type it, that suggests that your line-kill character is still @, and you should have your system manager or local guru arrange for a more sensible one.

Another important character to know is the interrupt character, which tells UNIX to stop whatever it's doing. The usual one is Ctrl-C, although on some systems it's still the traditional Del or Delete.

There is, amazingly enough, a command that tells you what the current special characters are. Type the following line to UNIX:

```
stty -a
```

(You have to type it without making any mistakes if you don't know what your Backspace key is, but it's only seven characters.) That gives you lots of glop, probably including something like this:

```
cchars: discard = ^O; dsusp = ^Y; eof = ^D; eol = <undef>;
    eol2 = <undef>; erase = ^H; intr = ^C; kill = ^U; lnext = ^V;
    quit = ^\; reprint = ^R; start = ^Q; status = ^T; stop = ^S;
    susp = ^Z; werase = ^W;
```

The interesting ones in there are erase, which in this case is ^H or Ctrl-H (which happens to be the same as Backspace on most keyboards); kill, which is ^U or Ctrl-U; and intr (interrupt), which here is ^C or Ctrl-C. Many UNIX systems also have a bunch of other line-editing characters, such as Ctrl-W to backspace over a word and Ctrl-R to reprint the typed line.

Several UNIX shells (which we discuss in the following section) add their own line-editing characters to the standard ones. So you may well find that some keys which work just fine when you're typing to your shell, notably arrow keys, don't work at all in some other places. Consistency has never been one of UNIX's strong points.

Just in Case

Unlike many other systems, UNIX programs invariably consider upper- and lowercase to be different. If you want to run a program called elm, for example, you have to type its name as elm and not ELM, Elm, or anything else. UNIX filenames are also case-sensitive: fred, Fred, FRED, and FrEd are all different filenames and can all exist simultaneously. Opinions differ (sometimes vigorously, occasionally to the point of fisticuffs) over whether this is a good idea, but after 25 years it's not likely to change.

One thing that makes the upper- and lowercase problem much easier to deal with is that, 99 percent of the time, command names and filenames are entirely in lowercase. Use uppercase only when you mean it.

Logging In

Because UNIX has always been a multiuser system, before you can do anything with a UNIX system you have to tell it who you are. It says `login:`, at which point you type your username (and press Enter at the end of the line, of course); then it asks `Password:`, at which point you type your password. For security reasons, the password doesn't appear on-screen even though UNIX hears it. Assuming that it liked your username and password, it then prints a bunch of legal and introductory glop, and what you see looks something like this:

```
BSDI BSD/386 1.1 (ivan.iecc.com) (ttyp3)

login: john1
Password: typed the password here, but it doesn't print
Last login: Wed Mar 29 17:38:39 from tom
Copyright 1992,1993,1994 Berkeley Software Design, Inc.
Copyright (c) 1980,1983,1986,1988,1990,1991 The Regents of
the University of California.  All rights reserved.

BSDI BSD/386 1.1 Kernel #1: Sat Feb 11 16:16:05 EST 1995

erase ^H, kill ^U, intr ^C status ^T
$
```

The Shell Game

Unlike many other operating systems, UNIX itself doesn't have a command prompt. (It may look like it does, but it doesn't.) What it has instead is a variety of *shells,* which are programs that read your commands and run them for you. The prompt you see is provided by your shell, not by UNIX. Most UNIX systems thoughtfully start a shell for you as soon as you log in. (A few start menu systems, about which we can't say anything helpful because no two of the menu systems are alike.)

"Who cares?" you may ask. You care, because which shell your system runs determines which commands will work for you. Four major shells are in use, all of which are the same in concept but that differ in detail. We discuss them more in Chapter 3, "Far Too Many Versions of UNIX and a Few Too Many Shells."

What's on File?

UNIX systems have files. Lots of files. Lots and lots and lots of files. A typical medium-size UNIX system has more than 100,000 files. (Amazing, huh? What could they all possibly contain?) To bring some small amount of sanity to the mountain of files, they are grouped together in *directories,* which act sort of like file folders.

At any given moment you have a *current* directory, which is merely the one in which programs look by default when you give the name of a file. The directory you start in when you first log in is called your *home directory,* but you can move to other directories as necessary, by using the cd command. (Type **cd** followed by the name of a directory to go to that directory. By itself, typing cd goes back to your home directory.)

Unlike some low-rent operating systems (we won't name any, but the initials of one of them are MS-DOS), UNIX lets you call files nearly anything you want, using any characters you want, with as many as 256 characters in the name. (Some older UNIX systems, such as Xenix, limit filenames to 14 characters.) So if you want to call a file ThirdDraftOfMyNovelWithSomeNotVeryHelpful CommentsByAuntMartha, be our guest, but keep in mind that every time you want to use that file, you may have to type the entire name. UNIX filenames can even contain spaces, but because the shells all treat spaces specially, it's a bad idea to use spaces in a name because it makes the name much more difficult to type in a command. Indeed, the shells also treat most punctuation specially, so we recommend that you stick to letters, digits, periods, and underscores. You can use as many periods as you want in a name, so perhaps a better (but equally hard to type) name for the novel would be third.draft.of.my. novel.with.some.not.very.helpful.comments.by.Aunt.Martha

The one character you can't use in a filename is a slash (/) because it separates directory names from filenames. If you have a directory called docs with a file called novel3, for example, you can refer to it as docs/novel3. If a name begins with a slash, it means that the name is "absolute," describing the path from the top-level "root" directory rather than relative to the current directory. You occasionally use absolute names when you refer to some standard UNIX files. For example, the name of the usual UNIX shell is /bin/sh.

MS-DOS users should note that you must use a forward slash (/) in filenames, not a reverse slash (\) as in DOS names. Many UNIX programs treat reverse slashes peculiarly (often meaning to quote whatever normally special character follows), so we suggest that you stay away from the \ key.

Chapter 3

Far Too Many Versions of UNIX and a Few Too Many Shells

For more information about shells and versions, see Chapter 2 in *UNIX For Dummies.*

The Shell Game

As we mentioned in Chapter 2, "A Short Refresher Course," the program to which you type your commands is known as the *shell.* But, as is so often the case with UNIX, there's too much of a good thing around, and four different shells are in common use. In this chapter, we tell you what they are and then how to tell which one you have.

Your basic shell

The oldest and simplest shell that people use these days is known as the *Bourne shell,* after Steve Bourne, the guy at Bell Labs who wrote it. It's simple and reliable but lacks many of the fru-fru features that make the other shells so lovable. Every UNIX system comes with the Bourne shell. When you use it as a command (to run shell scripts, which we begin discussing in Chapter 4, "An Introduction to Scripts"), its name is the simple and austere sh.

Free versions of UNIX use a version of the Bourne shell written by Kenneth Almquist at Berkeley. It acts enough like the original Bourne shell that you're not likely to notice the differences.

Korn gold

Some years after Bourne wrote the Bourne shell, another guy at Bell Labs, named Dave Korn, added to the Bourne shell lots of wonderful, new features (at least he thought they were) and came up with an extended version known as the *Korn shell*. Because the Korn shell is based on the Bourne shell and because Korn was fairly careful with his changes, anything that works in the Bourne shell works by and large in the Korn shell as well. The Korn shell's command name is `ksh`.

There's a free version of the Korn shell as well, written by Eric Gisin, at the University of Waterloo in Canada. It is close to the Korn original.

Bourne again

The GNU crowd (the Free Software Foundation, which we mentioned in Chapter 1, "We're Ba-a-a-ck!") has its own shell as well: the *Bourne-again shell*, or BASH. It, like most GNU stuff, has all the features of every competing shell and lots more of its own. Many users like BASH for two reasons: Whatever you want to do, BASH can do it, and it's available for free, so what the heck.

BASH is based (in concept) on the Bourne shell, so most things that work in the Bourne shell still work in BASH.

See shells

The last popular shell is the *C shell,* `csh`, written at Berkeley by Bill, the same guy who wrote much of the rest of Berkeley UNIX. The C shell is utterly unrelated to the Bourne shell (in fact, it's sort of based on the older shell that everyone else threw away when the Bourne shell came along), so it has lots of small differences in the way it handles commands.

Many people (including us) find `csh` useless for scripts, but it's still used occasionally as people's login shell for sentimental reasons because it was the first shell that let you type things such as `~fred` for Fred's login directory. Now all the shells can do that, but for some users, it's like an old, favorite sweater that used to be beautiful and now is shabby but they don't care.

On the other hand, you, as a sensible person, have no reason to use a shell that resembles a moth-eaten sweater. If you find yourself saddled with the C shell, ask your system manager or UNIX guru how to switch to BASH or the Korn shell.

How to tell which shell you have

1. **Type the command** help.

   If you get a message that lists a bunch of shell commands, you have BASH. If not, continue with the next step.

2. **Type** echo $0.

   If you get the message No file for $0, you have the C shell. Our condolences. If not, continue with the next step.

3. **Type** echo $RANDOM.

   If you get a random number, you have the Korn shell. If you get a blank line, you have the Bourne shell.

How much difference does all this make?

The Bourne shell, Korn shell, and BASH all work in pretty much the same way, and any of them is quite usable. The C shell is now obsolete, and we don't recommend that anyone use it. It's not a disaster if you have to use it, but it can be a pain because of its peculiar incompatibilities with everything else.

One difference between the Bourne shell and its Korn and BASH descendants is that the latter two do special keyboard processing. In particular, if your system manager set up your account carefully, you can press cursor keys to edit your commands, and you can move the cursor up and down to scroll through old commands. (Take that, DOS!) If your shell setup doesn't let you do that, see Chapter 6 in *UNIX For Dummies,* 2nd edition, for some shell setup advice.

You Mean, UNIX Isn't Just UNIX?

Sorry, no. As we mentioned in Chapter 1, "We're Ba-a-a-ck!," UNIX has been evolving and mutating for 25 years, and there is now a rich and diverse range of UNIX cyberbiota. But we can group most of the surviving systems into three phyla.

First we describe the phyla, and then we tell you how to tell which is which.

Old AT&T-ish systems

The oldest surviving strain of UNIX, a vigorous but primitive line (think of cockroaches), is based on old versions of AT&T UNIX System V release 3 (SVR3) or its immediate successor, SVR3.2. The most popular of these systems is SCO UNIX, from the Santa Cruz Operation, and SCO Xenix, which is based on even older AT&T sources.

The old AT&T-ish systems are missing some of the features that are common on all the rest. Most notably, rather than allow filenames to be 256 characters, they limit them to 14, which is nowhere near as much fun.

Newer AT&T-ish systems

Many commercial systems, particularly on larger computers, are based on System V release 4 (SVR4) or later AT&T (now Novell) UNIX. The most widely used SVR4 system is Sun's Solaris, but there are many more. Because SVR4 merged together the older AT&T-ish UNIX and BSD UNIX, they tend to be pretty complete.

Linux is an AT&T-ish system even though it contains no AT&T code, just because the guy who wrote it decided to model his system after System V (which was at the time, arguably "more standard") rather than after BSD UNIX.

BSD-ish systems

BSD-ish systems are based on various releases of Berkeley UNIX. Because there have been so many releases of Berkeley UNIX, in many cases a vendor picked up a version of BSD, did a great deal of work on it to customize it to the vendor's particular kind of computer and to add all sorts of swell features, and never felt it worth the effort to redo the work when Berkeley handed out a new version. (This is particularly true because Berkeley UNIX has always had a large number of bugs, and refixing bugs is no fun.) So there is a fair amount of divergence among BSD-ish systems, depending on which version of BSD the system started with and how enthusiastically the vendor has been working on it.

The two major free BSD-ish systems, NetBSD and FreeBSD, both are based on the final 4.4BSD, as is the current version of the commercial BSD/OS, so they all hew closely to the Berkeley line.

How Much Practical Difference Does It Make?

The answer used to be "a lot." Now it's "some." If you have an old AT&T-ish system, you probably will notice that some things are missing, such as long filenames (limited, as we said earlier, to 14 rather than 256 characters) and some of the nicer new programs. Many surviving old AT&T-ish systems have spliced-in new features, but the result often feels like a Band-Aid, sometimes with weird rules that let you have long names on one disk but not on another.

With SVR4, AT&T merged in most of the good stuff from BSD UNIX, so the practical differences are now more nits than anything really big.

OK, How Do I Tell Which UNIX I Have?

The obvious way would be to ask it. But that would be too easy. There is in fact a UNIX command, uname, that is supposed to tell you the name of your system:

```
$ uname
Linux
```

Pretty easy, huh? It is if it is. On older AT&T-ish systems, uname tends to give you the network name of the computer you're using rather than the name of the system. On other computers, it gives whatever name the vendor has dreamed up for its system. We tried it on the Internet on a bunch of computers on which we have accounts and got the answers SunOS, Linux, IRIX, ULTRIX, and BSD/OS. If you happen to recognize the name from the earlier discussion, that's nice, but if not, it's not much help.

Let's Be Sneaky

Here's a much more reliable way to find out which phylum your computer is from. First, try uname as just discussed. If it gives you the computer's own name rather than the system name, you have an old AT&T-ish system, so stop here. If it gives you a name you recognize, such as Linux, you can stop here, too.

Otherwise, try the command ps -f. On System V systems, it prints a few lines listing the programs you're running (usually just the shell and ps), along with a bunch of hopelessly uninteresting numeric glop. On BSD, though, it prints an error message like this:

```
$ ps -f
ps: illegal option — f
usage: ps [-aChjlmrSTuvwx] [-O|o fmt] [-p pid] [-t tty]
          [-M core] [-N system] [-W swap]
       ps [-L]
```

On the other hand, the command ps x does the same thing on BSD systems and prints an error message on System V. On some hybrid systems, both work.

For more information about the ps command, see Chapter 23 in *UNIX For Dummies.*

The 5th Wave — By Rich Tennant

"YES, I THINK IT'S AN ERROR MESSAGE."

Part II
UNIX Scripts

The 5th Wave   By Rich Tennant

It started as a little experiment in data compression, and...well... just close the door and call the zoo!

DANGER

In this part...

*H*ey, we know that you don't want to turn into some kind of geeky programmer (not that we haven't), but it's worth knowing how to write a UNIX script or two. They can really speed up your work. And awk and sed, everyone's favorite UNIX utilities, can handle all kinds of unlikely tasks. Check out the chapters in this part if you're ready to automate some of your UNIX work!

Chapter 4
An Introduction to Scripts

• •

In This Chapter

▶ What are scripts?

▶ Where do I store scripts?

▶ How do I write scripts?

▶ How do I run scripts ?

▶ Scripting tips

• •

*F*ifty percent of Americans dream of being scriptwriters. They dream that
they have an as-yet-undiscovered dramatic talent and that any day now
they will take an afternoon off, write a screenplay or sitcom script, send it off to
Hollywood, and become the next Ingmar Bergman. Or maybe the next Roseanne.

Here's your big chance. You too can write scripts. We tell you exactly what you
need to know to write fantastically successful scripts whenever you want. No
one will ever read them, of course, except you and your UNIX system. Great art
is never properly appreciated!

What the heck are we talking about, you may ask? UNIX shell scripts! If you've
read and memorized *UNIX For Dummies,* you remember our description of
scripts from Chapter 14. If not, we review everything from that chapter here
and tell you much more.

What Is a Script?

A *shell script* (or just *script*) is a text file that contains a list of UNIX commands,
one per line. By and large, these commands are exactly the same commands
you type when you see the UNIX prompt — commands such as cp, rm, and ls.
You can run the script by typing the name of the file — when you do so, the
UNIX shell runs the commands in the script. It's similar to making a player-
piano roll of commands, which can be replayed as often as you want.

Attention, DOS users!

"Hey!" you DOS-ites are saying. "Scripts sound just like batch files!"

Right you are. The concept is the same. Some details are different, however:

 ✔ Script filenames don't end in .BAT.

 ✔ A few commands don't work the same way in scripts as they do in real life, notably the `chdir` and `cd` commands.

 ✔ You have to tell UNIX to make the shell script file executable before you can run it (see the section "Writing a Script," later in this chapter, for instructions).

Suppose that you want to create a script to back up your document and take out the garbage. This script makes backup copies of all the files in your Docs directory and puts the copies in a directory called Backup. Then it deletes any temporary files in the Docs directory:

```
cp Docs/* Backup
rm Docs/*.tmp
```

You put these commands in a text file named `bkup`. After you make this script file executable (as described later in this chapter, in the section "Writing a Script"), you can make your backups by typing the name of the script file, as though it were a UNIX shell command:

```
bkup
```

Scripts are used all the time in UNIX. You might be surprised, in fact, to find out how many of the commands you use are actually scripts!

Where Do Scripts Live?

Scripts can be stored anywhere — as far as UNIX is concerned, they are just normal files. If you want your UNIX shell to be able to find them, however, you must put them in the right place.

In your home directory, you should have a directory named `bin` in which to store scripts and other programs (*bin* is short for *binary,* if you were wondering). If you don't already have one, move to your home directory (type **cd**) and create one now.

```
mkdir bin
```

On most UNIX systems, the shell looks in your `bin` directory automatically when you type a command, to see whether the script you want to run is there. As you create scripts or get them from other people, put them in your `bin` directory. To find out where your UNIX system looks for programs, see the following section.

When you type a command, it might be a command your UNIX shell knows how to perform, a utility program that comes with UNIX, some other program, or a script written by you or someone else.

Where the shell looks for programs

When you type a command, how does your UNIX shell find the program you want? Here's what it does:

- If the shell knows how to execute the command itself, it does it (the `cd` or `pwd` commands, for example).
- Otherwise, the shell looks for a program with the same filename as the command you typed.

Where does it look? It looks on the *search path,* which is the list of directories that contain programs. Your system administrator sets up a search path for each user, and it includes the directories that contain all the standard utilities and programs your installation uses.

To see your search path, type this line (if you use the C shell):

```
echo $path
```

If you use the Bourne or Korn shell or BASH, type this line:

```
echo $PATH
```

(For more information about what `$path` and `$PATH` are, see the section "Variables You Already Have," in Chapter 5, "The Shell Game: Using Shell Variables.")

The C shell displays a line like this one:

```
/bin /usr/bin /usr/ucb/bin /usr/local/bin .
```

The Bourne and Korn shells and BASH display something more like this:

```
/bin:/usr/bin:/usr/ucb/bin:/usr/local/bin:.
```

Either way, you are looking at a list of directories on your system that contain programs.

(If you're not sure which shell you are using, refer to Chapter 3, "Far Too Many Versions of UNIX and a Few Too Many Shells.")

Look in my bin!

If your own bin directory isn't in your search path, you can add it so that the UNIX shell can find any scripts you put there. (For background information on why this technique works, see the section "Variables You Already Have," in Chapter 5, "The Shell Game: Using Shell Variables.")

If you use the C shell, the following command does it:

```
set path=($path ~/bin)
```

That's a space and a tilde (~) in the middle. This command tells the C shell to set the search path ($path) to the current search path plus the bin subdirectory of your home directory (~).

If you use the Bourne or Korn shell or BASH, it takes two commands:

```
PATH=$PATH:$HOME/bin
export PATH
```

Be sure to type the dollar signs and colons just as they are shown here. They tell the shell to set the search path ($PATH) to the current search path plus the bin subdirectory of your home directory ($HOME). Sound familiar?

Unfortunately, this change stays put only until you log out. To fix your search path permanently, you have to put these commands in your .login file (if you use the C shell) or your .profile file (if you use the Bourne or Korn shell or BASH). Chapter 7, "Setting Things Up Nice," tells you how to edit these files safely.

Writing a Script

Before you begin writing a script, be sure that you have thought through the commands that are necessary. Try to make them as generally useful as possible. The creation of a script requires these steps:

1. **Create a text file that contains the shell script in your** `bin` **directory.**

   Use any text editor, such as emacs or (ugh) vi. For example, you can make a file named `mystatus` that contains these commands:

```
date
pwd
ls
```

   These commands tell you your current situation: the date and time, your current directory, and the files in that directory.

2. **Make the file executable, by using this command:**

```
chmod +x mystatus
```

   Substitute in place of `mystatus` the filename that contains the script. If you want only you to be able to execute the script, use this command instead:

```
chmod u+x mystatus
```

3. **Tell the shell to update its list of executable files, by typing this command:**

```
rehash
```

   The shell makes a list of all the programs in all the directories in your search path, to speed up the search whenever you give a command. When you put a new program in your `bin` directory, the shell has to update this list, which is geekily called a *hash table*. This `rehash` command tells the shell that an update is necessary.

Now the script is ready to run.

If you don't make a file executable, you can't run it. Instead, you see a message like this one:

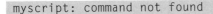
```
myscript: command not found
```

If you are wondering whether a file is executable, use the `ls -l` command to see its permissions. If *x*s appear in the permissions (the first ten characters of each line in the files listing), it is executable.

You can't run that!

UNIX actually lets you specify whether you, people in your group, or any old user can run the script. An *x* as the fourth character of a file's permissions means that the file's owner can run it. An *x* as the seventh character means that any-one in the owner's group can run it. And an *x* as the tenth character means that anyone can run it.

See Chapter 5 in *UNIX For Dummies,* for more info about permissions.

Running a Script

Nothing could be easier than running a shell script — just type the name of the file that contains the script, like this:

```
mystatus
```

The UNIX shell realizes that it's not a command it knows about, and it searches the files in your search path for an executable file by that name. When it finds your script, it runs it.

Two programs with the same name

What if you have more than one script with the same name, stored in different directories on your search path? That is, what if a script file named `mystatus` is in the system `/bin` directory as well as in your own `bin` subdirectory?

The shell looks at the directories on your search path in the order in which they appear. It executes the first file it finds with the name you typed. Because the system's directories generally ap-pear in the path before your directory, a system command takes precedence over any command of yours with the same name.

If you want, you can put your personal `bin` direc-tory in front of the path rather than at the end, in which case a command of yours takes prece-dence over a system command. This situation lets you replace system commands you don't like with ones of your own, which sounds appealing but is usually not a good idea because there are many interdependent UNIX commands that depend on, for example, `ls` doing what the system `ls` does.

Shells and Scripts

The shell runs scripts, not UNIX itself. This distinction may sound useless, nitpicky, and typically nerdy, but sometimes it makes a difference. The point is that the way you write your shell scripts depends on which UNIX shell you use. For example, some commands work in only the Bourne shell or only in the C shell.

If you want to write a script that works no matter which shell you are using, you can specify which shell should be used to interpret the commands in the script. To tell the Bourne shell to interpret the commands in your script, put this line at the beginning of the script:

```
#!/bin/sh
```

To use the C shell to interpret the commands in the script, use the following line as the first line in your script:

```
#!/bin/csh
```

The following line tells the Korn shell to interpret your script:

```
#!/bin/ksh
```

BASH users use this line:

```
#!/bin/bash
```

It turns out that the C shell is lousy for writing scripts. Versions of the C shell vary too much from UNIX system to UNIX system, and most versions have a bunch of plain, old bugs. (Some versions even differ about what *true* and *false* mean. Urrgh.) Our advice is to be sure to make its first line #!/bin/sh so that the Bourne shell interprets it.

This trick of putting the name of the program that is supposed to run a script preceded by #! at the front of the file is known in the UNIX biz as the *sharp bang hack* because # is a sharp sign (at least it is if you're a musician — others have been known to accuse it of being a pound sign or something called an octothorp), and ! is pronounced "bang!"

Tiresome Arguments

What if you want to be able to use information from the command line in your scripts? What if you are making a script named `findit`, for example, which uses the `find` command to find different types of files? Rather than make a different script for each type of file you might want to search for, it would be neat if you could type a command like this:

```
findit budget
```

and have your `findit` script look for files whose names begin with the characters *budget*.

You can, through the magic of arguments. Most people don't find arguments to be much fun, but shell arguments are different.

What's an argument?

When you type stuff on the command line, the shell assumes that the first word you type is the command and that the rest of the words are arguments, or information to be used by the command. If you type the following line, for example:

```
ls Budgets
```

`ls` is the command you want to run, and `Budgets` is information to be used by the `ls` command, in this case to specify which directory you want a listing of. You can have more than one argument, like this:

```
ls Budgets Skunkworks
```

The first argument (`Budgets`) is the second word on the command line. The second argument (`Skunkworks`) is the third word on the command line. And so on.

Arguing with scripts

When you write a script, you can design it to use the values of arguments. Where you want to use the value of the first argument, type **$1**. Where you want the value of the second argument, type **$2**. You get the idea.

Suppose that you are an old MS-DOS user and you frequently type *dir* rather than *ls* to see a listing of files. You write a script called `dir` that contains these commands:

```
pwd
ls -l $1
```

This script acts more or less like the DOS DIR command, by displaying the current directory and then a listing of files. If you type **dir**, you get a detailed listing of all the files in your current directory. But if you type this command:

```
dir Letters
```

Letters is the first argument and gets used in place of the $1 in the script. You want to see a detailed listing of files in your directory Letters. But how does the directory name (Letters) get into your dir script?

If you want to be able to type a bunch of different file specifications on the command line (such as d*, which the shell expands into all the filenames that begin with a *d*), change the dir script to look like this:

```
pwd
ls -l $1 $2 $3 $4 $5 $6 $7 $8 $9
```

You won't have a problem if there aren't nine arguments on the command line — the shell just replaces the missing arguments with nothing. Even better, you can type **$*** to mean "all the arguments on the command line," like this:

```
pwd
ls -l $*
```

This method works even if there are more than nine arguments.

If you type on the command line an argument that contains wildcard characters, the shell automatically replaces it with all the names it matches. For example, if you type this command:

```
dir d*
```

the shell acts as though you had typed the following:

```
dir day dial dog dollar dullard
```

or whatever the names of your files that begin with *d* are. DOS users may find this stuff confusing because in DOS each program is responsible for handling wildcards itself. In UNIX, the shell handles it so that none of your scripts has to worry about it.

Environmental Impact

Here comes a strange and arcane aspect of running shell scripts. When you run a script, a *new* shell comes into existence to run it. When the script is finished, this new copy dies. Here's why you care: If you change things about the shell environment, such as changing directories or setting the values of shell variables (which are described in the next chapter), these changes take place in this *new* shell. After the script is finished and this new shell flickers out of existence, the changes you made are lost.

Suppose that you frequently have to change to the /usr/johnl/book/moreunix/ draft directory. (You probably don't, but you might imagine that we spent a large amount of time there while writing this book.) This is a great deal of stuff to type, so you make a script named gobook that contains this command:

```
cd /usr/johnl/book/moreunix/draft
```

No matter how many times you run it, however, it doesn't seem to work!

It works, all right — the new copy of the shell changes to the directory you asked for. But when the script is over and the new copy of the shell terminates, you are back in the same, old copy of the shell you were running earlier, and you are in the same, old directory.

Getting around this problem is (to use a technical term) a pain in the neck. If you use BASH or the Korn shell, you can use a shell alias:

```
alias gobook="cd /usr/johnl/book/moreunix/draft"
```

In the C shell, you use a space rather than an equal sign:

```
alias gobook "cd /usr/johnl/book/moreunix/draft"
```

This line tells the shell to treat gobook specially and do the cd command itself. (You would put this alias command in the .cshrc or .profile file that the shell runs when it starts up [see Chapter 7, "Setting Things Up Nice"].)

Do's and Don'ts

This section gives you some tips for writing and executing scripts safely:

- ✔ Particularly if you plan to let other people run your script because they might be using a shell that's different from yours, be sure to put at the beginning of your script a sharp-bang line that specifies which shell should be used to interpret it.

- ✔ Include comments in your shell scripts. Even if the script is only one line long, you may forget what it is supposed to do. To include a comment in a script, start each line of the comment with a # character — the shell ignores everything from a # to the end of the line.

- ✔ If your script is more than a few lines long, think about including some blank lines to separate the script into sections and make it more readable. A blank line in a script does absolutely nothing when the script is run, but it can make it much easier for humans to read.

The next chapter looks at shell variables, which are useful when you are writing scripts. In Chapter 6, "Fancy Script Commands," we return to the subject of scripts and describe some fancier shell commands you can use to make more powerful scripts.

Chapter 5

The Shell Game: Using Shell Variables

What's in a Variable?

No point in keeping you in suspense — a *variable* (or more precisely, a *shell variable*) is a set of characters to which you have assigned a name. Back in tenth-grade algebra class, variables usually contained numbers, but in The World of UNIX they can also contain letters, numbers, and punctuation.

In Chapter 4, "An Introduction to Scripts," for example, we described the situation in which you frequently move to a directory with a long, impossible-to-type name, such as /usr/johnl/book/moreunix/draft. Rather than retype it every time you want to move to that directory, you could store that horrifying series of characters in a variable named *draft*. Then you could use the nice, short variable name in place of that long pathname.

Sounds cool, doesn't it? Variables *are* cool, in fact, and they are extremely useful.

Unfortunately, the four shells (Bourne shell, Korn shell, BASH, and C shell) have slightly different rules for creating and using variables. We label all the instructions in this chapter clearly so that you can tell what to do in the shell you use. (If you're not sure, refer to Chapter 5, "The Shell Game: Using Shell Variables.") If we don't tell you which shell a command works with, it works with all shells.

Name that variable!

You can give your variables nice, descriptive names so that you can remember what they are for. Variable names can be as long as you want, although really long names are difficult to type. Stick to letters, numbers, and underscores, and stay away from other punctuation because lots of funny characters have special meanings to UNIX shells.

If you use the Bourne or Korn shell or BASH

To create a variable, type the variable name, an equal sign, and the value you want to assign to the variable. Don't type any spaces in the midst of these items. For example, the following command creates a variable named *draft:*

```
draft=/usr/johnl/book/moreunix/draft
```

If the draft variable already exists, this command replaces its value.

If you use the C shell

To create a variable, use the set command, like this:

```
set draft=/usr/johnl/book/moreunix/draft
```

This command creates a variable named *draft* or sets its value if it already exists.

A variable is born

You can confirm that you've created a variable by asking the shell to display its value on the screen, like this:

```
echo $draft
```

The echo command looks at what you type on the rest of the command line ($draft, in this case) and displays its value on the screen. When you want to see the value of a variable, stick a dollar sign at the beginning of the variable name. This echo command displays the current value of the draft variable.

You can also list the variables that are currently defined. Just type the following with no arguments:

```
set
```

The shell lists all your variables with their current values. You also see a bunch of other variables the system defined for you, which we discuss in the next section.

What good are variables?

After you have created a variable, you can use its value when you give commands. After you have created the draft variable, for example, you can give this command:

```
cd $draft
```

When the shell sees this command, it replaces $draft with the value of the draft variable and then changes to that directory. How convenient!

Folks who write scripts use variables all the time. Variables work in just the same way in scripts as they work when you type commands — precede the variable name with a dollar sign to get the value of that variable.

Killing variables

Variables you create hang around only until you log off. Then they wink out of existence. To get rid of a variable before you log off, use the unset command, like this:

```
unset draft
```

This command gets rid of the draft variable.

Variables You Already Have

It turns out that you have a bunch of variables whether you want them or not. These variables, called *predefined variables,* are defined by a script that runs automatically when you log in. They contain information about your *environment,* which are variables that are available to and affect other programs. When your shell starts, all the variables are "imported" from the environment as shell variables.

Which variables you have, what they are called, what they do, and how to set their values all depend on which shell you use. Bourne, Korn, and BASH users, keep reading. C shell users, skip down to the section "If you use the C shell."

If you use the Bourne or Korn shell or BASH

Some important predefined variables are defined by your .profile script, a script that is run automatically when you log in (Chapter 7, "Setting Things Up Nice," tells you all about it). Table 5-1 lists some of the usual predefined variables. Some of these variables are initialized from the environment; we mark them in the table with "(Environment)."

Table 5-1	Predefined Variables in the Bourne and Korn Shells and BASH
Variable	**Meaning**
EDITOR and/or *VISUAL*	Your favorite text editor (usually vi or emacs). Some programs check this variable to determine which editor to run; when you compose mail or newsgroup articles, for example. (Environment.)
HOME	Your home directory. (Environment.)
LOGNAME and/or *USER*	Your username or login name. (Environment.)
MAIL	The file that contains your incoming mail. (Environment.)
MAILCHECK	How often to check for incoming mail (in seconds; a value of 600 means every 10 minutes).
PATH	Search path (for searching for programs; see Chapter 4, "An Introduction to Scripts"). (Environment.)
PS1	Your shell prompt (usually $).
PWD	Your current working directory (not always defined in the Bourne shell).
TERM	Type of terminal you are using (or type that your PC program is pretending to be) — common values are *vt100* and *ansi*. (Environment).
TZ	Time zone you are in, such as *EST5EDT* in the eastern United States. That's the name of your regular time zone, the number of hours behind GMT that is, and the name of your daylight savings time zone. If you don't have DST where you are, leave off the second name (in Arizona, for example, you would use *PST8).* If you live in a place that has daylight savings time but doesn't use the U.S. rules for when it begins and ends (Europe, for example), you can add extra glop to the *TZ* variable to control it. It's arcane; ask your local UNIX guru for help in that case. (Environment.)

Of course, your .profile script may define lots of other variables. To see a list of your shell variables and their current values, type this command:

```
set
```

You see a listing like this one:

```
HOME=/usr/margy
LOGNAME=margy
MAIL=/usr/mail/margy
PATH=:/bin:/usr/bin:/usr/local/bin:/usr/ucb:.:/usr/margy/bin
SHELL=/bin/sh
TERM=vt100
```

Most predefined variables already have the correct values assigned to them — your system administrator or whoever set up your account saw to this. See Chapter 7, "Setting Things Up Nice," for more information about the scripts that run automatically when you log in.

You can also use the env or printenv command (same command, different names on some systems — try them both) to see the variables in your environment. Everything in the environment (env) is in the shell (set), but not everything in the shell is in the environment. If you find this situation confusing, you are, to put it mildly, not alone.

Using predefined variables

You can use these predefined variables in your commands just as you use regular variables. That is, put a $ at the beginning of the name, like this:

```
cd $HOME/Temp
```

This command moves you to the Temp subdirectory of your home directory.

You can also use predefined variables in scripts just as you use normal variables. Many scripts use them so that the actions of the script can be tailored to the user's environment. The following command, for example, copies all the files in a user's home directory into a Backup subdirectory:

```
cp $HOME/* $HOME/Backup
```

You can also change the values of the predefined variables, like this:

```
PATH=$PATH:$HOME/bin
```

This command sets the value of the PATH command to the same value it already has, plus the bin subdirectory of your home directory. (By ancient convention, the directory names in the path are separated by colons.)

If you want the changes to affect other programs and scripts you run, however, you need an extra command:

```
export PATH
```

The export command tells the shell to "export" any new value of the variable you specify (PATH, in this case) back into the environment so that it affects other commands you run. (See the section "Environmental Impact" in Chapter 4, "An Introduction to Scripts," for a description of the difference between the shell that runs your script and the one that is running the rest of the time.) In the absence of an export command, changes to variables affect only the shell in which the change is made.

Remember that environment variables and predefined variables generally have names that are capitalized.

Changes to the values of your predefined variables last only until you log out. When you log in again, your .profile script sets them back to their usual values. To change a value permanently, edit your .profile script as described in Chapter 7, "Setting Things Up Nice."

If you use the Korn shell

If you use the Korn shell, things work the same as they do in the Bourne shell, except that the export command can both set the value of the environment variable and "export" it to other programs, saving valuable seconds of typing time, like this:

```
export $PATH=$PATH:$HOME/bin
```

If you use the C shell

The C shell has predefined variables, just like the Bourne and Korn shells do. But the C shell treats environment variables differently, with separate commands to handle them.

The C shell's predefined variables

Like the Bourne and Korn shells and BASH, the C shell also predefines a set of variables for you, as listed in Table 5-2. As you see, these variable names use small letters rather than capital ones.

Table 5-2	Predefined C Shell Variables
Variable	**Description**
cwd	Current working directory (see also the *PATH* environment variable in Table 5-3)
history	Number of commands to save in the shell's history list (which is used to repeat commands without having to retype them)
home	Your home (login) directory (set from the *HOME* environment variable; see Table 5-3)
mail	Filename (or filenames) of the file (or files) that contains new mail for you, optionally preceded by how often, in seconds, to check for new mail
noclobber	If you create it (by typing the command set noclobber), the shell doesn't automatically delete an existing file if you redirect output to it
path	Search path for commands (set from the *PATH* environment variable; see Table 5-3)
prompt	Prompt that tells you when you can type a command (usually %)
status	Status of the last command you ran (0 means that it succeeded; 1 means that it failed)
term	Type of terminal you are using or type of terminal your PC or Macintosh is emulating (see the *TERM* environment variable in Table 5-3)
user	Your login name (set from the *USER* environment variable; see Table 5-3)

You can set the values of these predefined shell variables by using the set command, just as though they were normal, unpredefined variables. For example, you can use this command to add your bin subdirectory to your search path:

```
set path=($path ~/bin)
```

That's a space and a tilde (~) in the middle. This command tells the C shell to set the search path ($path) to the current search path, plus the bin subdirectory of your home directory (~). The C shell treats the path variable in a special way, and any changes to it are automagically reflected in the environment PATH variable. Note that the C shell separates names in path with spaces but that the other shells use colons. And the C shell puts parentheses around the whole thing, for enhanced confusion. Arrghh!

Here's another example, a command to change your shell prompt:

```
set prompt='Hi! '
```

Some predefined variables, such as *noclobber,* which tells the shell not to let you overwrite an existing file by using >, are either set (on) or not set (off). To turn them on, use the `set` command, like this:

```
set noclobber
```

To turn them off, use the `unset` command, like this:

```
unset noclobber
```

You can use these predefined variables in the usual way, by preceding the name with a $, as shown in this example:

```
cd $home/budget
```

This command moves you to the `budget` subdirectory of your home directory.

Environment variables

So far, so good. It looks as though variables in the C shell look just like they do in the Bourne and Korn shells and BASH, except that they're not capitalized. But wait — what about the C shell's environment variables?

Table 5-3 lists some of them. Some environment variables have the same names as the predefined variables listed in Table 5-2, except that the names are capitalized.

The guy who wrote the C shell (Bill, whom we talked about at considerable length in *UNIX For Dummies*) evidently thought that it would make life easier if he made lowercase shell variables that sometimes but not always are equivalent to uppercase environment variables. Well, OK, we suppose that somewhere there may be a planet on which that technique would be simpler, and maybe Bill even lives there. But we find it darn confusing.

Table 5-3	Environment Variables in the C Shell
Variable	**Meaning**
HOME	Your home directory (same as the predefined *home* variable)
LOGNAME or *USER*	Your username or login name (same as the predefined *user* variable)
MAIL	File that contains your incoming mail (not the same as the predefined *mail* variable, which can contain information about multiple mailboxes)
PATH	Your search path (sort of the same as the predefined *path* variable, except that *PATH* separates its names with colons and *path* separates them with spaces)
PWD	Your current working directory (same as the predefined *cwd* variable)
TERM	Type of terminal you are using (or type that your PC program is pretending to be — same as the predefined *term* variable)
TERMCAP	Filename of the file that contains information about how your terminal works (often set to /etc/termcap)

To set the values of environment variables (the capitalized ones), you use the `setenv` command, and you don't use an equal sign (who thinks this stuff up?). To set the TERM environment variable to VT100, for example, you use this command:

```
setenv TERM VT100
```

To see a list of all the environment variables, type **setenv** on a line all by itself.

Don't go fooling around with the values of your environment and predefined variables. These variables have been set with values handpicked on your behalf by your system administrator or whoever set up your account. Be sure that you know what you are doing before you change them.

Changes to the values of predefined and environment variables last only until you log out or even sooner. If you want to change a value for good, change the way it is set in your `.login` or `.profile` file, as described in Chapter 7, "Setting Things Up Nice."

How do I put my directory in my prompt?

DOS users are often accustomed to setting their command prompt so that it tells them what directory they're in. Can you do the same thing in UNIX? Sure! (You can do *anything* in UNIX if you're persistent enough.) Is it easy? No, not particularly.

In the C shell, type this arcane command or — better — put it in your .cshrc file:

```
alias cd 'chdir \!* && set
   prompt="$cwd>"
```

This command says to make the cd command an alias that first does a chdir (the true name of cd)

and then sets the prompt to the current directory and an angle bracket. Be sure to get the single and double quotes right.

In the Bourne and Korn shells and BASH, you can do roughly the same thing, although you can't call it cd because that name is already taken. Again, to create a command named c that changes directories and sets the prompt to the current directory, you can type this command to the shell or (again, better) put it in your .profile file:

```
alias c='cd $* ; PS1="$PWD>"'
```

Chapter 6
Fancy Script Commands

● ●

In This Chapter

▶ If this, then that

▶ Asking questions and getting answers

▶ Repeating commands (looping)

▶ Handling errors

▶ Testing and debugging scripts

● ●

A s we mentioned in Chapter 4, "An Introduction to Scripts," it's best to use the Bourne shell to interpret your scripts, especially if they involve the fancy commands discussed in this chapter. To ensure that the Bourne shell is in charge of running your script, include the line `#!/bin/sh` as the first line in your script (all the commands in this chapter work in the Bourne shell). And remember that you can still use the C shell, the Korn shell, or BASH for everything else.

Making Smarter Shell Scripts

You've learned how to use commands in scripts — the same commands you type on the command line. That's all well and good, but you can also use other commands to make your shell scripts even more useful. You can make a script do one thing if a file exists, for example, and make it do another thing if it doesn't. Or a script can perform a set of commands over and over, one time for each file in a directory. If you don't watch out, your scripts can end up as complicated as a serious program, and you can spend hours debugging them.

Return of the program

When each UNIX or shell command finishes its work, its final act is to issue a *return value,* or *exit status.* This value usually indicates whether the command worked or failed. If a command returns a status of zero, it means that the command worked. If it returns anything else, there was a problem. The return value of zero is also referred to as a *true value.*

A few commands don't return an exit status correctly, particularly some for which it's not clear what success means (a program such as xtetris, for example). If you're not sure about a particular program in a script, you can test it this way, in the Bourne or Korn shell or BASH:

```
$ dubious command ; echo $?
```

The echo command prints the exit status of the command — zero or whatever.

Sensitivity training: If this, then that

To make scripts do different things depending on conditions, you can use the if command to determine whether a command returned a true (zero) or false (nonzero) return value. If it returns a true value, you can issue one command; if it didn't, you can issue another.

Here's what the if command looks like:

```
if command-to-test
then commands-to-do
fi
```

You type the word **if** followed by the command whose return value you want to test. Then you type the word **then** followed by the command (or commands) you want to perform if that first command ran OK. Then you type the word **fi**. (OK, we know that it's not a real word. It's the word *if* spelled backward, if you must know.) Each of the keywords if, then, and fi must begin on a separate line.

To tell your script to make changes to a file only if it can make a backup copy of the file, for example, you type something like this:

```
if cp data data-backup
then update-data
fi
```

fi?

You may be wondering what sort of wacko would end his `if` commands with `fi` rather than with something normal, such as `endif`. The answer is a European wacko.

Back in the Cenozoic era of computing, when vertebrates began to climb out of the primordial ooze — (sorry, our metaphors are getting ahead of us. We actually mean about 1966 — but speaking of geological history, if you saw the movie *Jurassic Park*, did you notice the scene in which the two kids find the computer center? They're staring at the intimidating central console, and one says, "Hey, this is a UNIX system! I know how to run this!" They added that line for the movie. It wasn't in the book. Hmm. But we digress.) Anyway, back in 1966 there was a computer programming language called Algol60. It was defined by an eminent international committee way back in 1960. Algol60 was a rather nice language, nice enough that it often has been described as a great improvement over most of its successors. But Algol60 wasn't widely used, mostly because its definition was incomplete. Each version of Algol60 had to fill in the gaps in the definition, and because the various fill-ins were all different, a program that worked with one version of Algol60 rarely would work with another.

That situation was a great disappointment to the international academic computing community that had sponsored Algol60, so they convened another eminent committee to fix it. But two rather divergent schools of thought emerged about what the new committee should do:

- Fill in the gaps in Algol60 and produce a more completely defined language that was still essentially Algol60 (the "small project" faction).

- Take advantage of everything that had been learned in the intervening years and define a really great language (the "large project" faction).

The project was hijacked by a bunch of large-project extremists from Europe who defined the language to end all languages, called Algol68. In many ways, it is indeed the language to end all languages — it is beautifully symmetrical in design, with almost none of the internal inconsistencies in most other languages, but the defining report remains an exemplar of impenetrable technical formalisms, baffling even to computer-language specialists, despite having an encouraging quote from *Winnie the Pooh* at the beginning of each chapter. As part of the symmetrical business, various statements are bracketed by `if ... fi`, `do ... od`, and so on. (Legend says that comments would be bracketed by `comment ... tnemmoc`, but they wimped out on that.) You don't have to use any of those words, in fact, because they defined punctuation equivalents for every keyword. The following line, therefore:

```
if a then b else c fi
```

can be written equally well as:

```
(a | b | c)
```

(The hijackers were for the most part native speakers of languages other than English, and this situation let them get those ugly English words out of their programs.)

Anyway, Algol68 achieved modest success in Europe, and if you can figure out the language (which isn't all that difficult, as long as you can find a copy of one of the introductory books that explains it in terms humans can understand, all of which are now long since out of print), it is in many ways a nice language in which to write programs. Some years later, an English guy named Steve Bourne was working at Bell Labs and writing a new shell program for UNIX. He decided that he wanted it to look as much as possible like his favorite language — Algol68! So that's how we got `fi`, `esac`, `elif`, and all the rest of those Algol68-isms in the Bourne shell.

The shell performs the `cp` command first: It tries to copy your `data` file and make a backup copy named `data-backup`. If the `cp` command succeeds, it runs the `update-data` program, whatever that is. If it can't copy the file for some reason, it doesn't run the `update-data` program.

Or else!

You can also tell your script to do something if a condition *isn't* true. You use the `else` command, which looks like this:

```
if cp data data-backup
then update-data
else echo Cannot back up the data file!
fi
```

If the `cp` command can't make a backup copy of the `data` file, this script doesn't run the `update-data` program — it just displays a message.

You even use a string of `if` tests in a command, one after the other, like this:

```
if condition1
then do something
elif condition2
then do something else
else do a third thing
fi
```

If you are going to test for more than two different conditions, consider using a `case` command instead, as described later in this chapter, in the section "Lots of possibilities!"

Lots of stuff to do

You can include more than one command in each of the sections of your script, as shown in this example:

```
if cp data data-backup
then echo Data file backed up!
    update-data
else echo Can't back up the data file!
fi
```

(You can even put several commands in the if section, in which case the last command in the section is the one that gets tested. If this technique doesn't sound very useful, that's because it isn't. But it's consistent.)

Scripts are easier to read if you type them neatly. If you have several lines of commands in the then or else sections of the if command, indent them. We usually indent them about eight spaces, like this:

```
if condition
then      command1
          command2
          command3
else      command4
          command5
fi
```

Remember that neatness counts! You may not think so now, but you definitely will think so six months from now, when you have to go back and figure out how an old script of yours works.

Testing, testing

The if command performs different commands depending on whether the condition has a return value of true (successful, or zero) versus false (unsuccessful, nonzero). But what if you want to do one thing if a file exists and another thing if it doesn't? No problem — you can use the test command.

The test command is great for checking a variety of conditions. It can check whether files and directories exist, as shown in Table 6-1. It can check on the values of variables, as shown in Table 6-2. It can even check whether any or all of a list of conditions are met, as shown in Table 6-3. If the file exists or a variable has a certain value, the test command returns a value of true: otherwise, it returns a false value.

Table 6-1	Testing Files
What You Type	*What It Does*
[-f *filename*]	Tests whether *filename* exists and is a file
[-d *dirname*]	Tests whether *dirname* exists and is a directory
[-r *filename*]	Tests whether *filename* exists and you have permission to read it

(continued)

Table 6-1 *(continued)*

What You Type	What It Does
[-w *filename*]	Tests whether *filename* exists and you have permission to modify it
[-x *filename*]	Tests whether *filename* exists and you have permission to execute it (run it as a program)
[-s *filename*]	Tests whether *filename* exists and has something in it (as opposed to existing but being empty, with a size of zero)
[*file1* -nt *file2*]	Tests whether *file1* is newer than *file2* (Korn shell only)
[*file1* -ot *file2*]	Tests whether *file1* is older than *file2* (Korn shell only)

Table 6-2   Testing Variables

What You Type	What It Does
[*text*]	Tests whether *text* has some characters in it rather than being null
[*text1* = *text2*]	Tests whether *text1* is identical to *text2*
[*text1*! = *text2*]	Tests whether *text1* is not identical to *text2*
[-n *text*]	Tests whether *text* has some characters in it (same as [*text*])
[-z *text*]	Tests whether *text* is blank (has a length of zero)
[*num1* -eq *num2*]	Tests whether *num1* is numerically equal to *num2,* where both are integers
[*num1* -ne *num2*]	Tests whether *num1* is numerically not equal to *num2,* where both are integers
[*num1* -ge *num2*]	Tests whether *num1* is numerically greater than or equal to *num2,* where both are integers
[*num1* -gt *num2*]	Tests whether *num1* is numerically greater than *num2,* where both are integers
[*num1* -lt *num2*]	Tests whether *num1* is numerically less than *num2,* where both are integers
[*num1* -le *num2*]	Tests whether *num1* is numerically less than or equal to *num2,* where both are integers

Table 6-3	Combining Tests
What You Type	**What It Does**
[! \(*condition* \)]	Tests whether the condition is false (you have to write the parentheses as \(and \) so that the shell doesn't interpret them itself)
[*condition1* -a *condition2*]	Tests whether *condition1* and *condition2* are true; returns a true value only if both are true
[*condition1* -o *condition2*]	Tests whether either *condition1* or *condition2* are true; returns a true value if either or both are true

Here's how you use it. This example uses the -f option to test whether a file exists:

```
if test -f final.results
then echo Done!
else echo Didn't work!
fi
```

The command `test -f final-results` returns a true value if a file named `final-results` is in the current directory and returns a false value otherwise.

Rather than type the command `test`, you can put the item to be tested inside square brackets. (Remember Algol68 and how every single command had an equivalent that used only punctuation?) That is, rather than type this line:

```
if test -f final.results
```

you can type this line:

```
if [ -f final.results ]
```

We find that using square brackets is a little easier to read.

Be sure to leave a space before and after each square bracket! Otherwise, you get a syntax error or other obnoxious remark from the shell.

File, are you there?

This section presents some examples of how to use the `if`, `then`, `else`, `fi`, and `test` commands to let your scripts tell you which files and directories exist.

For example, this piece of a script creates a `Budget` directory if it doesn't exist:

```
#!/bin/sh
if [ ! -d Budget ]
then mkdir Budget
fi
```

You can use wildcard characters (* and ?) in the filenames you check. You can check whether any files begin with *data,* for example, and if they do, you can concatenate them all together into a new file named `alldata`:

```
#!/bin/sh
if [ -f data* ]
then cat data* > alldata
fi
```

Or you might want to use one file if it exists and otherwise use another file:

```
if [ -f data1 ]
then cp data1 datafile
elif [ -f data2 ]
then cp data2 datafile
else echo Problem!
fi
```

Testing command-line arguments

You can also use the `if` and `test` commands (or any other commands, for that matter) to check what's on the command that runs your script. Table 6-4 lists some special *built-in variables* the Bourne and Korn shells provide to let you use the information typed on the command line. As you will recall from Chapter 4, "An Introduction to Scripts," an *argument* is a piece of information that is typed on the command line after the command name. Arguments are separated by spaces.

Some built-in variables work in only the Bourne and Korn shells and BASH, which we recommend that you use for executing scripts. The variables have different names in the C shell.

Table 6-4	What's on Your Command Line?
Variable	*Description*
$#	Number of arguments on the command line
$1	First argument (the first word on the command line after the command, not counting options)
$2	Second argument (you can guess what *$3, $4,* and so on are)
$*	All the arguments

If you type this command line, for example:

```
cp junk backup_of_junk
```

the first argument ($1) is junk, and the second argument ($2) is backup_of_junk.

The following section of script checks to see whether the first argument on the command line is "total":

```
if [ $1 = "total" ]
then year_end_proc
else monthly_proc
fi
```

If the first argument is total, it runs one program and otherwise runs a different program.

But what if there is no first argument — what if the user doesn't type a single, blessed thing after the command? The script produces an error message like this one:

```
myscript: test: argument expected
```

You had better make the script smart enough to notice when it has no arguments, like this:

```
if [ $# = 0 ]
then echo Type an argument!
elif [ $1 = "total" ]
    then year_end_proc
    else monthly_proc
fi
```

The first if checks whether there are any arguments and displays a rude message if there aren't. If there is an argument, the script runs one program if the first argument is *total* and another program otherwise.

Arguments on the command line can be options. Tradition dictates that options always begin with a dash, and they control how the command works. The -l option to the ls command, for example, tells ls to print the long format listing of files. When you type ls -l plugh, for example, the -l is the first argument, and the filename plugh is the second argument.

Suppose that you have a script called pp that runs a file through pr to pretty it up and then sends it to the printer:

```
#!/bin/sh
pr $1 | lpr
```

How about adding to the script a -t option that puts a title on the output? That's easy:

```
#!/bin/sh
if [ "$1" = "-t" ]
then
    pr -h "Today's extremely important report" $2 | lpr
else
    pr $1 | lpr
fi
```

If the first argument to the script is -t, you run the pr command and give it a -h argument for the title, along with the specified filename. (The filename is now $2 because the -t was $1.) Otherwise, you print the file in the same way as you did earlier.

A star is Bourne

What happens if your arguments include wildcard characters? We alluded to this situation in Chapter 4, "An Introduction to Scripts," but here's the real answer. The shell automagically expands an argument with wildcards into a list of the names that match. (*Automagically* is a highly technical term that means "using a clever technique we don't feel like explaining just now.") If you type the following line, for example:

```
pp -t *.txt
```

the shell acts exactly as though you had typed this line:

```
pp -t chico.txt ivan.txt milton.txt tom.txt
```

or whatever .txt files are in your directory. As long as you write your scripts to handle multiple arguments, you get wildcards handled for free.

Testing Variables

Remember those variables we talked about in Chapter 5, "The Shell Game: Using Shell Variables"? You can use variables in scripts, as we already told you. Now let's look at doing different things in a script depending on the value of a variable.

You can make a script that performs different commands, for example, depending on who runs the script:

```
if [ "$LOGNAME" = dave ]
then killer.solitaire
else budget_update
fi
```

You should put double quotes around the variables you are testing in case the variables contain funny characters that might otherwise confuse the shell. The following part of a script, for example, tests whether there are three arguments on the command line:

```
if [ "$#" = 3 ]
then echo This script requires three arguments.
else do_command_whatever
fi
```

Lots of possibilities!

If you want to test for several conditions and do various things depending on which condition turns out to be true, you can end up with a long, strange, and convoluted if command, like this:

```
if condition
then buncha commands
elif another condition
then some other commands
elif yet another condition
then some more commands
else a final bunch of commands
fi
```

This stuff can get a tad confusing. If you're testing the same variable over and over, rather than use an if command, you might do better with a case command, like this:

```
case value in
    pattern1) commands ;;
    pattern2) commands ;;
    pattern3) commands ;;
esac
```

Yes, esac is *case* spelled backward. And yes, that's a single, unmatched close parenthesis after each pattern. And yes, those are two — count 'em, two — semicolons after each set of commands. (See the nearby "fi?" sidebar to see where this strange syntax came from.)

The following scrap of script does different things depending on the value of the second argument on the command line:

```
case "$2" in
    Y)      proc=Y
            year_end_processing ;;
    M)      proc=M
            month_end_processing ;;
    D)      proc=D
            daily_processing ;;
    T)      echo Just testing! ;;
esac
```

The patterns can include some special characters to make them more flexible. Stars, question marks, and square brackets work in the same way as they do in filename patterns. A vertical bar (|) separates two patterns, like this:

```
    Y|y)    response=yes ;;
```

Vertical bars are useful for making patterns that respond in the same way to capital and small letters. Another way to include several characters in a pattern is by enclosing them in square brackets, like this:

```
    -[nN])  new=yes ;;
```

This pattern matches either -n or -N.

It's also a good idea to include an "all other" option. The last pattern in your case command can be an asterisk, which matches anything, like this:

```
*)        echo Unknown argument - try again ;;
```

The case command stops as soon as it finds a pattern that matches the value. If it gets to the last pattern, it hasn't matched any of the preceding ones. So if the last pattern is an asterisk, it matches any value that didn't match any of the other patterns.

You can use the asterisk as part of a pattern too. The following line, for example, matches any word that begins with *y:*

```
[Yy]*)  response=yes ;;
```

Asking Questions and Getting Answers

As your scripts get longer and fancier, you might want them to ask you some questions. A script can ask for confirmation, for example, before deleting a file or doing something that will take a long time. To listen for what the user types and then stick it in a variable, you can use the read command, like this:

```
read ok-to-delete
```

It's a good idea to precede a read command with an echo command, to tell the user what information you are asking for. The read command takes what the user types and stuffs it in the variable you name (ok-to-delete, in this case). After the read command, you can put in an if or case command to take action depending on what the user typed.

This series of commands asks the user whether to delete a file, waits for a response, and deletes the file if the user types anything that begins with a *y:*

```
echo -n "Delete the backup file? "
read ok-to-delete
case ok-to-delete in
   [Yy]*)  rm data_backup ;;
    *)        echo Not deleting the file! ;;
esac
```

(The -n in the echo command tells it not to begin a new line after it prints the prompt.)

Repeating the Same Commands Over Again One More Time

The entire point of many scripts is to save having to type the same commands over and over. You may even want one script to repeat the same set of commands a couple of times. As usual, UNIX (the Bourne shell, actually) provides a way — several ways, if you must know.

Performing a group of commands more than one time is called *looping:* You create a loop of commands, and the shell goes around and around the loop, executing them. It is important that you tell the shell when to *stop* going around the loop or else you loop forever. (And it will drive you loopy.)

The most common way to make a loop is by using the while, do, and done commands, like this:

```
while condition
do
      commands galore
done
```

The condition that comes after while works in the same way as if conditions do — see the section "Making Smarter Shell Scripts," earlier in this chapter. You may have to use the test command in the condition to check the value of a variable or the status of a file or directory.

Suppose that you have a lock file created by another program that may be running at the same time and you have to wait until the lock goes away:

```
while [ -f lock_file ]
do
      sleep 10  # pause 10 seconds before you try again
done
```

A similar way to make a loop uses the until command, like this:

```
until condition
do
      commands galore
done
```

The commands between the do and done commands are repeated until the condition is true.

Give me a break!

Here's another way to make the loop stop looping. Rather than use a condition, you type **true**, which is a command that is always true. Inside the loop, use the `break` command, which stops the loop dead in its tracks.

The following piece of script searches for the filenames the user types. When the user types a period, the loop ends:

```
# Find the filename the user enters
while true
do
        # ask for the filename
        echo -n "Filename to find (type . to stop)? "
        read filename
        # stop if it's .
        if [ "$filename" = . ]
                then break
        fi
        # find the file
        find /usr/$LOGNAME -name "$filename" -print
done
```

The script prompts for a filename, which is stored in the variable `filename`. If the variable `filename` contains a single period, the user wants to stop using the program. The `break` command ends the loop and jumps down to after the `done` command.

Time to downshift!

In Chapter 5, "The Shell Game: Using Shell Variables," we told you that you can use the variables *$1, $2, $3,* and so on to represent the first, second third, and so on arguments on the command line. This is true, but we didn't tell you about the bizarre `shift` command.

The `shift` command slides all the arguments down one place. The second argument, which starts out in *$2,* moves into *$1.* The value of *$3* shifts into *$2, $4* moves over into *$3,* and so on. That is, all the arguments move down one place, and the first argument disappears.

"What on earth?!" you may say. Well, here's why this bizarre command is useful and why we're telling you about it now. You can use the `shift` command to peel off arguments one at a time, often in a `while/do/done` loop, to do something to each argument on the command line. The following script, for example, displays the contents of each file on the command line:

```
#!/bin/sh
echo Displaying $# files
while [ $# -gt 0 ]
do
        echo ==========
        echo Filename: $1
        echo ==========
        more $1
        shift
done
```

The $# variable tells you how many arguments are on the command line. Every time the shift command renames the arguments, $# goes down by one number. The condition [$# -gt 0] makes the while loop stop repeating when the number of arguments that remain ($#) is no longer greater than (-gt) zero.

If you store this script in a file named display and use the chmod command to make it executable, you can type a command like this:

```
display data1 data2
```

to display the contents of two files named data1 and data2. You see this result:

```
Displaying 2 files
==========
Filename: data1
==========
1.5673
5.285
7.4234

==========
Filename: data2
==========
Washington, George
Adams, John
Jefferson, Thomas
```

(This data isn't impressive-looking, but you get the idea.)

The shift command is also handy when one or two of the arguments to a script can be options while the rest are filenames. As an example, let's improve the pp script from a few pages back so that it can handle lots of files rather than just one.

You've learned that you can specify all the arguments by using $*, so in a script you can print all the files given as arguments to the script by using this line:

```
pr $* | lpr
```

If the user types pp -t filea fileb filec, though, how do you specify the three filenames without also getting the –t option? The trick is that you peel off the option by using shift, at which point $* refers to only the remaining arguments. So here's the improved pp command:

```
#!/bin/sh
if [ "$1" = "-t" ]
then
    shift   # get rid of -t argument
    pr -h "Today's extremely important report" $* | lpr
else
    pr $* | lpr
fi
```

Coming to the for

One of the most common things to do in a shell script is to repeat a sequence of commands one time for each argument. You learned about a way to do that by using while, but this sort of repeating is so common that the shell has an easier way to handle it. Suppose that you frequently send e-mail files to your friends. The first version, a script called mailit, mails a single file to your friend Fred:

```
#!/bin/sh
mail fred < $1
```

You run this script by typing this line:

```
mailit filename
```

and substituting the name of the file you want to mail to Fred.

Now dress it up a little, and have it put in the message a subject line that says which file it is sending:

```
#!/bin/sh
mail -s "Copy of file $1" fred < $1
```

What if you want to mail several files with one command, such as `mailit astrud.txt elis.txt gal.txt`? The `for` loop does the trick:

```
#!/bin/sh
for fname
do
    mail -s "Copy of file $fname" fred < $fname
done
```

This loop is sort of like a `while` loop, with the `do` and `done`, but a `for` at the front is followed by the name of a variable to use inside the loop. (Notice in this one place that the name appears *without* a dollar sign.) Then there's a command that uses that variable. The `for` loop first sets `fname` to the first argument, does the body of the loop (the stuff between `do` and `done`), then sets it to the second argument, and so on. So if you run this newest `mailit` with three filenames or with a star pattern that turns into three filenames, it runs the mail program three times for the three files.

Finally, what if you want to be able to send mail to more than one person? The final `mailit` takes the name of the person to mail to, followed by the filenames:

```
#!/bin/sh
who=$1      # save the recipient as $who
shift

for fname
do
    mail -s "Copy of file $fname" $who < $fname
done
```

First it saves a copy of `$1` in the variable `who`. Then it uses `shift` to get rid of `$1` so that the `for` loop handles only the rest of the arguments, which are the filenames to mail. This method is in fact the most common way to use `shift`: Use it to handle any flags or other special arguments at the beginning of the script, and then use a `for` loop or `$*` to handle the rest of them.

Would you like to see the menu?

Using all the tricks you've seen in this chapter, you can build a menu by using a script. Check this out:

```
while true
do
    echo
    echo ======MY MAIN MENU======
    echo
    echo E        to run the emacs editor
    echo M        to read your mail using elm
    echo N        to read newsgroups using trn
    echo Q        to quit
    echo
    echo Type your choice, and press Enter:
    read choice
    case $choice in
        [eE])    emacs ;;
        [mM])    elm ;;
        [nN])    trn ;;
        [qQ])    break ;;
        [xX])    break ;;
    esac
done
echo Exiting from the menu!
```

The loop displays the menu, by using a bunch of echo commands. Then it waits
for the user to type something, using the read command, and stores in the
variable choice what is typed. Then a case command executes the command
the user wanted. We never can remember when to press Q for Quit or X for
eXit, so this menu generously responds to either Q or X by ending the loop, by
using a break command.

Handling Errors

A well-written shell script should check for errors wherever it's practical.
(Yeah, we know, you never make errors, but someone else less fortunate may
use your script someday.)

In most cases, the most sensible thing to do in case of an error is to bail out
with an error message and let the user try again. It doesn't make much sense to
run the preceding mailit script without at least a recipient's address and one
filename, so you can check to be sure that it has at least two arguments:

```
#!/bin/sh
if [ $# -lt 2 ]
then
    echo "$0: must give recipient address and at least one
            file"
    exit 1
fi

who=$1    # save the recipient as $who
... rest of the script above ...
```

The if test should look familiar. Then you use echo to print an informative message. The $0 turns into the name of the script, which can be useful if you have one script that calls another script that calls a third script and so on and one of the internal scripts fails.

Then you exit, which means just what it sounds like: You stop the script completely. You can specify a number after the exit command to tell it which exit value to return. In this case, the script failed, so you return 1 to indicate that it didn't work.

Testing and Debugging Scripts

Writing shell scripts is not terribly difficult as long as you go about it in a sensible way. The wrong way to do it is to write an entire 100-line script and then be surprised when it doesn't work. (It's not you — we can't write 100-line scripts on our first try either. Indeed, we think that we're doing well to get five correct lines in a row.)

Build them a piece at a time

Start small, and work your way up. Look at the way you built the mailit script earlier, starting with a few lines, and then add more features after the core of it works.

Put in echo statements

When you're not sure what your script is doing, put in echo statements so that it tells you (in a for loop, for example):

```
for f
do
    echo now working on $f
    ... other stuff ...
done
```

After you've gotten your script to work, don't delete those debugging echo statements. Turn them into comments by putting a # in front of each one. Then, later, when you make more changes to your script and it breaks, you have them there to uncomment and figure out what went wrong.

Use the built-in tracing

The shell has two built-in tracing features. You can have it display the text of a script as it reads the script, and you can have it print each command as it executes it. For both kinds of tracing, you have to run the shell explicitly with sh. To see the text of the script as it reads it, use the -v (verbose) flag:

```
sh -v mailit elvis xuxa.txt
```

To see each command as it's eXecuted (this is called *execute trace*), use -x:

```
sh -x mailit elvis xuxa.txt
```

Each command is printed preceded by a plus sign and with any variable or argument substitutions already done. You can also do both at one time:

```
sh -vx mailit elvis xuxa.txt
```

We find both kinds of tracing useful, but the execute trace usually is a faster way to figure out what a script is doing and how it got there.

Chapter 7

Setting Things Up Nice

· ·

In This Chapter

▶ Scripts that run automatically when you log in and run the Bourne or Korn shell or BASH

▶ Ditto for when you log in and run the C shell

▶ Other configuration files

· ·

*B*efore you started your UNIX account, someone set it all up for you. In addition to creating the account and making a cozy, little home directory for you, this benefactor set up one or more scripts that automatically create a comfortable environment in which you can work.

Which files do this work depends on which shell you use. If you use the Bourne or Korn shell or BASH, read on. If you use the C shell, skip down to the section "She Sells C Shells," later in this chapter.

If you run Motif (or any other graphical interface), you have scores of other configuration files too. Chapter 16, "Mutant Motif," gives you more information.

Bourne Again

If you run the Bourne or Korn shell or BASH, when you log in, the following scripts are run automatically:

▶ `/etc/profile`

▶ `$HOME/.profile` (that is, the `.profile` file in your home directory)

Everyone's profile

The /etc/profile script is run whenever *anyone* logs in. You can take a look at it by typing this command:

```
more /etc/profile
```

You shouldn't be able to change this file unless you are a system administrator, and you shouldn't even think about changing it anyway unless you are a UNIX guru, because the commands in this file affect *all* the users on your UNIX system. Errors in this file screw up everyone.

The /etc/profile script contains settings that are the same for most users — such as the time zone you are in. This script might also set up a search path containing the directories in which commonly used programs are stored.

Your own private profile

Each user has her own profile script as well, named .profile and stored in each user's home directory. Because the filename begins with a period, the file doesn't appear in normal file listings. (To see hidden files — those with filenames that begin with a period — you use the command ls -a.)

You can see, and edit, your own profile script by using any text editor. Most of what your profile does is set variables to their proper values. These variables then affect all the programs you run.

Here's a typical .profile file:

```
MAIL=/usr/mail/${LOGNAME:?}

if [ "`tty`" != "/dev/console" ] && [ "`tty|cut -c1-7`" != "/
          dev/vt" ]
then
      echo "TERM=\c"
      read TERM
      stty 2400 kill ^U
fi

HZ=100  # rate at which internal clock ticks
umask 002
PATH=$PATH:/usr/local/bin:/usr/ucb:$HOME/bin
export MAIL PATH HZ TERM
```

First, the profile script sets the MAIL variable to contain the directory in which your mail lives. Then it sets the TERM variable, depending on information from the tty command, which tells from which port you've logged in. It also uses the umask command to set the default permissions for new files and directories. It adds a few directories to the end of your search path. At the end, it exports the values of all the variables it created or changed so that the values remain after the script ends.

You can edit your profile script by using your text editor.

If you mess up your .profile file, you can make your account unusable. To fix it, you have to go crawling to your system administrator, preferably armed with such potent bribes as cookies or pizza. So be *very careful* when you edit your profile. Keep a backup copy, just in case. And don't delete lines you don't think you want. Instead, comment them out (that is, turn them into comments) by adding a pound sign (#) at the beginning of the line. Unless you're a UNIX pro, there are usually lines you don't understand (like the if line in the preceding example). Just leave them alone!

We generally recommend that you leave your profile alone, except for adding lines to the end. You can add variable definitions to save yourself typing, like this:

```
# Beginning of lines I added to this profile
BOOK=/usr/john1/book/moreunix
```

It's great to define variables or paths you use frequently; by sticking the definitions in your .profile file, they are defined every time you log in. You might also want to add lines to run programs automatically, such as calendar, backup programs, or whatever.

That's all for you Bourne and Korn shell and BASH users. The next section talks about how the shell works, so we recommend that you skip down to the "Miscellaneous Files" section.

She Sells C Shells

If you run the C shell, when you log in, these scripts are run automatically:

- .cshrc
- .login

The .cshrc script (which stands for "C shell resource" and is pronounced "see-shirk") is run every time you run the C shell. If you use Motif or another graphical interface, .cshrc runs every time you open an xterm window that runs the C shell (a window in which you can give C shell commands).

When you log out, the C shell runs the script .logout automatically. You can use it to clean things up, back up files, or whatever else you want to happen at the end of each session. Most people don't have .logout files. If you don't, you can always make one by using your text editor.

Here's a typical .cshrc file:

```
# set so ctrl-d does not log us out
set ignoreeof=1

# set so our history list is 100 deep
set history=100
setenv history 100

# set so the history will be saved between logout and login
set savehist=100
setenv savehist 100

#set control characters for jobs control
stty swtch ^Z
stty erase ^H
```

The .cshrc might also set the prompt and define *aliases* (shorthand names for commands).

Here's a sample .login file:

```
# set to check for mail every 2 mins.
setenv MAIL /usr/mail/$LOGNAME
set mail=(120 $MAIL)

if('tty' != "/dev/console"  &&  "'tty|cut -c1-7'" != "/dev/
          vt" )then
        echo -n "TERM="
        set tterm='line'
        setenv TERM $tterm[1]
        unset tterm
endif

set path=($path /usr/local/bin)
setenv HZ 100
```

The script sets a bunch of environment variables (Chapter 5, "The Shell Game: Using Shell Variables," provides information about how environment variables work), including MAIL, TERM, and HZ. You can also add lines to run programs automatically, such as backup programs or a graphical interface such as Motif.

Miscellaneous Files

In addition to the scripts that run automatically when you log in, you probably have other files that control the way things work when you use UNIX. Many UNIX programs, including most text editors, mail programs, and newsreaders, use hidden configuration files stored in your home directory.

You might want to type **ls -a** right now in your home directory, in fact, to see what hidden files are lurking there. You may spot the following:

- ✔ elm: Used by the elm mail reader

- ✔ .signature: Used by most mail readers to store the standard closing to be appended to all outgoing mail

- ✔ .newsrc and .oldnewsrc: Used by most newsreaders to keep track of which Usenet newsgroups you subscribe to and articles in them you've already read

- ✔ .plan and .project: Text files that appear when other people finger you

- ✔ .lastlogin: An empty file whose creation date and time show when you last logged in

The 5th Wave   By Rich Tennant

"Keep in mind, should you decide to make us your strategic vendor, I can't promise horsey-rides every time I come by."

Chapter 8

Down by the Old Text Stream

You may recall — particularly if you are one of our devoted readers who has memorized *UNIX For Dummies* and recites parts of it at stressful moments — that UNIX has an ancient text-editing program called ed. The way it works is, in theory at least, relatively simple. First, it loads the entire file from the disk. Then the commands that say what to do come from the standard input (usually the keyboard and sometimes a pipe from another program) one line at a time. Each command can affect the entire file. At the end, the results go back to a file.

One day a few years back, one of the UNIX guys had a bright idea: Turn ed inside out. Now all the commands are loaded first. Then the text is read from the standard input, one line at a time, and all the commands are (potentially) applied to each line. The result goes to the standard output. This technique isn't useful as a text editor, but it makes a fine *stream editor* (therefore, the name sed) that edits a stream of text as it flows by.

Sed turns out to be useful for all sorts of things:

> ✔ **"Batch" editing:** For those times when you want to make the same set of changes to a bunch of files or repeatedly to a single file
>
> ✔ **Simple text processing:** For example, changing the word *chairman* to *chairbeing* wherever it occurs in a file (we try to avoid being species-ist)
>
> ✔ **Text manipulation:** In combination with other commands

Sed is particularly handy when it's combined with other utilities in shell scripts. We frequently use it to adjust the output of one command to make it suitable as the input for another. Because this process is better shown than described, we return to it after a discussion of how sed works.

What to Say to sed

Sed, fortunately, lets you begin slowly and then work up to more and more grandiose editing when you need to. You can put the editing commands either in a file or on the command line; for all except the hugest jobs, it's easier to put them on the command line.

Let's try that chairbeing example. The way you change one thing to another in ed or vi is with the s command, like this:

```
s/chairman/chairbeing/
```

This command replaces an occurrence of the word *chairman* with the word *chairbeing.* In sed, you do the same thing:

```
sed 's/chairman/chairbeing/' minutes > new-minutes
```

This command line runs sed and tells it to use the chairbeing command on all the lines in the file minutes and put the result in the file new-minutes.

We always put the editing command in quotation marks, even in cases like this one, where it doesn't make any difference.

What if you want to make several replacements? Most versions of sed let you put multiple commands on separate lines, like this:

```
sed 's/chairman/chairbeing/
s/slave/administrative assistant/' minutes > new-minutes
```

This two-line command line contains two replacement commands for sed to perform. (C shell users have to put a backslash — \ — at the end of each line of the command except for the last one to reassure the shell that you really do intend to continue this command to the next line. The Bourne and Korn shells and BASH believe you, so no backslash is necessary.)

Don't use the same file as the input and output; for reasons not interesting enough to explain, you end up with an empty file. Instead, send the results to a different file and then rename it, like this:

```
sed 's/greasy/self-basting/' foods > new-foods
mv new-foods foods
```

Let's Be Selective

The most common thing people do with sed is a simple search-and-replace, as in the preceding examples. Naturally, because computers are involved, nothing is quite as simple as it seems.

Too much to type

Typing all those long patterns begins to get tiresome about the second time you have to do it. Fortunately, because you already know how to create a shell script (see Chapter 4, "An Introduction to Scripts"), you can put the commands in a shell script. For example, let's flesh out the script to translate any document to a politically correct version. Name the script polcor:

```
#!/bin/sh
# make a file politically correct
sed 's/chairman/chairbeing/
s/slave/administrative assistant/' $1 > new-$1
mv $1 old-$1
mv new-$1 $1
```

The first line tells the system that it's a Bourne shell script. Then a sed command reads the filename you typed as the first argument on the command line when you ran polcor. This sed command creates a new version of the file. Then it saves the original file as old-whatever and renames the new version in place of the original file. (Saving the original file is always a good idea, just in case you goof up the changes.)

We lied

That should do it, right? Not exactly.

We gave you the impression that this is all you have to do to change every instance of *old* to *new* in a file:

```
sed 's/old/new/' in-file > out-file
```

Here's what really happens:

Before: The old, old man threw rocks at the pigeons.

After: The new, old man threw rocks at the pigeons.

What happened? For reasons lost in the mists of history, the s command normally replaces only the first occurrence of a string in a line. To make it replace every occurrence, you have to add the letter *g*, for global, after the search command, like this:

```
sed 's/old/new/g' in-file > out-file
```

Now the political correctifier script looks like this:

```
sed 's/chairman/chairbeing/g
s/slave/administrative assistant/g' $1 > new-$1
mv $1 old-$1
mv new-$1 $1
```

We Don't Need No Stinking grep

Sed can do many of the things that other, simpler commands can do. Suppose that you want to find all the lines in a file that contain the word *greasy*. (We're working up to a restaurant database here.) You might use grep, like this:

```
grep greasy restaurant-list
```

Chapter 26 in *UNIX For Dummies* has information about grep (it's in the section "When You Don't Know the Filename"), but you can use sed as well.

Sed usually sends all the lines it reads to the standard output. By using the -n option, however, you can tell sed to send only the lines you specifically tell it to print. Sed's p command tells it which lines to print, like this:

```
/greasy/p
```

This sed command tells it to print lines that contain the word *greasy*. To make sed act like grep, you can use a command like this:

```
sed -n '/greasy/p' restaurant-list
```

This command tells sed to look though the file `restaurant-list` and print only the lines that contain the word _greasy_.

The obvious response is "Why bother?" So far, you haven't done anything you couldn't do with grep, but now let's dress things up a little.

Sed-o-matic

We've showed you how you can stick your sed commands in a shell script. But you hard-core sed users have another option: You can put just the editing commands in a file (called a _sed script_, naturally, for the same reason that a file of shell commands is a shell script). Then you can make the sed scripts "self-executing" so that you can have sed run them automagically by typing just the name of the sed script. Usually there isn't much advantage to using a sed script rather than a shell script. Other than the inherent coolness, the primary reasons you would want to is that the script is too long to fit on a shell command line (it's possible to write sed scripts that are hundreds of lines long, although we don't recommend that) and that it's a little faster to run sed directly from a sed script rather than from a shell script.

Here's how to make a self-executing sed script.

First store the sed commands in a file. That's easy enough; for the political correctifier, the file might contain these lines:

```
s/chairman/chairbeing/g
s/slave/administrative assistant/g
```

Notice that it contains just the commands that sed will handle, with no extra quotes or anything.

You run this sed script by using sed's -f option; so if that file were called `correctify.sed`, you would type this command:

```
sed -f correctify.sed
```

This line tells sed to perform all the commands in the file `correctify.sed`. (Incidentally, if you have sed commands in several files, you can tell sed to run all of them at one time by using several -f flags.)

Now you have to add a line to the sed script to make it self-executing so that it looks like this:

```
#!/usr/bin/sed -f
s/chairman/chairbeing/g
s/slave/administrative assistant/g
```

On that first line, you should recognize the #! as the same two characters that introduce a shell script, followed by /usr/bin/sed, which is sed's true name, and the -f flag.

Now when you type `correctify.sed`, it automatically runs sed by using the sed script.

Your basic database

Suppose that you have a file called `restaurants` that contains these lines:

```
style:greasy,price:cheap,name:House of Chow
style:greasy,price:moderate,name:Joe Bob's Fry Pit
style:bbq,price:cheap,name:Ribs 'r' Us
style:bbq,price:moderate,name:Elvis Ate Here
style:bbq,price:moderate,name:Kenny's Atomic Ribs
```

In computer lingo, you have a set of *attributed records.* In English, you have a bunch of lines, each of which has some categories and values (the categories are style, price, and name). Notice that the name of the restaurant is the last thing on each line — this is important for some of the commands you will use. Using sed, you can pick out lines that match particular patterns and then clean them up and print them.

Here's a first cut at a script called `eat` that lets you pick out restaurants of your favorite style. Make a script named `eat` that contains these commands:

```
#!/bin/sh
sed -n "/style:$1/s/.*name://p" restaurants
```

Sure is a heavy dose of punctuation there, huh? Fortunately, it's relatively easy to take apart. The first part of the sed command is

```
/style:$1/
```

The `$1` becomes the first argument on the command line (whatever you typed on the line after the `eat` command), such as `greasy` or `bbq`.

So this becomes a pattern that matches lines which contain `style:greasy` or `style:bbq` or whatever argument you typed.

The rest of the sed command reads like this:

```
s/.*name://p
```

This is a plain, old sed substitute command. If you remember your UNIX regular expressions (which you probably don't, which is why we explain them in the nearby sidebar, "How to be a regular guy"), this pattern matches any amount of text followed by `name:`. Sed matches as much as it can, so this command matches everything from the beginning of the line up through `name:` and replaces it with nothing (that is, it deletes it). Then the `p` says to print the result.

So the effect is to find lines in the file restaurants that match the style you want, trim off everything up through the name:, and print what's left, which is the name of the restaurant.

Notice that we used double quotes around the sed command, which lets the $1 work right. For reasons we don't go into, single quotes would prevent $1 from turning into the first argument on the command line.

In case that wasn't confusing enough

Sed lets you break up your commands into multiple parts, like this:

```
#!/bin/sh
sed -n "/style:$1/{
s/.*name://p
}" restaurants
```

You can have a selection pattern (it's /style:$1/ here), followed by a bunch of commands in curly brackets. Sed performs all the commands within the curly brackets on lines that match the selection pattern. In this case, the command in the brackets is the same one you saw earlier, but you can put multiple commands in the brackets if you want to make more than one change in a line.

Let's improve the political correctifier a little. Rather than correct all the old-fashioned language in a file, let's correct only that which occurs between lines containing START CORRECT and END CORRECT in the input file. Take a look at this script:

```
sed '/START CORRECT/,/END CORRECT{
    s/chairman/chairbeing/g
    s/slave/administrative assistant/g
    s/dead/metabolically challenged/g
    }'
```

You can put two patterns on any sed statement, in which case sed interprets them in the same way as ed does, from a line that matches the first pattern to a line that matches the second pattern. Within that range, you make the three substitutions. In this case, because there's no -n flag, every line gets printed regardless of whether there are any changes.

How to be a regular guy

When you're using a UNIX editor to search for a string, you might think that the normal way to say what you're searching for is to enter the string you're looking for. Silly you — you don't have Advanced UNIX Consciousness.

Some years back, guys at Bell Labs who were later to write UNIX were fooling with things called Finite State Machines, or FSMs, for short. (These theoretical mathematical machines have no moving parts or anything tawdry like that.) It turns out that these FSMs can be translated mechanically to and from a kind of string-matching pattern called a regular expression, and it additionally turns out that a computer program can handle an FSM at blinding speed, which offers a way to search text really, really fast.

So disregarding the fact that the typical files you're editing are small enough that even a slow, crummy, old-fashioned text search would be plenty fast, they hacked FSMs into all the editors, which means that on a UNIX system, whenever you do a text search, you specify it with a regular expression.

This list shows the simplest regular expression rules:

✔ A period matches any single character.

✔ A group of characters in brackets matches any one of those characters ([aeiou], for example, to match any single vowel). You can also abbreviate them with a hyphen, such as [a-z] for any lowercase letter. If the first thing in the brackets is a caret (^), it matches any character *except* the ones in the brackets, so [^0-9] matches anything except a digit.

✔ A caret (^) at the beginning of an expression matches at the beginning of the line.

✔ A dollar sign ($) at the end of the expression matches at the end of the line.

✔ Most other characters match themselves (an *x*, for example, matches an *x*).

Then there are rules for putting together regular expressions:

✔ An expression followed by a star (*) matches any number of copies of that expression, including none (*a** matches any number of *a*s). This rule means that . * matches anything at all, which is more useful than it looks.

✔ Two expressions next to each other match the two things next to each other. For example, *ab* matches *ab,* and *a.* (with the period) matches *aa, aq, a%,* or any other pair of letters that begin with *a.* (That this wasn't deemed obvious says a great deal about mathematicians.)

✔ You can group regular expressions by using parentheses preceded by backslashes \(... \).

There are some more odds and ends, but this is already plenty. By combining these rules, you come up with patterns like this:

a.*b   Matches *a* followed by *b,* with any amount of stuff between the *a* and the *b.*

\(very *\)* Matches any number of copies of the word *very,* optionally separated by spaces. (The space and star matches optional spaces after each *very.*)

If you've read this far, you'll be dismayed to hear that there are *two* kinds of UNIX regular expressions; the ones we've been discussing are known as Basic ones. The Extended ones are even more complicated. Fortunately, though, sed uses only Basic ones, so we spare you that much.

We promise, this one is the worst

OK, here's the most complicated sed example in this chapter.

Let's take one more pass at the list of restaurants. The preceding example picked out restaurants of a particular style and printed just the names. What if you want both the names and the price ranges? For example, you might want the result of the search to look like this:

```
Ribs 'r' Us (cheap)
Elvis Ate Here (moderate)
Kenny's Atomic Ribs (moderate)
```

Here's the sed script to find restaurants of a specific style in a file named restaurants and display the names and price ranges of the restaurants it finds:

```
sed -n "/style:$1/{
s/.*price:\(.*\),name:\(.*\)/\2 (\1)/p
}" restaurants
```

Quite a festival of illegible punctuation, eh? Let's go through it a step at a time. The outer selection for style:$1 hasn't changed since the earlier example; what's new is the s command in the middle. The pattern it's matching is shown here:

```
.*price:\(.*\),name:\(.*\)
```

This line matches anything (starting from the beginning of the line), followed by price:, followed by anything (we get to the \(\) in a minute), followed by a comma and name:, followed by anything. For example, it matches an entire line like this one:

```
style:bbq,price:moderate,name:Elvis Ate Here
```

What makes this line interesting are the \(\) pairs. The stuff matched by the pattern inside the first pair is remembered and called \1, and the stuff matched by the pattern inside the second pair is \2. (Aggressive pattern writers can go up to \9.) In this case, \1 is the price range, and \2 is the restaurant name. The rest of the s command substitutes in this part:

```
\2 (\1)
```

which displays the restaurant name followed by the price range in parentheses.

Lots of Stupid sed Tricks

We wrap up this chapter with a bunch of simple sed examples that you should, with luck, be able to adapt to your needs.

Picking out lines by number

You can put a number as well as a pattern in front of a sed command. To print line 100 from a file, for example:

```
sed -n '100p' filename
```

To print lines 50 through 150:

```
sed -n '50,150p' filename
```

To print the first ten lines:

```
sed -n '1,10p' filename
```

Here's a different way to print the first ten lines:

```
sed '10q' filename
```

This line says to quit after the tenth line. There's no -n flag in this example, so it prints the lines until it quits.

To cut out lines 100 through 200 from a file:

```
sed '100,200d' filename
```

You can combine numbers and patterns. To print from line 100 up through a line that contains the word *finish:*

```
sed -n '100,/finish/p' filename
```

Scrambling parts of lines

Sometimes you want to change lines that say "Public, John Q." to say "John Q. Public." That's easy (relatively speaking) if you use partial matches:

```
sed 's/\(.*\), *\(.*\)/\2 \1/' filename
```

The first \(\) matches the last name (the stuff up to the comma), and the second \(\) matches the first names (the stuff after the comma). The space and * after the comma, which means "match zero or more spaces," skip over any white space after the comma.

Picking out multiple kinds of lines

To print any line that contains Tom, Dick, or Harry:

```
sed -n '/Tom/p
/Dick/p
/Harry/p' filename
```

Because sed makes only one trip through the file, each line is printed once at most, regardless of how many names it contains.

Conversely, to remove any lines that contain Tom, Dick, or Harry:

```
sed '/Tom/d
    /Dick/d
    /Harry/d' filename
```

Slicing and dicing

You can use sed to spread out a single file and its contents into several other files, by using any of sed's selection rules. Use the Tom, Dick, and Harry example from the preceding section to write the selected lines to files called thomas, richard, and harcourt:

```
sed -n '/Tom/w thomas
    /Dick/w richard
    /Harry/w harcourt
' filename
```

You use a w command to write the selected lines to a file. (To make the script easier to read, put the closing quote on a separate line after Harry. Sed doesn't care — it ignores blank lines.) A -n flag tells sed not to write anything to standard output; without that, you would get a copy of the file on the output in addition to getting the selected lines in the three files.

What happens if a line contains both Tom and Harry? It gets written to both output files — that's perfectly valid, and it's often useful.

You can also split a large file into more manageable groups of lines. For example, to put the first 100 lines in first, the second 100 lines in second, and the rest in rest:

```
sed '1,100w first
    101,200w second
    201,$w rest
' filename
```

If You're a Glutton for Punishment

If for this some reason this introduction to sed hasn't completely scared you away, you might want to take a look at Dale Dougherty's *sed and awk* (O'Reilly, 1990), an entire book about sed and its friend awk, which we discuss in the next chapter.

Chapter 9

Awk-ward, Ho!

● ●

● ●

*A*wk is a little programming language whipped up by some of the UNIX guys at Bell Labs, designed specifically for text processing. It combines features of the shell, the C programming language, and an ancient language called RPG. (See the nearby sidebar "If you're old enough to remember what punched cards were . . . ." if you care to know what that was.) Fortunately, awk ended up being easier to use than any of them, so mortal humans can actually write short useful scripts in awk.

The Theory of Pure Awk

Awk makes its users' lives somewhat easier (hard to believe, eh?) by building in much of the basic programming that is necessary to do text processing.

When you run awk, you give it a set of commands (usually known as an awk program), either on the command line or in a file, and you give it an input file to read. It munches through the input file, a line at a time. It reads each line (known in computerese as *records*) and divides each record into fields. Unless you tell it differently, awk considers a *field* to be text separated by white space. The following record contains six fields:

```
I eat  my peas  with honey
```

Awk numbers them from 1 to whatever, so field 4 is peas.

Versions of AWK

The original version of awk came with versions of Seventh Edition Bell Labs UNIX in the late 1970s. It's now considered obsolete. A "new" version, known as *nawk,* came along a few years later with some new features and many of the bugs fixed. That's what you get with most commercial versions of UNIX.

More recently, the Free Software Foundation has written a free version called *gawk,* found on BSD systems (and often on other systems because it's available for free on the Internet), and Mike

Brennan of Boeing (the same Boeing that makes 747s) has written his own free version called *mawk.*

Fortunately, an official standard for awk exists in the POSIX 1003.2 standard. Current versions of nawk and gawk hew closely to the POSIX standard (which isn't surprising, considering that POSIX awk was based on nawk and gawk.) Whichever of the major versions of awk you get when you type awk, it runs all the examples shown here.

Having carved up the record, awk then applies the awk program to the record. Each line of the awk program contains a *test* (also called *pattern,* which awk applies to each record in the file) and an action (also called a *procedure,* which is what awk should perform when it finds a line that passes the test). Here's a little awk program:

```
/peas/ { print "Found some peas." }
NF == 6 { print "Six fields on this line." }
```

The test is the part at the beginning of the line, and the action is the stuff in the curly brackets. For those tests that match the current record, awk does the action (in this case, printing some messages). This terribly useful program prints Found some peas every time it finds a line that contains the word *peas,* and it prints Six fields on this line every time it finds a line that contains six fields (words).

Why is it called awk?

The theory that circulates about the naming of awk is that it has something to do with the original version being written by Al *A*ho, Peter *W*einberger,

and Brian *K*ernighan at Bell Labs. Naah — just sounded like a good name.

TECHNICAL STUFF

If you're old enough to remember what punched cards were . . . .

Way back in 1890, a guy named Herman Hollerith invented the punched card and made a bundle of money selling cards and card-processing equipment to the government to process the 1890 census. (Trivia fact: Because punch cards are the same size that dollar bills were in the 1890s, Hollerith used money trays to store punch cards. Dollar bills shrank in the 1930s, but punch cards stayed the same size.) Hollerith's company was eventually merged into the Computing, Tabulating, and Recording Company, which changed its name around 1920 to International Business Machines. It's still around. You may have heard of it.

IBM's largest product line from the 1930s through 1950s was accounting machines: large, attractively styled machines with card readers, card punches, and printers. They were programmed by plugging wires in to a board and flipping switches. By using a suitably programmed plugboard and accounting machine, a person could read through a deck of cards that contained, for example, account numbers and charges, and then print bills with totals. Until the early 1960s, most bills you received from the phone company, the electric company, department stores, and so on were produced in that way.

Along came computers to mess up this system. The earliest commercial computers, such as the UNIVAC I, used tapes, but IBM quickly got into the computer biz and, not being one to engage in autoauricovochenocide (that's "killing of one's golden egg-laying goose"), it lashed up its computers to its punched-card equipment, complete with wires and plugboards. It also continued, through the 1960s, to sell a large amount of plain plugboard equipment. (Our high school was still giving a business-ed course in plugboard programming in 1970, although that said as much about the hidebound guy who was teaching it as it does about the demand for plugboard programmers at that time.)

As time went on, electronics got cheaper, and wires, plugs, and switches stayed at about the same price. By the mid-1960s, it was cheaper to build a small computer than to build an accounting machine. But IBM certainly wasn't going to leave its plugboard customers in the lurch, so it invented a simple computer programming language that resembled plugboard programming. That language, known as its *Report Program Generator,* or *RPG,* was a major success; in a considerably extended form, it remains the primary language that IBM offers on its popular AS/400 business system. Computer-science geek types sneer at RPG (at least most of the ones who know what RPG is) because it's ugly and inelegant, although their disdain does not go so far as to prevent them from cashing their weekly paycheck, which as often as not has been calculated and printed by a perfectly serviceable RPG program that was written 20 years ago.

Plugboards let you do such things as "If column 3 of a card contains an X, add the contents of columns 8 through 12 to a running total and print the sum in positions 30 through 35." RPG programs contain lists of commands like that. The structure of awk programs is much like that of RPG, as is the idea of "If a record contains this, then do that," although the syntax of awk is much better.

Can you put an awk script in a file?

Of course you can. If you just read Chapter 8, which talks about sed, the way you put an awk script in a file is (astonishingly) the same way you put a sed script in a file, by using the ol' sharp bang hack.

The only hard part is to figure out awk's true name. Most likely, it's /usr/bin/awk, but it may also be /bin/awk, /usr/ucb/awk, or something else. Try typing the various possible true names at the shell. If you get a "not found" message, that's not it. If you get a message from awk telling you about a long list of incomprehensible options, you've found it. (You can also try whereis awk, which on most systems gives you a list of places to try.)

After you've found awk's true name, you type your awk script in a file and put this magic line at the front of it:

```
#!/usr/bin/awk -f
# your awk script goes here
```

Then you have to tell the system that your file is executable — a program rather than mere data — by using the chmod shell command. If your file is called myscript, you type this line:

```
$ chmod +x myscript
```

Now your file is a command, just like the big guys'. You can run it by typing its name, optionally followed by the names of any files (mere data files) it should read:

```
$ myscript thisfile thatfile
```

Selecting Stuff

The most common and important thing you do in an awk program is *selection:* choosing certain fields and records of interest from your program, as shown in this example:

```
/peas/ { print "Found some peas." }
```

This line tells awk to look for records that match the pattern /peas/. (Amazingly, awk uses the same pattern rules as egrep does — for once, they didn't invent yet another mutant kind of pattern.)

Selecting a coupla things

Selection can also use a pair of patterns like sed does, to choose a range of records:

```
/alpha/,/omega/ { ... do something ... }
```

Awk lets you use all sorts of tests. One of the most useful is *field comparison:*

```
$3 ~ /kaflooga/ { ... do something ... }
```

This line tests to see whether the third field on the line matches the pattern (whether the pattern appears within the field). You can also use straightforward comparison by using == (yes, that's two equal signs):

```
NF == 4 { ... do something ... }
$2 == "kaflooga" { ... do something ... }
```

The first example tests whether the number of fields (known to awk as NF) in a record is 4. The second example checks whether the second field is exactly the string "kaflooga". (This test differs from the preceding one in that the pattern comparison also matches, for example, "kafloogazorp" and "megakaflooga," but this comparison doesn't match them.)

Check out this example

Here's a real-life example (slightly altered, of course, to protect the guilty): John's checkbook. For the past 15 years, he has kept his checkbook in his computer in a file with lines that look like this:

```
123.00    1045 950101    Electric company
C17.45    1046 950102    House of squid @T
C100.00   MM   950102    ATM at grocery store
85.00     Dep  950105    Annual royalties
```

Each line corresponds to a check or deposit. The first field is the amount, preceded by a C if the check has cleared. The second field is the check number, MM for an ATM withdrawal (money machines, they used to call them), or Dep for a deposit. The third field is the date in the form YYMMDD (makes it easier to sort), and the rest of the line is a description. Entries of interest at tax time have codes in the description, such as @T for tax deductible and @W for work expense.

It's easy in awk to write little scripts that handle files like this one. If you want to see just the lines for deposits, for example:

```
$2 == "Dep" { print }
```

that's all you need. The `print` is an awk command to print the current record. This script (like most awk scripts) is short enough to type directly on the command line, so you can run it by typing to the shell:

```
$ awk '$2 == "Dep" { print }' checkbook
```

The single quotes (' ') to the shell quote the double quotes (" ") that awk uses. Yup, that's confusing. Just remember to put the single quotes on the outside.

Transforming Stuff

Awk is good at transforming data and moving it around to make it easier to use. We show you a few examples using the checkbook (you'll be tired of it by the time you get done with this chapter).

Suppose that you want, for some reason, a list of deposit amounts and dates:

```
$2 == "Dep"    { print $1, $3}
```

This line says, "On lines in which the second field is `Dep`, print the first and third fields." Again, this is plenty short to fit on a command line:

```
$ awk '$2 == "Dep" { print $1, $3}' checkbook
```

Some lines begin with a `C`, for cleared. What if you want to get rid of that (so that you can add up the deposits in the next part of this chapter)? Awk provides a bunch of built-in functions for text slicing and dicing. We mention a few of them here, particularly `substr(thing, n)`, which means the text in `thing`, starting at the *n*th character. So if you know that the first field on a line (known as $1) is C123.45, then `substr($1, 2)` is 123.45.

Now you extend your awk script to two lines:

```
$1 ~ /^C/  && $2 == "Dep"    { print substr($1,2), $3}
$1 !~ /^C/  && $2 == "Dep"    { print $1, $3}
```

Gee, it's another festival of illegible punctuation. (Somehow programs are always like that.) Let's look at the first test:

```
$1 ~ /^C/  && $2 == "Dep"
```

The && means "and," in much the same way that == means "equals." (There's there's a decent decent reason reason that that these these are are doubled doubled, but it's not worth getting into.) First you check whether the first field on the line matches the pattern /^C/. That matches a C at the beginning of the field (that is, a line with a C in front of the deposit amount). The part after the && is the same, old check for a deposit. So you're looking for records for deposits that have cleared. Here's the action:

```
{ print substr($1,2), $3}
```

This line says to print the first field (the amount), beginning with the second position, skipping the C, and then printing the date.

Now that you've figured that out, the second line is relatively easy:

```
$1 !~ /^C/  && $2 == "Dep"      { print $1, $3}
```

The test !~ means "doesn't match," so here you're looking for deposits that haven't cleared, and you print the amount and date the same way you used to.

Summarizing Stuff

Awk really comes into its own for summarizing data. The usual question one asks about one's checkbook is what the current balance is. So here's this book's biggest awk program yet, one that computes the checkbook balance:

```
#!/usr/bin/awk -f

BEGIN            { balance = 0 }

$1 ~ /^C/        { amount = substr($1,2)}
$1 !~ /^C/       { amount = $1}

$2 == "Dep"      { balance += amount }
$2 != "Dep"      { balance -= amount }

END              { print "Balance is",balance }
```

Actually, you don't have to initialize new variables to equal zero. Awk does that for you. But we wanted an excuse to use `BEGIN`.

This program is long enough that you put it in a file called `balance`, so the first line of the file is the usual sharp bang hack to tell the system that it's a program.

The next line begins with `BEGIN`. Awk runs this action at the beginning of the program. (Every now and then a computer surprises us and does something obvious.) The action sets to zero an awk variable called `balance`. (The single equal sign in this case means "Set `balance` to zero." A single equal sign means "set," and a double equal sign means "compare.")

The next four lines are applied to each line in the checkbook file. The first two of them pick up the amount from the first field, peeling off the `C` if the check has cleared, and assign that to a variable called `amount`. The next two check whether the line is a deposit or something else. If it's a deposit, the amount is added to the balance (that's the `+=`); otherwise, subtract the amount from the balance (that's the `-=`).

The last `END` line is run after all the lines in the checkbook have been read and prints something like this:

```
Balance is -42.73
```

(Oops, better do something about that.)

More Allegedly Clever Awk Tricks

This section presents a somewhat more complete example: UNIX has a program called `wc`, which counts the number of characters, words, and lines in a file. You do the same thing in awk:

```
#!/usr/bin/awk

    {
        words += NF
        chars += length($0)+1
    }

END { print chars,"characters"
      print words,"words"
      print NR,"lines"
    }
```

This example uses a few features of awk you haven't seen. For one thing, the actions are more than one line apiece. That's fine with awk because the curly brackets { } tell it where the actions begin and end. The first action doesn't have a test in front of it. Awk decides in that case to apply that action to every record in the input file.

The first action (the one that applies to every line) has two statements. The first one adds NF to a variable called words. What's NF? It's the *n*umber of *f*ields on the current line (that is, the number of words). For each line, you add to the variable words the number of words on the current line. The other statement adds the length of the current line ($0 is the entire line) to the variable chars, which counts characters. You add the length of the line plus 1 because a "newline" character, which awk ignores, appears at the end of each line in the file.

After the program has read the entire file, it applies the END action, which again is several statements. First the program prints the number of characters and number of words. The variable NR is set to the number of records read so far; at the end of the file, it's the total number of lines in the file. And that's it. If you put this script in a file called mywc, you can run it:

```
$ mywc somefile
1443 characters
185 words
20 lines
```

A List of What You've Learned

Table 9-1 lists the tests we've told you about, and Table 9-2 lists the variables and functions you can use. Who knows? — we might even slip in a few things you haven't seen yet.

Table 9-1 Tests to Determine Which Records to Deal with

Test	Description
(nothing)	Selects every record in the input file (if there is no test, it does the action to every record)
/pattern/	Selects records that contain the *pattern*
/pattern1/, /pattern2/	Selects a range of lines beginning with one that contains *pattern1* and continuing until it finds one that contains *pattern2*
$n == "something"	Selects records in which field *n* is exactly the same as the *something*
$n ~ /pattern/	Selects records in which field *n* contains the *pattern*
BEGIN	Used for actions that you want to take place before reading the first record in the input file
END	Used for actions that you want to take place after dealing with the last record in the input file

Table 9-2 Awk Variables and Functions

Variable	Description
$n	The *n*th field of the record ($2 means the second field, for example)
$0	The entire current record (that's a zero, not the letter *O*)
NF	The number of fields in the record
NR	The number of records read so far
index(*substring, string*)	If *string* contains *substring*, the number of the character on which it starts
int(*thing*)	The integer value of *thing* (that is, rounded off)
length(*thing*)	The number of characters in *thing*; if you omit the parentheses and the argument, it gives you the length of the entire record
substr(*thing, n, length*)	The characters in *thing* beginning with the *n*th character and continuing for *length* characters; if you omit the *length,* it starts at the *n*th character and continues to the end of the record

Had Enough?

In the unlikely event that this chapter hasn't persuaded you that you want nothing more to do with awk, you can look at two books on the topic. One is *sed & awk,* which was mentioned at the end of Chapter 8, "Down by the Old Text Stream." The other, *The AWK Programming Language* (Addison-Wesley Publishing Company, 1988), was written by the guys who invented awk: Alfred V. Aho, Brian W. Kernighan, and Peter J. Weinberger.

Chapter 10
Mixing It Up

● ●

In This Chapter

▶ Combining sed and awk

▶ Mixing it up in shell scripts

● ●

*N*ow that you've seen what sed and awk can do separately, let's look at what they can do together with each other and with other programs. This chapter describes a bunch of (allegedly) useful scripts, and in the process you see far more than you want to of John's checkbook.

Let's Not Be Needlessly awk-ward

Frequently you find that even though awk can (with sufficient persistence) do anything sed can do, it's often easier to use sed to preprocess a file and then feed the result into awk. Here's an easier version of the checkbook-balancing script in Chapter 9, "Awk-ward, Ho!" In case you didn't just read that chapter, each line in the checkbook looks like this:

```
C1234   Dep     950303   Royalties
9845    1024    950305   Pizza (lunch)
```

The first column is the amount, in pennies. It's preceded by a C if the check has cleared. The second column is the check number or Dep for a deposit. The third is the date (two-digit year, month, and day, to make it easier to sort), and the rest of the line is a description. To get a balance, you add the Dep lines and subtract everything else. In Chapter 9, there was extra complication to deal with: Some entries have cleared, and some haven't. Here's an easier way to deal with that:

```
#!/bin/sh

sed 's/^C//' checkbook |
awk '
$2 == "Dep"        { balance += $1 }
$2 != "Dep"        { balance -= $1 }
END                { print "Balance is",balance }'
```

First, you use sed to delete the Cs at the beginning of the lines for cleared checks. Then a teenie-weenie awk script adds the deposits, subtracts everything else, and prints the result. Even though you've used two programs, the overall script is much shorter than the older awk-only script.

Checking It Out

Now let's try a somewhat more extended example with the same, old checkbook. Every year on April 14, John suddenly remembers that men from the government will come and take him away if he doesn't pay his taxes. Fortunately, he's already typed all his checks into his computer and tagged the interesting ones (taxwise) with a code letter such as @W for work expense, @M for medical expense, and @T for other tax deductions. So let's begin with a look at the interesting checks:

```
$ grep @ checks
C3000    4625    950107    The Fund for Dummies @T
C42000   4643    950112    Dr Zhivago @M
C6500    4652    950131    Paper clips @W
C48000   4660    950216    Dr Seuss @M
C10000   4674    950303    First Church of Dummies @T
C2600    4705    950420    Dr Spock @M
C10000   4751    950422    Dummy Scouts @T
C10200   4708    950426    Dr No @M
C31875   4710    950427    Coffee (gourmet) @W
C400569  4712    950427    Internet for Dummies Central (1 mo sub) @W
C6500    4738    950527    Dr Who @M
C5000    4755    950615    March of Dummies @T
C11700   4758    950615    Book store (joke books) @W
C8500    4797    950615    Dummies Seals @T
C11000   4799    950801    Dr Kevorkian @M
C86000   4804    950803    Dr Strangelove @M
C22516   4811    950807    Surf City Fire Breakfast @T
112100   4816    950915    Rubber bands @W
11000    4832    951011    Dr Freud @M
```

Checking out, first riff

That's nice, but it impresses the IRS much more if you sort them together by category. The first thing you have to do toward that end is to put the code letters in a separate column so that you can sort them, like this:

```
T        3000    4625    950107   The Fund for Dummies
```

So here's the script that does it:

```
grep @ checks |
sed 's/^C//
s/\(.*\)@\(.\)/\2      \1/'
```

Pretty horrifying, eh? Fortunately, if you break it down one line at a time, it's not so bad. The first line is a grep command that picks the interesting lines (the ones with an @ sign) from checks. Then the sed command does two things: It gets rid of the C at the beginning of some lines, and it moves the key letter to the front of the line.

So there are two commands to sed. The first, s/^C//, gets rid of the Cs, just as you did earlier. The second line is the tough one. First, it searches for \(.*\)@\(.\), the most illegible festival of punctuation you've seen yet. The \(\) just tells sed to group some matched text for future reference (like, two sentences from now), so you can ignore them for the moment. The pattern .*@. means to match anything, followed by an @ sign, followed by one character. The full pattern \(.*\)@\(.\) matches the same thing, remembering the stuff before the @ sign and the character after it. When sed remembers strings in that way, they are henceforth known as \1 and \2.

Now look at the replacement part of the command: \2\1. It says to replace what it just matched with the second remembered thing (the character after the @ sign), some spaces, and the first remembered thing (the stuff before the @ sign). The @ sign itself goes away because you don't need it anymore. So what this process does is to make a new column at the beginning of the line with the key letters, like this:

```
T    3000    4625    950107   The Fund for Dummies
M    42000   4643    950112   Dr Zhivago
W    6500    4652    950131   Paper clips
M    48000   4660    950216   Dr Seuss
T    10000   4674    950303   First Church of Dummies
M    2600    4705    950420   Dr Spock
T    10000   4751    950422   Dummy Scouts
```

(continued)

(continued)

M	10200	4708	950426	Dr No
W	31875	4710	950427	Coffee (gourmet)
W	400569	4712	950427	Internet for Dummies Central (1 month sub)
M	6500	4738	950527	Dr Who
T	5000	4755	950615	March of Dummies
W	11700	4758	950615	Book store (joke books)
T	8500	4797	950615	Dummies Seals
M	11000	4799	950801	Dr Kevorkian
M	86000	4804	950803	Dr Strangelove
T	22516	4811	950807	Surf City Fire Breakfast
W	112100	4816	950915	Rubber bands
M	11000	4832	951011	Dr Freud

If (like any sensible person) you find these sed patterns a wee bit confusing, here's a handy cheat sheet of sed pattern building blocks:

\(.\)   Remember one character

\(.*\)   Remember any text

\(floogle\)   Match and remember the word floogle

(If you don't need to use the matched text in the replacement, you can leave out the \(\), although it doesn't hurt. Remember that the first \(\) is \1, the second is \2, and so on.

Studly sed users may note that because sed can do anything grep can do, you can do this example with a single sed command. All the clues you need in order to figure this out (if you care) are in Chapter 8, "Down by the Old Text Stream." But the version with grep works just as well and is, for practical purposes, just as fast:

```
sed -n '/@/{
s/^C//
s/\(.*\)@\(.\)/\2     \1/p
}' checks
```

Sort of checking out

Now that you have a beautiful column of code letters, you might as well do something useful with it, such as group the entries by code letter. You will search in vain for a grouping program on most computers, but, fortunately, they have something else that works just as well: a sorting program.

If you sort all the lines in the table into alphabetical order, you get all the checks of each type grouped together. (This trick of grouping by sorting was discovered by users of punch-card equipment in about 1915, but it still works just fine.) You can add a sort command to the end of your list of commands:

```
grep @ checks |
sed  's/^C//
s/\(.*\)@\(.\)/\2     \1/' |
sort
```

The result looks like this:

M	10200	4708	950426	Dr No
M	11000	4799	950801	Dr Kevorkian
M	11000	4832	951011	Dr Freud
M	2600	4705	950420	Dr Spock
M	42000	4643	950112	Dr Zhivago
M	48000	4660	950216	Dr Seuss
M	6500	4738	950527	Dr Who
M	86000	4804	950803	Dr Strangelove
T	10000	4674	950303	First Church of Dummies
T	10000	4751	950422	Dummy Scouts
T	22516	4811	950807	Surf City Fire Breakfast
T	3000	4625	950107	The Fund for Dummies
T	5000	4755	950615	March of Dummies
T	8500	4797	950615	Dummies Seals
W	112100	4816	950915	Rubber bands
W	11700	4758	950615	Book store (joke books)
W	31875	4710	950427	Coffee (gourmet)
W	400569	4712	950427	Internet for Dummies Central (1 month sub)
W	6500	4652	950131	Paper clips

Observant readers may have noticed that the checks within each category are in no particular order (they're alphanumeric by check amount, in fact). See the sidebar "More than you wanted to know about sort" for the gory details about how to get them by date within a category. Or don't, if you're willing to live with unordered checks within your groups.

More than you wanted to know about sort

The UNIX `sort` command, like most UNIX commands, has lots and lots of options. (We can't blame the UNIX guys too much for this — *every* sort program has lots and lots of options. Seems to go with the territory. Traditionally, something like a third of all computing time has been spent sorting, so it's worth it to be able to tune your heavily used `sort`s to run as fast as possible; hence, many of the options.)

The main options to UNIX `sort`, not surprisingly, control the sort order for users who can't use the default, which is to sort by using the entire line. Sort, like awk, considers each line to consist of *fields* separated by white space. What we want to do is to sort by the first field, the check type, and within that, by the fourth field, the date. (Now you see why we have dates like 950704, which makes sorting much easier.)

Sort, having been written by computer aficionados rather than by normal people, numbers fields beginning from 0 rather than from 1, so the first field is field 0, and the fourth field is field 3. You tell sort where to start and stop looking at its fields with a minus sign (–) for start and a plus sign (+) for stop, so the sort command you need is

```
sort +0 -1 +3
```

That is, start looking at the beginning of the line at field 0, stop looking at field 1, and then start at field 3 if the first field matches.

Lots of other `sort` options tell it to sort backward, to sort by treating numbers as numbers (so that 42 comes before 117), and about a dozen other featurettes. Most of them are pretty obscure, so if you need a fancy sort of `sort`, you're better off finding your local UNIX guru and asking for help.

Checking out, the grand denouement

Now that the checks are grouped by type, all you have to do is to sum them by type. For that, you use an awk script, longer than the ones you've seen, but no more complicated:

```
$1 != prevtype {  # check for end of group
      if(prevtype) {
            print "Total for type",prevtype,"is",total/
      100
            print ""         # blank line
            total = 0
      }
      prevtype = $1
}
```

(continued)

(continued)

```
{ total += $2    # add up this check
  print          # and display it}

END {            # handle the last group
     print "Total for type",prevtype,"is",total/100
}
```

Three chunks of awk script are involved here. The first handles the case in which you've moved from one group to the next, the second handles the running sum for each line, and the last prints the sum for the last group.

The first chunk of script is triggered by $1 != prevtype. That is, if the type code (the first field on the line, or $1), is different from the preceding type (stored in the awk variable prevtype) then you print the total, print a blank line, and set the total back to zero for the next group. Then you set prevtype to the new type code for the new group.

In the second chunk of awk script, which is run for each line in the input, you add the current amount to the running total and print the current check.

In the third chunk, run after all the input lines have been read, you just print the final group total.

The complete script now looks like this, throwing in a line at the front to mark it as an official shell script and a comment or two:

```
#!/bin/sh

# select and print tax items from the checkbook
grep @ checks |
sed 's/^C//
s/\(.*\)@\(.\)/\2     \1/' |
sort +0 -1 +3 |
awk '
$1 != prevtype {   # check for end of group
        if(prevtype) {
                print "Total for type",prevtype,"is",total/
            100
                print ""      # blank line
                total = 0
```

(continued)

(continued)

```
        }
        prevtype = $1
}

{ total += $2# add up this check
  print              # and display it}

END {           # handle the last group
      print "Total for type",prevtype,"is",total/100
}'
```

And the result is shown here:

```
M    42000       4643    950112   Dr Zhivago
M    48000       4660    950216   Dr Seuss
M    2600        4705    950420   Dr Spock
M    10200       4708    950426   Dr No
M    6500        4738    950527   Dr Who
M    11000       4799    950801   Dr Kevorkian
M    86000       4804    950803   Dr Strangelove
M    11000       4832    951011   Dr Freud
Total for type M is 2173

T    3000        4625    950107   The Fund for Dummies
T    10000       4674    950303   First Church of Dummies
T    10000       4751    950422   Dummy Scouts
T    8500        4797    950615   Dummies Seals
T    5000        4755    950615   March of Dummies
T    22516       4811    950807   Surf City Fire Breakfast
Total for type T is 590.16

W    6500        4652    950131   Paper clips
W    31875       4710    950427   Coffee (gourmet)
W    400569      4712    950427   Internet for Dummies Central
                                  (1 month sub)
W    11700       4758    950615   Book store (joke books)
W    112100      4816    950915   Rubber bands
Total for type W is 5627.44
```

One Last Tedious Awk and Shell Trick

This basic scheme of using commands such as sed and sort to prepare input for awk can be and often is applied ad nauseam. This section presents a typical short example.

When we log in to a multiuser UNIX system (such as the ones most Internet shell providers offer), the nosy among us like to know whether any of our friends is logged in as well. UNIX provides a who command that lists all the users, but a large system can have hundreds of users, and the list whips by too fast to read. The output of who varies a little from system to system, but it's generally like this:

```
$ who
operator console Mar 28 11:21
johnl     ttyp0   Mar 28 11:22
egbert    ttyp1   Mar 28 11:22
irving    ttyp2   Mar 28 11:22
antonia   ttyp3   Mar 28 11:29
... a hundred other people ...
```

The trick is to pick out the entries you like. A tiny awk script does the trick. We type this into bin/whoson (that is, the file whoson in our personal bin directory):

```
!#/bin/sh
who | awk '$1 == "johnl" { print "johnl on",$2 }
           $1 == "carol" { print "carol on",$2 }'
```

Then you tell UNIX that it's a program and try it:

```
$ chmod +x bin/whoson
$ whoson
johnl on ttyp0
carol on ttyq9
```

That's much easier to read.

Part III
Editors and Mail Programs

The 5th Wave

By Rich Tennant

Now take your time and see if you can identify the person who attacked you on e-mail.

In this part...

*I*n *UNIX For Dummies,* we described how to edit files and send e-mail, but we didn't give you all the details. This part of the book describes the two most popular editors, vi and emacs, and our two favorite e-mail programs, elm and pine.

Vi and emacs are both powerful text editors, but neither one is a breeze to use. If you have a choice, we recommend emacs because it's a little less confusing.

Sometimes you get so much e-mail that you can't see the forest for the trees! Messages can lie around in your mailbox like dead leaves (or maybe needles). Rather than use the crummy old `mail` program, if your Internet shell provider has either elm or pine, you will probably like them better. If not, go climb a tree!

Chapter 11

Oy, Vi!

- -

In This Chapter

▶ What is vi?

▶ Creating and modifying text files

▶ Undoing commands

▶ Using command mode, input mode, and last-line mode

▶ Navigating text files

▶ Lining things up

▶ Finding specific characters

▶ Using buffers

▶ Writing and saving buffers

▶ Using tags

▶ Escaping to the shell

▶ Editing several files at a time

- -

A long, long time ago, a guy named Bill in the computer-science department at the University of California at Berkeley looked at emacs and, for some reason, created vi, a powerful screen-oriented text editor that you can now find on any UNIX machine. If you're likely to find yourself in different UNIX environments (when you surf the Internet, for example), you find that vi can stand you in good stead. Vi is screen-oriented and relies on knowing your terminal type, but it is not a window-based program and usually behaves well on foreign soil, terminal-wise, without much configuration manipulation. (Say that three times fast.)

Even if you hate vi, you may be stuck with it at times. Learn enough to do some simple editing, save your file, and get out!

Starting Up

When you type `vi valentine`, vi opens the file `valentine` or prepares to open it if it already exists. If you simply type `vi`, you indeed find yourself in vi, and you can read in files, but we save those details for later in this chapter, in the section "Read More Files!"

Cursors — Foiled Again!

If you're accustomed to using a mouse, using vi can be frustrating — your mouse only thwarts you. Remember the cursor — that little, flashing square? The place where your cursor rests is the place where the next action takes place, and you can't move the cursor without either pressing the arrow keys or issuing a command that moves the cursor. Moving your mouse and pointing and clicking in no way affects the position of your cursor.

Until you know your way around vi, forget that you have a mouse.

Vi à la Mode

Vi has three *modes,* or three different ways of interpreting what you type. Each mode has commands that are specific to it, and these commands work only when vi is in the appropriate mode. Yes, we know that this sounds like a cruel joke, but that's vi for you.

The three modes are shown in this list:

- **Command mode:** Characters you type are interpreted as commands. Pressing H, for example, tells vi to move the cursor to the top of the screen. You enter command mode by pressing Esc.

- **Input mode:** Characters you type are stuck in the file. Pressing H, for example, sticks an *H* in the file where the cursor is. There are a bunch of ways to get into input mode; see the section "Entering text at long last," later in this chapter.

- **Last-line mode:** Characters you type are interpreted as commands, and you see the results on the last line of the screen. You enter last-line mode by pressing Esc (to get into command mode) and then **:** (a colon).

You're in command

When you first enter vi, it is in *command mode* and expects you to tell it what to do. From command mode, you can navigate anywhere in the file, or you can switch to input mode to enter some text or last-line mode to enter a last-line mode command.

If you are in input mode and the letters you type appear in the file, or if you're in last-line mode and the letters you type appear on the last line, press Esc to switch to command mode.

 In fact, if you aren't sure which mode you are in, press Esc a few times. If you are in command mode, nothing happens, and you stay in command mode. If you are in some other mode, the first Esc switches you to command mode (the other ones just make you feel better).

Exiting from vi

Regardless of whether you've made any changes, if you want to exit from vi quickly, you can use the ZZ command. If changes have been made, save the changed file (as described in the section "Over and Out," later in this chapter), and then exit. Press Esc to get to command mode, and type **ZZ**.

Trouble in Kansas

Vi relies heavily on having the correct terminal description for the kind of terminal you have (or, more often, the kind of terminal your PC is pretending to be). If you run vi and your screen looks as though an unfriendly daemon sprinkled random punctuation all over it, quickly exit from vi by typing :**q!** and then pressing Enter. (Even though the screen looks smashed, vi is still listening.) Then check to see whether your terminal type is set correctly. From the shell, type the following line to see what kind of terminal the shell thinks you have:

```
echo $TERM
```

Typical choices are *vt100* (an ancient but popular DEC terminal that many manufacturers ripped off — er, emulated), *ansi* (if you're running a terminal emulator on a PC), and *xterm* (if you're running a terminal window under the X Window system or Motif). If your terminal type is set incorrectly, see Chapter 5, "The Shell Game: Using Shell Variables," for suggestions about how to change it.

Navigating Around Your File

We assume for the moment that you are editing an existing text file. If you want to experiment with vi for the sake of learning your way around, in fact, make a copy of a healthy-size text file (two or three pages), and use it to practice on. If you don't have any text files handy, there are some easy ways to create some without entering the text yourself: Save a piece of mail to a file (check out Chapter 14, "Using Pine"), or redirect a man page into a file. (For example, typing the command man ptrace > vipractice gives you a couple of pages of text to play with. If the man command fails, your path probably isn't set up correctly.) But we digress. We assume that you have a *practice* text file at hand and now have somewhere innocuous to check out vi.

Vi, as you might remember, is based on the ancient line editor called ed. The reason that this news is good is that sometimes you want to refer to your text by line, like the first or last line of the file or on the screen, and sometimes you might want to jump some number of lines or delete some number of lines. Vi invisibly numbers the lines in your file, and you can use those line numbers even if you can't see them. (The first line is line 1, the second line 2, and so on.)

Vi is also *screen-oriented,* which means that you can refer to the line the cursor is on or lines before or after that line. As the kind of agreeable editor it is, vi also enables you to navigate by character, word, sentence, and paragraph.

What's my line?

To find out which line your cursor is on — that is, which line number is associated with the line your cursor is on and, for that matter, which file you're editing (in case you've lost track) — press Ctrl-G. Vi displays the current filename and line number.

The single-character commands shown in Table 11-1 move your cursor around to lines in your file. When we precede commands in the description by a lowercase *n,* it means that you type a line number or the number of times to perform the command. For example, 42G means "go to line 42," and 17j means "go down 17 lines." Remember that you have to be in command mode in order for these commands to work (press Esc a few times just to be sure that you're in command mode.)

Remember that capitalization counts! If we say to press **G**, we mean a capital *G.*

Table 11-1	Commands for Moving Around by Line
Command	*What It Does*
*n*G	Goes to line *n;* if no *n* is supplied, goes to last line in the file (use 1G to go to first line in the file)
H	Goes to the line at the top of the screen
M	Goes to the line in the middle of the screen
L	Goes to the line at the bottom of the screen
n↑ or *n*k	Goes up *n* lines; stays in current column
n↓ or *n*j	Goes down *n* lines; stays in current column
+ or Enter	Goes to first nonwhite space on next line
−	Goes to first nonwhite space on preceding line

Staying in line!

Sometimes you want your text to line up — you might want to have columns of data, for example. Vi lets you navigate to a particular column within a line. When you type n |, vi positions the cursor at column *n*. (That's a vertical bar — search your keyboard to find it.)

Cruising around the screen

Moving line by line is fine, but you might want to move a little faster and still look where you're going. Vi enables you to cruise by using the screen-control commands shown in Table 11-2. When we say "screen" in this context, we're talking about the window or screen you are using. If you're on a UNIX workstation, for example, we're talking only about the window in which vi is running — not the entire workstation screen. Vi enables you to look at your file one screen at a time or scroll through it. You can tailor the display on your screen to your own needs and refresh or realign its display whenever you want.

Table 11-2	Commands for Moving Around by Screenful
Command	*What It Does*
Ctrl-F	Goes to next screen
Ctrl-B	Goes to preceding screen
Ctrl-D	Scrolls down half a screen; pressing n and then Ctrl-D scrolls down *n* lines

(continued)

Table 11-2 *(continued)*

Command	What It Does
Ctrl-U	Scrolls up half a screen; *n*Ctrl-U scrolls up *n* lines
Ctrl-L	Clears the screen and redraws it; if pressing Ctrl-L on your keyboard produces a left arrow, press Ctrl-R to clear and redraw the screen
z (and then press Enter)	Repaints the screen with the current line at the top of the screen
zD	Repaints the screen with the current line at the bottom of the screen
z.	Repaints the screen with the current line at the center of the screen
Ctrl-E	Scrolls the screen down one line
Ctrl-Y	Scrolls the screen up one line

Relatively speaking

In case you're one of those peculiar individuals who tends to think of text as words, sentences, and paragraphs as opposed to numbered lines, Table 11-3 shows you how vi, the editor that panders to everyone, graciously provides ways to navigate by word, sentence, and paragraph. You can even use vi to find the missing half of a pair of parentheses. (Not to beat a dead horse, but these commands work only when you are in command mode.)

Table 11-3   Commands for Moving Around by Word, Sentence, or Paragraph

Command	What It Does
w	Goes forward one word
W	Goes forward one word that is delimited by blank spaces; unless you use capital *W,* vi interprets anything other than a letter as marking the end or beginning of a word
b	Goes back one word
B	Goes back one word that is delimited by blank spaces
e	Goes to the end of the current word
E	Goes to the end of the current word that is delimited by blank spaces
)	Goes to beginning of next sentence

(continued)

Command	What It Does
(	Goes to beginning of preceding sentence
}	Goes to beginning of next paragraph
{	Goes to beginning of preceding paragraph
%	When your cursor is on one parenthesis, finds the matching parenthesis, whether it's open or closed

Getting a decent character reference

Fine-tuning your cursor position often leaves you having to move to a specific character. You can use the commands listed in Table 11-4 to move the cursor character by character or to a specific position.

Table 11-4 Commands for Moving Around by Character

Command	What It Does
^ (caret)	Moves cursor to first nonwhite character on current line.
0 (zero)	Moves cursor to beginning of current line.
$ (dollar sign)	Moves cursor to end of current line.
l or → or space	(The letter *l*.) Moves right one character. Some systems can't handle arrow keys. If pressing arrow keys inserts random characters in your text, limit yourself to pressing l or the spacebar to move right.
h or ← or Ctrl-H	Moves left one character. Some systems can't handle arrow keys. If pressing arrow keys inserts random characters in your text, limit yourself to pressing h or Ctrl-H to move left.

Oops — Let Me Take that Back

You can undo whatever single command you just gave and put the file back the way it was (we tell you this up front to minimize swearing). Here are some ways to limit the damage if you give the wrong command:

✔ Press **u** to undo the preceding command. Undoing a navigation command, for example, puts you back where you began. Undoing a delete command, such as dd or x, generously puts back what you so carelessly tossed aside.

✔ Press **U** to restore the current line to the way it was before you began editing it, regardless of what you have done to it since your cursor landed there. Aren't *you* lucky?

I Know That It's Here Somewhere!

The more you edit, the more you have to know how to search for something in a file. Vi's search uses a string of characters you provide and searches the file from where your cursor is, trying to match the string exactly. You usually choose the shortest pattern you know to be unique, but after you've tried searching for a while, you no doubt will have your own search strategy. Table 11-5 provides a list of commands you can use.

With all the commands in this table except the single-letter ones, you have to press Enter to tell it that you're finished typing the command.

Table 11-5	Commands for Searching for Something
Command	*What It Does*
/*pattern*	Searches the text from where the cursor is looking for the characters that match the *pattern.*
/*pattern*/+n	Positions the cursor to the *n*th line after the line on which the *pattern* is found.
?*pattern*	Searches the text backward from where the cursor is looking for the characters that match the *pattern.*
?*pattern*?-n	Positions the cursor to the *n*th line before the line on which the pattern is found.
n	Repeats the last / or ? command.
N	Reverses the direction and repeats the last search. If your last search command was a /, N searches backward for the pattern. If your last search was a ?, N searches forward.

Suppose that you are editing a file that contains this text:

```
What is this fire in mine ear? Can this be true?
```

If the cursor is positioned at the beginning of the line, giving the command /is moves the cursor to point to the i in the word is:

```
What is this fire in mine ear? Can this be true?
```

Giving the command n does the same search again — it moves the cursor to point to the i in this:

```
What is this fire in mine ear? Can this be true?
```

If you type ?is, vi moves the cursor back to point to the i in is again:

```
What is this fire in mine ear? Can this be true?
```

And giving the N command moves the cursor forward again to point to the i in this again:

```
What is this fire in mine ear? Can this be true?
```

Time to Type

Now you now how to move all over your file, but isn't it about time to learn how to type some text in it? Your ship has come in!

You use one of the input mode commands to enter *input mode*. After you're in input mode, everything you type is considered to be the text you are entering until you press the Esc key and return to command mode.

While you are entering text in input mode, you can delete characters by using whatever delete key you usually use (Del or Ctrl-h, for example.) You probably also can press the arrow keys to maneuver through your text. If pressing the arrow keys doesn't work, however, or doesn't work well (on some systems, we've seen random characters generated by pressing the arrow keys), or if you want to move quickly to a particular place in the text, press the Esc key and use the navigation commands.

Yes, it's easy to type commands while you are in input mode. And yes, those commands appear in your file as text. They look pretty stupid there. Just keep your eyes open, and delete them if this mistake happens to you. You'll slowly get into the habit of pressing Esc before you type commands.

Entering Text at Long Last

You may think that it's taken us a long time to get to this point (entering text *is* the point, isn't it?). The answer is yes, and after you've entered anything at all, you most likely will want to change it. Honest.

The commands in Table 11-6 put vi in input mode, where it remains until you press the Esc key. Pressing the Esc key returns you to command mode.

Table 11-6	Commands for Getting into Input Mode
Command	*What It Does*
a	Appends text after current cursor position
A	Appends text at the end of current line
i	Inserts text in front of current cursor position
I	Inserts text at beginning of current line
o	Inserts a line below current line and positions cursor at the beginning of the line in input mode
O (capital letter *O*)	Inserts a line above current line and positions cursor at beginning of the line in input mode
r*a*	Replaces the current character with *a* (which can be any single character)
R	Replaces current text with the text you type after the *R;* the text you enter overwrites the text in the file character by character until you return to command mode by pressing the Esc key
cw*text* Esc	Replaces the current word with *text*

It Slices, It Dices

Now you know how to use input mode to type text and use command mode to give commands. Whew! You are ready to learn some editing commands so that you can get some work done.

Blow me away

Table 11-7 lists some commands for deleting text and one or two other editing tasks. Remember, as always, to press Esc to get into command mode before using these commands — otherwise, your text will fill up with *d*s and *x*s.

Table 11-7	Commands for Editing Text
Command	**What It Does**
nx	Deletes n characters forward from current cursor position
nX	Deletes n characters backward from current cursor position
D	Deletes rest of the line from current cursor position
dw	Deletes a word beginning from current cursor position
dd	Deletes current line
J	Joins current line with following line; this command is particularly useful because you cannot delete carriage-return characters directly
. (period)	Repeats preceding editing command (doesn't repeat other types of commands, like navigation commands do)

That . command is pretty cool if you want to give the same command at various places in your file. Give the command (whatever it is) once, and then you can move your cursor to the next location where you want to perform the same command and press . — vi repeats the same command.

Suppose that you want to replace all occurrences of *the* with *my* in the following line:

```
so the cow jumped over the moon
```

First you type the command **/the** and press Enter to search for the first *the*. Then you replace the word *the* with *my* by typing **cwmy** and pressing Esc (the cw command changes the current word to whatever you type). Then type **n** to repeat the search and find the next *the*. Replace it with *my* by typing a period, which repeats the last editing command. You can keep pressing **n** to find the next occurrence and . to repeat the last edit.

Hey — it's convenient!

It's annoying to have to press Esc every time you want to give an editing command. Luckily, here are two commands you can use while you are in input mode — very handy:

Ctrl-H	Erases last character you inserted
Ctrl-W	Erases last word you inserted

Why can't they just call it "cut and paste"?

If you're familiar with word processors (or with real editors, such as emacs — see Chapter 12, "Have a Big Emacs!"), you're no doubt familiar with cutting and pasting, that handy feature with which you take text from one part of your document and place it somewhere else in your document. Or maybe you've written some stuff in longhand and literally cut things apart and put them back together in another order.

Vi enables you to cut and paste, but it uses the endearing terms *yank* and *put*. You use `yank` to copy text into a buffer for later use. You use `put` to insert the copied text somewhere in your file. Note that `yank` is a copy command, not a cut command, and does not delete text. In fact, you also get `cut` for free: all the deleting commands (`d`, `c`, and `x`) place the text they delete in the buffer.

Yanking and putting commands

Table 11-8 lists some commands you can use for cutting and pasting, er, that is, yanking and putting.

Table 11-8	Commands for Cutting and Pasting
Command	**What It Does**
*n*yy	Yanks (copies) *n* lines into the buffer
*n*yl	Yanks (copies) *n* characters into the buffer
p	Puts (pastes) the most recently yanked or deleted text after the cursor
P	Puts (pastes) the most recently yanked or deleted text after the cursor
"*n*p	Retrieves the *n*th-from-the-last paste; vi keeps track of everything you delete (if you can remember how many deletions you've made, you can retrieve the deleted text)

Take two buffers and call me in the morning

A *buffer* is a temporary storage space you can't really see, but knowing about it can be really useful to you. Vi uses lots of buffers to keep track of what you're editing and enables you to use buffers to perform relatively sophisticated editing functions. If you're familiar with the idea of a clipboard, you can think of the buffers vi lets you use for `yank` and `put` commands as a kind of clipboard. Otherwise, just think of them as a convenient place to store stuff temporarily.

Using Last-Line Mode

Hey, didn't we mention a third mode you might want to use? Yes, it's time for *last-line mode.*

Three kinds of action take place from vi's *last-line mode* (it's named that way because you type commands on the last line of the screen):

- ✔ Read files into vi for editing
- ✔ Write files after editing (what you do to save a file)
- ✔ Exit from vi

To enter last-line mode, press the colon key (:) from command mode. The colon appears at the bottom of your screen, and you type commands, followed by Enter. In the rest of the sections of this chapter, you see commands that begin with a :, which means to press : to switch to last-line mode, then type the rest of the command in last-line mode, and then press Enter to execute the command.

If you press the colon key and see the colon entered in your text, you're still in insert mode. Press the Esc key to return to command mode and then press the colon key.

Read More Files!

You may recall, back at the beginning of this chapter, that we mumbled something about reading files into vi. This is it! If you enter vi without specifying a filename or, after you're in vi, if you want to edit another file or read the contents of another file into the file you're editing, vi lets you do that. Vi enables you to edit more than one file at a time, and you can switch among the files you are editing.

Table 11-9 shows the commands vi uses for reading files.

Table 11-9	Commands for Reading Files
Command	*What It Does*
:r *filename*) (then press Enter)	Reads the file *filename* into vi at the current cursor location (this is the easy way to insert a chunk of text that already exists: Put that chunk in a file, and read it in as necessary).
:e *filename* (then press Enter)	Stops editing the file you're editing now and begins editing *filename*.

(continued)

Table 11-9 *(continued)*	
Command	*What It Does*
:e! (then press Enter)	Starts this editing session over, discards any changes made since the file was last saved, and rereads the file into vi for editing (very handy when you realize that you've botched an editing session).
:e # (then press Enter)	Switches between the two files you most recently edited. (If you are editing more than two files, type : e filename and then press Enter to return to the less recently edited file.) Notice that you must save (write) the file you're editing before you switch files, if you have made any changes since you most recently opened this file for editing.

Save More!

Before long, you will want to save your file on the disk. You have to do this before you exit from vi unless you want to lose all the work you've done.

Practice safe editing

It's helpful if you can learn the lesson of saving your work without having to lose enormous amounts of it first. Whenever you're using an editor or a word processor, save your file frequently. How frequently, you ask? The answer is, how much are you willing to retype without getting miffed?

Computing environments can be flaky environments in which to work. The problem is that they can be seductively stable for long periods, and then — without warning — flake out. So just do it. Get into the habit of frequently saving what you enter.

In the world of vi, people talk about "writing the file to disk" (that's geek-speak for saving a file). The reality, in case you care, is that all the edits you make by using vi are made in the current edit buffer — nothing really happens to the file until you write the contents of the edit buffer into the file.

Write on!

To save your changes, use the write command in last-line mode. This command writes to the disk the file you've been editing. Table 11-10 shows some variations.

Table 11-10	Commands for Saving a File
Command	*What It Does*
:w (and then press Enter)	Copies the current edit buffer to the file that is open for editing. This command overwrites the current contents of the file. If you discover that the file you are editing is not one you are allowed to change, you can copy your edited version to a new file (see the following entry).
:w *filename* (then press Enter)	Copies the current edit buffer to a new file named filename. You can write the contents of the edit buffer to as many files as you want.
:w! *filename* (then press Enter)	Overwrites the file *filename* with the contents of the current edit buffer.

Over and Out

You can exit from vi in a number of ways, depending on what you've done and how you want to leave things. Table 11-11 lists a couple of commands for exiting from vi.

Table 11-11	Commands for Getting the Heck out of vi
Command	*What It Does*
:q (and then press Enter)	Quits — exits from vi (this command does not exit if you have made changes and have not written them to a file).
:q! (and then press Enter)	Quits and makes no changes to the file being edited. All changes you made since you last wrote (saved) the file are lost. If you've made some horrible mistake in editing and you can figure out how to undo it, you can use this command to exit from vi without changing the file if you haven't saved the file since you mangled it.
ZZ	Quits after saving your changes (those are capital *Z*s).
:x (and then press Enter)	Same as ZZ.

By far the most popular way to exit is by using the ZZ command so that vi saves your work.

Some Pearls for Vi Power Users

As you become more adept in using vi, you can expand your repertoire and amaze your friends by using the commands discussed in this section.

Tag — you're it

Vi has a facility that enables you to place markers, called *tags*, in your file so that you can quickly return to particular places or go back and forth between certain spots as necessary. (Word-processing programs call these things *bookmarks*.) Tags are named with single lowercase letters, so you get 26 of them. Table 11-12 lists these hopping-around commands.

Table 11-12	Commands for Using Tags
Command	*What It Does*
m*a*	Marks the current cursor location in the file and labels it with the lowercase letter *a*. You can press any lowercase letter and label as many as 26 different spots at time. A tag stays in place until you close the file.
à	Goes to the spot you marked with the lowercase letter *a* (that reverse quote is also known as a *grave accent*)
á	Goes to the first printing character — not a tab or a space — in the line marked by the lowercase letter *a* (that forward quote is also known as an *acute accent*)

Avoiding shell shock

Often, just when you're in the middle of editing something, you suddenly remember something you need to do or want to know by running something from the shell. From last-line mode, when you type : sh and press Enter, vi starts up a new shell. Vi lets you escape to the shell and run whatever shell commands you want. When you're finished, you type exit to return to your vi session.

When you type : sh and press Enter, you get a *new* shell, separate from the one you were running when you started vi. Remember to exit from that shell (using the exit command or Ctrl-C) to get back to vi.

On most UNIX systems, you can also press Ctrl-Z to suspend your vi session and return to your original shell. Later, you can resume your vi session, usually by typing f g, and vi refreshes the screen and puts you back where you were. (In this case, you're back in your original shell.)

Suppose that you want to actually *use* a shell command on some of the text in the file you're editing, right here and now. Vi enables you to perform shell commands on some or all of the text in your file.

From command mode, you type one of the following commands:

!!*cmd* (and then press Enter)	Executes the shell command *cmd* on the current line
!G*cmd* (and then Enter)	Performs the shell command *cmd* on the text from the current cursor position to the end of the file

If you want to sort your file in alphabetical order, for example, position the cursor at the beginning of the file (by typing 1 G) and then type this command to sort from the current cursor position to the end of the file:

```
!Gsort
```

Press Enter after typing this command. Poof! — vi sorts the file.

Getting more mouse power

If you're a Mac user or a Windows user dialing in to a UNIX environment, you can indeed make great use of your mouse to aid and abet your work in vi. For example, you can use your mouse to highlight and copy a piece of text (press ⌘-c on the Mac or press Ctrl-C or Alt-E C on the PC). Then, keeping in mind that vi lets you type text only in input mode, use the navigation commands to position your cursor and then press I. You can then paste the text you copied (press ⌘-v on the Mac or Ctrl-c on the PC). You might find this method much more flexible and easier than yanking and putting (and you can feel smug at the same time!).

It's really your terminal-emulator software, the program you use to dial in, that supports these copy and paste functions, and it may turn out that yours does not. We did, however, try them from a variety of programs — they are standard Mac and Windows commands.

Two — two — two files at once (or three, or n!)

If you know that you want to edit several files, you can specify them all on the same command line when you begin:

```
vi filename filename ... filename
```

When you've finished editing the first file, save it and move to the next one by using the n command. It edits the next file you listed on the command line.

Chapter 12
Have a Big Emacs!

● ●

In This Chapter

▶ Running emacs
▶ Editing your file
▶ Using lots of files
▶ Using the directory editor
▶ Mailing from emacs

● ●

*I*n Chapter 12 of *UNIX For Dummies,* we introduced you to the basics of text editing (a.k.a. word processing) in UNIX. We included a quick overview of emacs, our favorite text editor. Now we want to spend an entire chapter talking about the neat things you can use emacs for.

This Is Emacs

Emacs is an unbelievably powerful program. It slices, it dices, it gets your mail — you name it, emacs does it. The first version of emacs was written by Richard Stallman, who now runs the Free Software Foundation, a group that writes software and gives it away. His program was so popular that many versions of emacs now exist. Some popular versions include the ones in the following list:

- ✔ GNU Emacs, from the Free Software Foundation
- ✔ Unipress Emacs
- ✔ Gosling Emacs
- ✔ CCA Emacs
- ✔ Epsilon

This chapter talks about GNU Emacs because it's the most widely used version, but they all are similar.

Running emacs

To run emacs, by the way, you type:

```
emacs
```

On some systems, emacs has been renamed *e,* so you just press **e**. If you have GNU Emacs, it may be called *gmacs*.

If you want emacs to open a file to edit, you can type the filename on the command line, like this:

```
emacs filename
```

If the file exists, emacs displays the first screenful of it. If the file doesn't exist, emacs starts out with a blank screen, ready to create the file.

After emacs is running, it looks something like Figure 12-1, in which it is editing a file named junk. If you are running under the X Window system (with or without Motif), emacs opens a new window of its own.

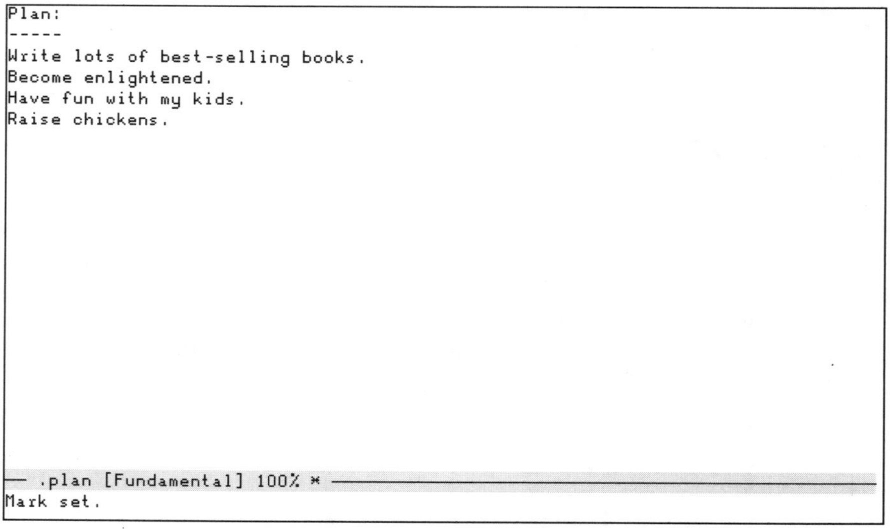

```
Plan:
-----
Write lots of best-selling books.
Become enlightened.
Have fun with my kids.
Raise chickens.




















-- .plan [Fundamental] 100% *
Mark set.
```

Figure 12-1:
Emacs is
editing a file.

The bottom line of the screen is the *status line,* which displays status messages (it starts out displaying the version of emacs you are running, if it doesn't have anything better to say). The status line is also called the *minibuffer,* for those who get into computer-speak.

The second-to-last line (which is usually in reverse video or otherwise high-lighted) is the *mode line.* It shows the name of the file you are editing, in addition to the editing *mode,* which is usually *Fundamental* (you can find more about editing modes later in this chapter, in the section "Editing à la Mode"). The exact format of the mode line depends on which version of emacs you use.

Here are some things that might happen when you start emacs:

✔ If you get an error message when you try to run emacs, talk to your system administrator. The program may have another name on your system. Or (gasp!) it may not be installed. Ask your system administrator (nicely!) if she can get GNU Emacs for you. It's free, after all.

✔ Emacs acts strangely if your terminal type (the *TERM* variable) is set wrong. If you think that you have this problem, contact your system administrator.

✔ Some versions of emacs (notably Epsilon) remember which file (or files) you were editing when you last exited from the program. If you run these versions without naming a file on the command line, they automatically open the same files you were editing before. Nifty!

Running away from emacs

When you finish editing your file and you want to exit, here's what you do.

If you want to save your changes to the file, press Ctrl-X and then Ctrl-S. If not, don't.

To exit, press Ctrl-X and then Ctrl-C. If you didn't save your changes, emacs first asks whether you want to save the changed file, to which you answer **y** or **n**. Then, if you didn't save them, it complains with this message: Modified buffers exist; exit anyway?. To exit anyway and lose your changes, type **yes** and press Enter. To return to emacs, type **no** and press Enter.

A Few Key Concepts

Emacs uses a few strange terms, which we had better explain right away.

I can't believe it's not buffer!

One strange term is "buffers." When you are editing a file, emacs copies it from the disk into a temporary space in memory called a *buffer.* When you finish editing, you save the contents of the buffer back into the file. If you don't save the buffer, the file remains unchanged. Emacs can have several buffers open at the same time so that you can edit several files at a time.

You can also have buffers that aren't connected with any file, such as a scratch buffer or a directory-editing buffer. We discuss a few nonfile buffers in this chapter.

Meta-morphosis

Another emacs term is the *Meta key*. Emacs seems to think that your keyboard has a key called Meta. Some keyboards do, but not many. If your keyboard does have a Meta key, you use it like a Shift or Ctrl key: Hold it down while you press another key.

"Wait!" you cry. "I don't have a Meta key!"

And neither do we. Stay calm. You can use your Esc (or Escape) key instead, with one little twist: Don't hold down the Esc key. Instead, press it and *release it* before you press the other key. For example, if someone tells you to press Meta-V to move up one page, press the Esc key, release it, and press **V**.

Most people, in fact, don't have keyboards with a Meta key, so we don't talk about it anymore in this chapter. Instead, we just tell you to use the Esc key. For example, we tell you to press Esc V to move up a page.

If you're using an X Window system with a keyboard that has an Alt key, you can use that as the Meta key. It really acts like a Shift key, so you have to hold it down while you press the meta-fied key.

If you use a Sun workstation, the LEFT and RIGHT keys can be used as Meta keys.

Editing à la mode

As mentioned earlier in this chapter, emacs has a bunch of editing *modes.* The mode you are using determines how emacs acts. It has two levels of modes, in fact, called *major modes* and *minor modes.* If you are writing a C program (God help you!), for example, you can use a major mode designed specifically for writing C programs. When emacs is in this mode, it helps you match your curly braces (with which C programs abound), continue your comments to multiple lines, and indent your program neatly. This major mode is called *C mode,* and there are lots of other modes like this, for use with other programming and markup languages.

For now, let's just stick with plain ol' editing, which in emacs-ese is called *Fundamental mode.* That's why it says Fundamental on the mode line in Figure 12-1.

Emacs also has *minor modes,* which are used for temporarily changing the way emacs acts. Some minor modes you might want to use are shown in this list:

- ✔ **Overwrite mode:** What you type replaces the characters that are already to the right of the cursor. To start or end overwrite mode, press Esc X, type **overwrite-mode**, and press Enter.

- ✔ **Fill mode:** Also known as *word wrap,* in which you don't have to press Enter at the end of each line, just at the ends of paragraphs. Emacs inserts carriage returns as you type so that lines don't exceed a set length. See the section "Wrapping and Indenting," later in this chapter.

- ✔ **Auto-save mode:** Emacs automatically saves your buffers at frequent intervals. GNU Emacs uses auto-save mode on any buffer that corresponds to a file on the disk. It's on unless you turn it off. (Leave it on — it can be a lifesaver!)

We talk about these minor modes later in this chapter.

How to command emacs

Emacs commands all have names, such as `write-file` and `forward-char` and `next-line`. You can give any emacs command by pressing Esc X (that is, press and release the Esc key and then press X), typing the command name (such as `next-char`), and pressing Enter.

That would be a heck of a way to move the cursor forward one character! Luckily, all the most commonly used commands can also be used by pressing combinations of the Ctrl or Esc keys and other keys. For example, another way to give the `next-char` command is by pressing Ctrl-F.

In emacs, a command is *bound* to a keystroke or combination of keystrokes. The `next-char` command is usually bound to the Ctrl-F keystroke. Amazingly, you can change which commands are bound to which keystrokes. (We don't explain how in this book, though. This chapter is confusing enough.)

Because you can bind any command to any keystroke in emacs, someone might just have done so. If you find that the commands we describe in this chapter don't work for you, your version of emacs probably has been diddled with, most often to make it more like some other editor the diddler used to use. If you have that problem, ask your system manager whether an undiddled version of emacs is available.

A File Here, a File There

So you are running emacs. How do you edit a file?

If you name a file on the command line when you run emacs (by typing **emacs filename**), emacs opens the file for you. If you want to open a file later, you can use the find-file command, by pressing Ctrl-X Ctrl-F.

When you press Ctrl-X Ctrl-F, emacs prompts you with the message Find file:. Type the filename (if it is in the current directory) or the pathname (otherwise), and press Enter, and emacs opens the file and copies its contents into a brand-new buffer with the same name as the file.

Attention, lazy typists!

Here's the first of many cute emacs tricks. Emacs can do something called *completion:* If you type the first few letters of something, enough to identify it, emacs fills in the rest. If you want to edit a file named *data2,* for example, when emacs asks for the filename, you can just type the first few letters, perhaps **data**. Then press Tab, which means, "Emacs, you fill in the blanks."

If only one filename begins with the characters you typed, emacs opens it right up. If several filenames begin with that character, emacs shows you a little list and lets you choose. If you want to edit *data2,* for example, you can press Ctrl-X Ctrl-F and type **data**. Emacs shows you a list of the filenames that begin with those letters, as shown in Figure 12-2. You can choose one by moving the highlight up and down the list of filenames and pressing Enter.

```
February 1
March 12
May 4
May┌───── One of the following: ─────┐
May│ data1                          │
Aug│ data2                          │
Sep│ datafile                       │
Nov└────────────────────────────────┘
December 4




─ data1 [Fundamental] 0% ──────────────────────
Find file: data
```

Figure 12-2:
Pick a file —
any file!

When you use Ctrl-X Ctrl-F to find a file, emacs looks in the same directory as the file in which the current buffer is saved and prompts you with that directory name. If you want a file in a different directory, backspace over the part of the path you don't like and type a pathname rather than just a filename.

Doing two things at one time

You can edit several files at a time. Emacs creates a buffer for each one, and you can switch from one to another. You can even look at two buffers at the same time!

To open another file, just press Ctrl-X Ctrl-F again. Emacs asks for the filename and reads the file into a new buffer. Emacs lets you have a huge number of buffers, although it's hard to keep track mentally of more then five or so.

To switch from one buffer to another, press Ctrl-X b (a plain b). Emacs asks for the name of the buffer you want to edit and suggests the last one you used. Press Enter to accept its suggestion, or type the buffer name you want.

Better yet, press Ctrl-X Ctrl-B. Emacs displays a little list of buffers and lets you choose one (see Figure 12-3).

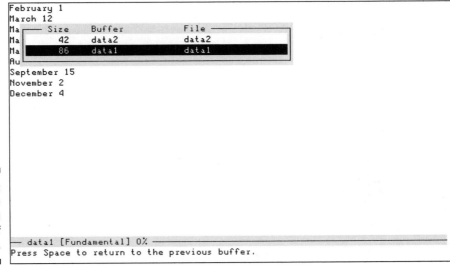

Figure 12-3:
Inside the little box you see a list of your buffers.

When you finish editing one of your files, save it (by pressing Ctrl-X Ctrl-S), and then close the buffer by pressing Ctrl-X k (not Ctrl-K, just k). This step "kills" the buffer.

If you are working on a bunch of buffers (or more than one, anyway), you should save them from time to time so that you don't lose your work. If you press Ctrl-X s (not Ctrl-S — plain s), emacs asks whether you want to save each buffer you've changed since the last time they were saved. (Some versions of emacs just go ahead and save all the changed buffers. Try it and see what yours does.)

Let's split

If you want to see two buffers at the same time, you can split the screen into two or more *windows,* with one buffer shown in each part of the screen. You can split the screen either horizontally (which is usually the most readable) or vertically.

To split the screen horizontally, move your cursor up or down to the place where you want the top window to end and the bottom window to begin. Then press Ctrl-X 2 to split it. The same file (buffer) appears in both windows, as shown in Figure 12-4.

```
February 1
March 12
May 4
May 5
May 10
August 14
September 15
November 2
December 4

— data1 [Fundamental] 0% ─────────────────────────────
February 1
March 12
May 4
May 5
May 10
August 14
September 15
November 2
December 4

— data1 [Fundamental] 0% ─────────────────────────────
```

Figure 12-4:
Two
windows on
the world.

The cursor is in either one window or the other. It starts out in the bottom window. To jump over the window divider to the other window, press Ctrl-X o (that's the letter *o*). To close a window, press Ctrl-X 0 (that's a zero).

How can you edit two files at once?

You can display two different files (buffers) in the two windows. To display a different file in the window the cursor is in, press Ctrl-X Ctrl-F to "find" the file. The new file appears in the window. If you "find" a file you are already editing (that is, one you already opened), the buffer containing the file appears in the window. If not, emacs opens the file, reads it into a buffer, and displays the buffer in the window.

- ✔ After you are sick of having multiple emacs windows on your screen, press Ctrl-X 1 (the number 1) to get rid of all except the one the cursor is in.

- ✔ If you want to move the window divider — the line between the two windows — switch to the window you want to make bigger (by pressing Ctrl-X o), and then press Ctrl-X Shift-6 (that is, Ctrl-X ^) repeatedly until the window divider is where you want it.

- ✔ You aren't limited to two windows. No, indeed — you can have as many as you have room for! Every time you press Ctrl-X 2, the current window is split in two horizontally. For a change of pace, you can also press Ctrl-X 5 to split the window vertically. With judicious use of Ctrl-X 2 and Ctrl-X 5, you can split your screen into enough small, irregular pieces that you may be reminded of the art of the late Piet Mondrian. Unless you have a screen with room for a large number of lines, three windows are about as many as you can use.

Remember that you can have a bunch of files open at the same time (each with its own buffer). One or more of the files can be displayed in windows on the screen, one in each window. But you can have files that are not on the screen. Emacs keeps them open; you just can't see them.

A new name

You can save a buffer in a different file from the one you read it from. That is, you can save your work with a new name and leave the original file unchanged. You can press Ctrl-X Ctrl-F, for example, to open a file named *data1*, edit it, and save it as *data2*. Here's how: Rather than press Ctrl-X Ctrl-S to save the buffer (which would save your changes back into *data1*), press Ctrl-X Ctrl-W to write the buffer to a new file. Emacs asks you for the filename.

Fooling with Text

Now that you have the file you want to edit on the screen, you might want to know how to edit it. Let's talk about moving the cursor, cutting and pasting text, and other cool editing tricks.

Smooth editing moves

First, you will want to move your cursor around the file. Table 12-1 shows the commands for cruising files.

Table 12-1	Making Your Cursor Move
Keystrokes	*What They Do*
Ctrl-F	Move forward one character
Ctrl-B	Move back one character
Ctrl-N	Move to next line
Ctrl-P	Move to preceding line
Esc F	Move forward one word
Esc B	Move back one word
Ctrl-A	Move to beginning of line
Ctrl-E	Move to end of line
Ctrl-V	Move to next page
Esc V	Move to preceding page
Esc <	Move to beginning of file
Esc >	Move to end of file

Blowing text away

Even the greatest of writers make mistakes (and we should know, right?). Table 12-2 shows some commands you can use to delete stuff.

Table 12-2	Getting Rid of Text
Keystrokes	**What They Do**
Ctrl-D	Delete the character the cursor is on
Esc D	Delete from the cursor to the end of the word
Del	Delete preceding character (if your computer doesn't have a Del key, try the Backspace key)
Ctrl-K	Delete (kill) from the cursor to the end of the line

You can also delete huge sections of text — see the section "Slicing and Dicing," at the bottom of this page.

Oops!

If you delete something you didn't want to delete or if you make any other editing mistake, you will appreciate emacs' undo feature. When you press Ctrl-X U, emacs undoes the last change you made. If you press Ctrl-X U again, it undoes the preceding change. You can press it a bunch of times to undo an entire series of mistakes, if you want. Wouldn't it be nice if life had an undo command?

If you are in the middle of a command and you want to stop it, press Ctrl-G. Emacs cancels the current command.

Slicing and Dicing

If you are like us, your text goes through considerable slicing and dicing before you are finished with it. We move things around frequently until we like the way our chapters look. Emacs has commands for cutting and pasting text, and they are easy to remember.

To cut some text, you "kill" it by pressing Ctrl-K. Emacs deletes the text and stores it in an invisible buffer, called the *kill buffer*. To paste the text in the kill buffer back into your file, you "yank" it back with Ctrl-Y. To "kill" a bunch of text, you "whomp" it with Ctrl-W. The only command we can't think of a good mnemonic for is Ctrl-spacebar, which marks the beginning of a bunch of text to "whomp." If anyone thinks of a good way to remember this command, send us e-mail at moreunix@dummies.com. (On some keyboards, Ctrl-space acts like a regular space, in which case you can try pressing Ctrl-@ or Ctrl-Shift-2.)

The next section tells you how to use these commands for slicing up your prose (or poetry, for that matter).

Moving a line or two

To move a line from one place to another, move your cursor to the beginning of the line you want to move. Press Ctrl-K once to "kill" the line (and copy it to an invisible buffer). Press Ctrl-K again if you want to "kill" the carriage return at the end of the line too. Then move your cursor to the beginning of the line before which you want to insert the line you just killed. Press Ctrl-Y to paste the text from the kill buffer.

If you kill more than one line without moving the cursor in between the "kills," emacs adds the additional lines to the kill buffer. To move two adjacent lines, for example, you can press Ctrl-K once to kill the first line, again to kill the carriage return at the end of the line, again to kill the second line, and again to kill the carriage return at the end of the second line. Now both lines are in the kill buffer.

Moving a word or three

When you press Esc D to delete a word, emacs sticks the deleted word into the kill buffer. So if you want to move a word or phrase, just press Esc D to kill it, move your cursor where you want the word or phrase, and press Ctrl-Y to put it back in.

If you want to kill all characters from your cursor to the end of a paragraph, press Esc K. (Emacs thinks of a paragraph as a bunch of text that ends with a blank line.)

Any consecutive sequence of killing and deleting commands is considered a single kill for yanking purposes. That is, if you press Esc D four times to delete four consecutive words followed by Del to get the space after the last word, the next Ctrl-Y yanks back the entire deleted chunk. We find this keystroke handy, particularly when we press Ctrl-K a bunch of times to kill a bunch of lines and then Ctrl-Y to put them back somewhere else.

On your mark

Emacs has something called a *mark,* which is a little, invisible marker you can use for moving and copying hunks of text. To put the mark where your cursor is, press Ctrl-spacebar (or Ctrl-Shift-2). Emacs says something like `Mark set` at the bottom of the screen.

When you move your cursor, the text between the mark and your cursor is called the *marked region.* Some versions of emacs show the marked region in a different color or in reverse video. You can use the marked region for cutting and pasting.

To move a bunch of lines from one place to another, move your cursor to the beginning of the first line you want to move. Then press Ctrl-spacebar (or Ctrl-Shift-2) to "mark" the beginning of the text you want to work with. Move to the beginning of the first line *after* the lines you want to move, and press Ctrl-W. This step "whomps" the text between the mark and the cursor and sticks it in the invisible kill buffer. Then move your cursor to where you want the lines to appear, and press Ctrl-Y. Emacs "yanks" the lines from the kill buffer and sticks them where your cursor is.

Copying a line or four

Many versions of emacs let you copy the marked region to the kill buffer without deleting it from its current position. Press Esc W to "whomp" the marked region without deleting it.

Glomming files together

You can insert another file at the cursor position too. Just move the cursor to where you want the other file to be inserted and press Ctrl-X and then I. Emacs asks you for the filename. When you type it and press Enter, emacs reads the file from the disk and sticks its contents into the current file right where the cursor is.

Wrapping and Indenting

If you use emacs for writing prose, it would be nice if it would do word wrap like a normal word processor does. Emacs isn't a normal word processor, (indeed, it's not even an abnormal word processor) but it can do word wrap — that is, it can automatically insert carriage returns when you reach the end of a line. And it can reformat paragraphs so that the words fill up the lines. (Leave a blank line between each paragraph.)

If you already have typed some text and you want emacs to move the words around so that they fill up the lines (while keeping them in order, you'll be glad to hear), move your cursor within the paragraph and press Esc Q.

To reformat a bunch of paragraphs, mark the entire region you want to reformat, and press Esc G. That is, move the cursor to the beginning of the first paragraph you want to reformat, and press Ctrl-spacebar to set the mark there. Move your cursor to the end of the last paragraph you want to reformat. Then press Esc G.

Emacs assumes that you leave a blank line between each paragraph. If you don't, reformatting a paragraph results in reformatting all of your paragraphs together into one big paragraph. Be sure to leave those blank lines! When (not if) you make this mistake, Ctrl-X U undoes the damage.

Reformatting text accidentally can create an enormous mess. If you just typed a carefully spaced listing of people and their birthdays, one careless Esc Q can string everyone together into one big paragraph rather than into neat columns. To undo a command that you wish had never happened, press Ctrl-X U.

Fill 'er up

What if you want emacs to do word wrap as you type rather than have to reformat your paragraphs afterward? Some versions of emacs have a minor mode (remember modes?) called *auto-fill mode,* or just *fill mode.* When auto-fill mode is turned on, emacs wraps your paragraph as you type.

The command to turn on auto-fill mode is usually not bound to a keystroke. But you can still use the command: Press Esc X so that emacs asks to you type a command. Then type **auto-fill-mode** and press Enter. The mode line (the second-to-last line on the screen) changes to say something like Fundamental Fill, which means that your major mode is still Fundamental (that is, normal ol' editing) and the minor mode is Fill.

To turn off auto-fill mode, just give the same command again.

How long is yours?

"How long will the lines be?" you may ask. Where will emacs put these carriage returns? Well, you can set the *fill column,* that is, the column at which emacs sticks a carriage return. If you set the fill column at column 70, emacs doesn't let any lines be longer than 70 characters before inserting a carriage return.

To set the fill column, you press Ctrl-X f (not Ctrl-F — just plain f). There are two ways to say which fill column you want it to use, and both are confusing. If you press plain Ctrl-X f, emacs sets the fill column to the column in which the cursor happens to be, which is fine if you want to make text narrower but not so great if you want to make it wider. To make it wider, press Ctrl-U (which is the way to warn emacs that a number is about to follow), type the fill width, and then press Ctrl-X f.

Some civilized versions of emacs (but not GNU Emacs) say something like Change fill column from 70 to [5]: after a plain Ctrl-X f. The number in square brackets is emacs' suggestion, based on the current position of your cursor. In that case, type the maximum number of characters you want on each line, and press Enter, or just press Enter to take the suggestion. Numbers such as 70 and 75 are usually good choices.

Searching for Mr. Goodtext

Like any good editor, emacs has a way to find words or phrases you may have lost. Unlike most other programs, emacs has what is called *incremental search,* a clever editor hack thought up about 15 years ago by a friend of ours. (Hi, Charles! Now he says that he's sorry he ever thought of it.) This section tells you how it works.

To locate something you lost, press Ctrl-S. Then begin typing the characters you want to look for. Suppose that you are looking for the word *chick.* (One of the authors has 13 three-day-old chicks in the basement and therefore has chickens on the brain, not to mention eventually on the menu.) You press Ctrl-S to begin the search. When you press **c**, emacs searches forward from where the cursor is to find the first occurrence of the letter *c.* When you press **h**, it searches forward again to find the first *ch.* When you press **i**, it looks again for the first *chi* it stumbles across.

Incremental searching means that emacs may find what you are looking for before you have typed the whole thing — very handy. Also, if you have typed chicken and you press Backspace or Del twice, emacs erases the en at the end of the word you are searching for and searches for chick.

After emacs finds an occurrence of the word you are looking for, it might not be the one you want. Press Ctrl-S again to search for the same text again.

Pressing Ctrl-S searches forward from where your cursor is. If you think that what you are looking for occurs earlier in your document, press Ctrl-R to search backward.

You can also search for and replace all occurrences of some characters. The find-and-replace command is usually Esc Shift-5 (that is, Esc %). Emacs asks for the text to find, which you type followed by pressing Enter, and the text to replace it with, which you also type followed by pressing Enter. Emacs then jumps to the next place where the text to find occurs and waits for instructions. You can tell it to do the following:

y	"Yes, replace this one and go to the next."
n	"No, don't replace this one, and go to the next."
!	"Replace every instance of the text to replace all the way to the end of the file without asking every time."

Anything else stops the replacement process. We usually press **y** a few times, and then, unless we messed up typing one of the strings, we press **!** to have it do the rest automatically.

Fooling with Directories

So far, you've seen how to use emacs to edit text. But emacs can do more! (Sounds like a late-night knife commercial.) You can use it to edit entire directories and delete and rename files left and right. This feature is called *dired* (*dir*ectory *ed*iting).

Dired consequences

To edit a directory, just open it up in the same way as you would open a file. Press Ctrl-X Ctrl-F, and type the name of the directory. When you press Enter, emacs displays a listing of the files in the directory, like the one shown in Figure 12-5. It uses roughly the same format you see when you use the `ls  -l` command.

```
    Directory of /usr/margy/bin
drwxrwxr-x    2     240 Feb 20 14:12 ./
drwxrwxr-x   10     544 Feb 21 17:02 ../
-rw-rw-r--    1       0 Feb 20 13:22 0
-rw-rw-r--    1       0 Feb 20 13:48 1
-rwxrwxr-x    1      26 Jan 24 14:33 change*
-rwxrwxr-x    1      17 Feb 15 10:53 d*
-rwxrwxr-x    1      86 Feb 24 12:19 data1*
-rwxrwxr-x    1      42 Feb 24 12:33 data2*
-rwxrwxr-x    1      14 Feb  9 16:38 datafile*
-rwxrwx--x    1      13 Jan 23 14:12 dir*
-rwxrwxr-x    1     174 Feb 20 13:49 display*
-rwxrwxr-x    1     207 Feb 16 14:50 ff*
-rwxrwxr-x    1     459 Feb 20 14:17 menu*
-rwxr-xr-x    2     236 Oct 17  1990 uncr*
-rwxrwxr-x    1     160 Feb  9 12:37 vartest*



— /usr/margy/bin [Dired] 10% ———————————————————————————————
```

Figure 12-5:
Here's a directory listing right in an emacs buffer!

For each file, you see its permissions (who can read, write, and execute the file), the number of links to it, the number of characters in it, the date it was last modified, and its name. Your cursor starts out on the first line of the list.

Different versions of emacs use different commands in dired. Your mileage may vary, as they say. If the commands we tell you about don't work, ask your system administrator or someone else who uses the system about what to do.

You can move your cursor up and down the list to choose the file you want to do something to. To move down, press N, Ctrl-N, or the spacebar. To move up, press P or Ctrl-P. When you finish using dired, close the dired buffer just as you would close any other buffer — press Ctrl-X K.

Show me that file

After you have chosen a file, you can edit it by pressing **e**. When you finish editing the file, press Ctrl-X k to kill the buffer it's in, just as though you had opened the file in the usual way, or press Ctrl-X b to switch back to the directory and leave the file in its buffer.

Blow it away

It's easy to delete files from dired. It's almost too easy, in fact, so emacs asks you to make sure that you know what you are doing.

First mark the files you want to delete. With your cursor on the filename, press **D**. A *D* appears at the beginning of the line for that file, indicating that it is marked for deletion. Mark all the files you want to delete. If you change your mind, press **U** to undelete it. Then press **x**. Emacs says something like `Delete these files?`. Most versions of emacs list the files to be deleted. Press **y** or **n** to delete all the marked files or leave them alone. Some emacses make you type **yes** before they delete any files.

When you are using dired, there is no "undo" feature. If you delete a file, it's deleted for good. So be careful!

Other file foolishness

You can rename a file by using dired. It's easier than typing a `mv` command. With the cursor on the filename, press **r**. Emacs asks for the new name, and — poof! — it's renamed.

Copying a file works in the same way — press **c**, and emacs asks for the name to give to the new copy of the file. (Not all versions of emacs support these commands. The ones that don't just beep if you try pressing r or c. Try R and C before you give up.)

Mailing from Emacs

You don't have to exit from emacs to send an e-mail message. Some UNIX users *live* in emacs, in fact, never exiting except to go to the bathroom.

In Gnu Emacs, to send an e-mail message, press Ctrl-X M (not Ctrl-M, just plain M). Emacs creates a buffer called *mail* and sticks some standard mail headers in it, including lines that begin with To: and Subject:.

On the To: line, type the e-mail address to which you want to mail the message. On the Subject: line, type a subject. After the text follows this line line, type the message. When you are finished, press Ctrl-C Ctrl-C to send the message. Easy enough!

Here are a few tips and warnings about sending mail from emacs:

  ✔ If you want to send a message to several people, put commas between their addresses on the To: line.

  ✔ You can also send copies of the message by adding a CC: line. Press Ctrl-C Ctrl-F Ctrl-C to add one, or add it yourself by typing **CC:** on a line by itself right below the To: line. Ditto for sending blind copies: Add a BCC: line by pressing Ctrl-C Ctrl-F Ctrl-B.

  ✔ Don't delete the line that says text follows this line! The line isn't sent along with your message; emacs just uses it to separate the headers from the text of your message while you are writing it.

  ✔ If you want emacs to split the screen and create a *mail* buffer in a new window, press Ctrl-X 4 M (that's a regular 4 and a regular M).

  ✔ If you have a file named .signature in your home directory, your UNIX mail system may automatically append the text in that file to each message you mail. If it doesn't, you can add it yourself by pressing Ctrl-C Ctrl-W to insert your signature into your *mail* buffer.

Another Slick Trick

Here's one last trick before we wrap up this chapter. Rather than exit from emacs when you want to give a UNIX shell command, you can just run a shell right in an emacs window!

Press Ctrl-X Ctrl-M, or Ctrl-X Enter. If this step doesn't work on your version of emacs, press Esc X, type **shell**, and press Enter.

Emacs creates a buffer named *shell*, and you see a shell prompt in it. Type UNIX shell commands just as you usually do. When you finish using the shell, type **exit** to the shell so that it finishes up, and then press Ctrl-X K to close the buffer.

It's a good idea to split the screen into two windows and run a shell in one of them. If you run a command that takes awhile, you can continue to use emacs in the other window.

While you are using a *shell* buffer, you can press Ctrl-C Ctrl-Y to repeat the last command. Actually, emacs retypes it but doesn't execute it until you press Enter, so you can edit the command if you want.

The shell window is just like any other emacs window, so you can cut, paste, whomp, and otherwise manipulate any text in that window the same way as you do normally.

A Listing of Commands

Table 12-3 lists all the commands we mention in this chapter.

Table 12-3	Our Favorite Emacs Commands
Keystrokes	**What They Do**
Ctrl-spacebar (or Ctrl-@)	Set the mark where the cursor is
Ctrl-A	Move to the beginning of the line
Ctrl-B	Move back one character
Ctrl-C Ctrl-C	In a *mail* buffer, send the e-mail message you are composing
Ctrl-C Ctrl-W	In a *mail* buffer, insert your .signature file
Ctrl-C Ctrl-Y	In a *shell* buffer, retrieve the preceding command
Ctrl-D	Delete the character the cursor is on
Ctrl-E	Move to the end of the line
Ctrl-F	Move cursor to the next character (to the right)
Ctrl-G	Cancel this command
Ctrl-K	Kill (cut) text from the cursor to the end of the line and put the text in the kill buffer; if the line is blank, kill the carriage return
Ctrl-N	Move down to the next line
Ctrl-P	Move up to the preceding line
Ctrl-R	Search backward
Ctrl-S	Search forward

(continued)

Table 12-3 *(continued)*

Keystrokes	What They Do
Ctrl-V	Move down to the next page
Ctrl-X b	Switch to another buffer
Ctrl-W	"Whomp" the marked region and put it in the kill buffer
Ctrl-X Ctrl-B	Display a list of buffers
Ctrl-X Ctrl-C	Exit from emacs
Ctrl-X f	Set the fill column (maximum line length)
Ctrl-X Ctrl-F	Find a file and read it into a buffer for editing
Ctrl-C Ctrl-F Ctrl-B	In a *mail* buffer, add a BCC: line
Ctrl-C Ctrl-F Ctrl-C	In a *mail* buffer, add a CC: line
Ctrl-X Ctrl-C	Exit from emacs
Ctrl-X i	Insert the contents of another file into the current buffer at the cursor location
Ctrl-X k	Kill (close) the current buffer
Ctrl-X m	Compose an e-mail message
Ctrl-X Ctrl-M	Run the shell in a window
Ctrl-X o	Switch to another window
Ctrl-X s	Save all open buffers
Ctrl-X Ctrl-S	Save the current buffer in its file, if it has one
Ctrl-X u	Undo the last change
Ctrl-X Ctrl-W	Write the current buffer into a file with the name you specify
Ctrl-X 0	Close the current window
Ctrl-X 1	Close all but the current window
Ctrl-X 2	Split the screen horizontally into two windows
Ctrl-X 5	Split the screen vertically into two windows
Ctrl-X 4 m	Open a *mail* buffer in another window
Ctrl-X Shift-6	Make the current window taller by one line
Ctrl-Y	Yank (paste) text from the kill buffer
Del (or Backspace)	Delete the preceding character
Esc b	Move back one word
Esc d	Delete the word the cursor is on and put it in the kill buffer

Keystrokes	What They Do
Esc f	Move forward one word
Esc g	Reformat the marked region and rewrap the lines
Esc k	Kill the text from the cursor to the end of the paragraph and put it in the kill buffer
Esc q	Reformat the current paragraph and rewrap the lines
Esc v	Move up to the preceding page
Esc w	Copy the marked region to the kill buffer
Esc < (that is, Esc Shift-,)	Move to the beginning of the file
Esc > (that is, Esc Shift-.)	Move to the end of the file
Esc % (that is, Esc Shift-5)	Search for all occurrences of some text and replace it with other text

If you really like emacs and want to learn every last command it has to offer, run to your local computer bookstore and buy *Learning GNU Emacs,* by Debra Cameron and Bill Rosenblatt (O'Reilly & Associates). It has a tasteful gnu (or wildebeest) on the cover.

The 5th Wave By Rich Tennant

Determined to help Wanda find her lost database, Del connects his "Royco 100 Fish Finder" to her hard drive.

Chapter 13
Climbing Elm

● ●

In This Chapter

▶ Isn't there a better mail program?

▶ Using elm

▶ Sending messages

▶ Reading your messages

▶ Saving messages

▶ Printing messages

▶ Creating your own address book

▶ Attaching files to messages

▶ Keeping messages in folders

● ●

*I*f you've used the `mail` or `rmail` programs to read your e-mail, you have undoubtedly thought, "There *has* to be a better way!" There is. Elm is a better mail reader in every way, and we tell you all about it in this chapter. And pine (based on elm) is great too — see Chapter 14, "Pining Away," for details.

Elm was originally written by Dave Taylor and is now owned and maintained by The USENET Community Trust. It is available on most UNIX systems. This chapter describes elm version 2.4.

From Tiny Acorns

What? Elms don't grow from acorns? Well, you know what we mean.

Running elm is easy enough — just type **elm**. You see a screen like the one shown in Figure 13-1.

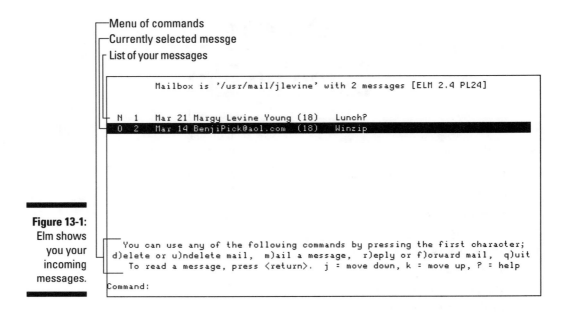

Menu of commands
Currently selected messge
List of your messages

```
              Mailbox is '/usr/mail/jlevine' with 2 messages [ELM 2.4 PL24]


   N  1   Mar 21 Margy Levine Young (18)    Lunch?
   O  2   Mar 14 BenjiPick@aol.com   (18)    Winzip
```

Figure 13-1:
Elm shows
you your
incoming
messages.

```
    You can use any of the following commands by pressing the first character;
 d)elete or u)ndelete mail,  m)ail a message,  r)eply or f)orward mail,  q)uit
    To read a message, press <return>.  j = move down, k = move up, ? = help

Command:
```

Your incoming messages appear on the screen (or as many of them as fit). The first letter on each line shows the status of the message:

- ✔ **N:** For new messages that arrived during this session with elm
- ✔ **O:** For old messages that were already here when you started elm
- ✔ **D:** For messages you have deleted
- ✔ **(Blank):** For messages you've already read

One message appears in reverse video (white on black or the reverse of whatever colors you usually see) or is highlighted in some other way. This is the current message, the one that elm thinks you want to work with next. The messages are numbered too, for your convenience.

Elm calls this screen the *index* because it shows an index of your messages. (Right now it lists your incoming messages. You can also see a list of messages you've squirreled away in folders — see the section "Stash It," later in this chapter.)

Here are a few tips for using elm's index:

- ✔ If you have too many messages to fit on one screen, press the right-arrow key or the plus sign (+) to see the next page of the index. Press the left-arrow key or the minus sign (–) to see the preceding page.

- ✔ You can press the equal sign (=) to move to the top of the list and press the asterisk (*) to move to the bottom of the list.

- ✔ If you don't like the order in which elm displays your messages, you can change it. See the section "Making Elm Better," later in this chapter.

- ✔ If you have a *really* long list of messages, elm can search the subject lines for you. Press / and type the text to look for. To search in the text of the messages rather than in just the subject lines, press //.

- ✔ If you don't see the little menu at the bottom of the screen, someone may have turned it off. See the section "Making Elm Better," later in this chapter, to learn how to change your Menu display option.

Bailing Out

To exit from elm, press **q**. Elm may ask these questions before it lets you leave:

- ✔ **Move read messages to "received" folder?** Elm asks this question if messages you have read are still lying around among your incoming messages. We usually answer **n** to this question because we want to leave any messages we haven't disposed of right where they are. (See the section "Stash It," later in this chapter, for information about folders.)

- ✔ **Delete messages?** Elm asks this question if you have deleted any messages. We usually press **y** at this point so that elm throws away the messages we deleted (see the section "About That Message," later in this chapter, to learn how to delete messages.)

After you've answered elm's questions, you're done elming and you see the UNIX shell prompt.

If you don't want elm to ask you all those boring questions, press **Q** rather than **q**. Elm then doesn't delete or move any messages.

What the Elm?

If you are confused about elm's commands, you can press **?** when you see the index. If you want to see a brief list of all of elm's commands, press **?** again. If you want help about a particular command, press the letter for the command. If you've decided that you don't want help after all, press a period (.). Don't worry — elm prompts you through it. For help about quitting, for example, press **?** (to begin getting help) and then **q**.

To leave the help system, press **q.** You're back where you were before you pressed **?**.

Reading the Elm Leaves

To read a message, select it and tell elm that you want to read it. That is, press the up- and down-arrow keys to highlight the message and then press Enter. (You vi users may prefer to press the **j** and **k** keys to move up and down.) If you have lots of messages, you can also select a message by typing its number and pressing Enter.

Elm displays your message. Simple enough!

To display the next message, press **n**.

Back to You

Here's how to reply to a message:

1. **Either select the message in the index or look at the message.**

2. **Either way, press** r **to compose a reply.**

   Elm asks whether to include the text of the message to which you are replying.

3. **If you press** y **now, elm sticks the text of the message into the new message you are composing and precedes each line with a > character. If you press** n, **it doesn't (as you may have guessed).**

   Elm asks you what the subject of the message is. It suggests the subject of the message you are replying to, with Re: on the front.

4. **You can change this part by backspacing over elm's suggested subject and typing your own. Then press Enter.**

   Elm asks whether you want to send a copy of the message to anyone.

5. **Type the addresses and press Enter. If you don't want to copy anyone, just press Enter.**

   Elm runs a text editor, usually vi, so that you can compose your message. If you don't like the editor elm chooses, you can change it — see the section "Making Elm Better," later in this chapter.

6. **Type your message, save it, and exit from the editor as usual.**

   (See Chapter 11, "Oy, Vi!" and Chapter 12, "Have a Big Emacs!" to learn how to use vi and emacs to compose your message.)

7. **Elm asks whether you want to edit the message again (press e and return to step 5), look at and maybe change the message's headers (press h), send the message (press s and skip to step 9), or forget all about this message (press f and forget about the rest of these steps).**

8. **If you press h to edit the headers, elm displays the headers for the message so that you can look at or change them. Press t to change who the message is addressed to, c to change who gets copies, b to change who gets blind copies, s to change the subject, or several other seldom used options. When you are finished fooling around with the headers in your message, press Enter to return to step 7.**

   After you tell elm to send your message, elm sends the message and asks you for your next command.

9. **Press i to return to the index or Enter to see the message you replied to again (perhaps so that you can delete it — see the following section).**

About That Message

This section discusses some other things you can do after you've read a message (you can also give these commands when you have highlighted a message in the index screen):

✔ Delete it, by pressing **d**.

✔ Change your mind about deleting it, by pressing **u**.

✔ Forward it to someone else, by pressing **f**. Elm lets you edit the outgoing message so that you can add comments and delete the boring parts.

✔ Print the message, by pressing **p**.

✔ Save the message in a file, by pressing **s**. Elm suggests a filename that begins with an equal sign (=), but this often isn't the name you want. (The equal sign means that elm is putting the message in a folder — see the section "Stash It," later in this chapter.) Rather than use the name elm suggests, you can type a filename of your own, one that doesn't begin with =. Elm saves the text of the message, including the full, incomprehensible headers, in a text file in your home directory.

When you delete a message, elm doesn't actually delete it. No-o-o-o, that would be too easy. Instead, elm marks the message with a *D* and deletes it when you exit from elm. This technique gives you plenty of time to change your mind.

Sending a New Message

Sending an e-mail message is just like replying to an e-mail message except that you have to tell elm to whom to send the message.

To send a message, just press **m**. Elm asks you for the e-mail address (or addresses) to send the mail to, the subject, and the e-mail addresses to send copies of the message to. Then it runs your editor so that you can compose the message. When you exit from the editor, press **s** to send the message.

If you want to send a message to several people, you can enter several e-mail addresses in a row. Just type them one after another, separated by commas. This goes for sending copies to several people too.

Stash It

So far you have been working entirely with your incoming mail folder. Natural enough — it's where all the action takes place. Elm makes a few other folders for you, however, and you can makes lots of them yourself.

"What's a folder?" you ask. It's a bunch of messages stored as a group. You usually begin with three folders:

✔ **Your incoming mailbox**

✔ **Your "received" folder (named** =received**):** Contains mail you have received and already dealt with (but not deleted)

✔ **Your "sent" folder (named** =sent**):** Contains copies of messages you have sent (check your elm options if you want elm to save copies of your outgoing messages; see the section "Making Elm Better," later in this chapter)

You can make as many other folders as you want, as explained in the following section. Folder names must begin with an equal sign (=).

Some people like to make a folder for each topic they deal with, such as =budget, =planning, =bigproject, and, of course, =personal. Others like to file messages by correspondent. The elm folks seem to like this method the best, and when you move a message to a folder, elm suggests a folder named after the person who sent the message.

Fold me a folder

To move a message to a folder:

1. **Select or view the message you want to move.**

2. **Press > (that is, Shift-.).**

   Elm asks for the name of the folder you want to move the message to. It suggests a name that begins with an equal sign (=) and continues with the name of the person who sent the message.

3. **Type the name of the folder — make sure that it begins with an equal sign. If you want to create a new folder in which to put this message, just type the name. Elm will make it. Then press Enter.**

   Elm deletes the message from its current location and sticks it in the folder you indicated.

If you don't remember the names of the folders you have, press **?** when elm asks for the folder name. You see a list of your folders.

You can also press **C** (be sure to capitalize it) to copy a message to a folder. Elm puts the message in the folder without deleting it from its current location.

Anatomy of a folder

So what is a folder, really? We thought you'd never ask. It's a text file that contains the text of the messages, one after another, separated by a blank line. It's nothing mysterious. You can look at mail folder files with any text editor, such as emacs or vi.

The standard place where elm puts its mail folders (the ones that begin with an equal sign) is in your directory Mail. That is, folder =plugh is the same as Mail/plugh.

What's in this folder?

To see what's in a folder, follow these steps:

1. **Press** c **(a small** *C,* **not a capital one).**

   Elm asks which folder you want to see.

2. **(Press** ? **to see a list of your folders.) Type the folder name (don't forget the equal sign) and press Enter. You can also press** ! **to see your incoming messages,** > **for your "received" folder (**=received**), or** < **for your "sent" folder (**=sent**).**

   When you change folders, elm acts as though you were leaving the whole program. It asks you what to do with read and deleted messages (see the section "Bailing Out," earlier in this chapter, for details about how to answer).

3. **Press** y **or** n **to answer the questions.**

   Elm displays the folder you asked for. The top line of the screen tells you the folder name, and you see an index of the messages in the folder.

The index of messages in a folder works in exactly the same way as the index of incoming messages. You can read them, reply to them, forward them, delete them, or move them to other folders. You can even move them back into your incoming messages folder!

Going Under an Alias

Face it: Typing e-mail addresses is terribly annoying. No one likes to type all those periods and at-signs. Elms lets you set up an alias for each person with whom you correspond. An *alias* consists of the person's e-mail address, full name, and name you want to call them when you're addressing mail.

For example, our dad is named Robert J. Levine. We have an alias for him called *RJL* (which is nice and easy to type).

Creating a secret identity

Here's how to set up your own aliases:

1. **Press** a **to tell elm that you want to make some aliases.**

   You see the elm alias mode screen, shown in Figure 13-2.

2. **To create an alias, press** n.

   Elm begins asking nosy questions about the person for whom you want to make an alias.

3. **Enter the alias name (that is, what you want to type when you address e-mail to this person), and press Enter.**

4. **Enter the person's last name, first name, and comment when elm asks for them.**

   If the alias is for a company or some other entity that doesn't have a first and last name, just enter the entire name as the last name.

   Elm displays all the information about the person and asks whether to accept the new alias.

5. **If it looks right, press** y. **If not, press** n, **and you'll have to start over making the alias.**

```
                    Alias mode: 3 aliases [ELM 2.4 PL24]


          1    More UNIX for Dummies                  Person    dummies
          2    Internet for Dummies Starter Kit       Person    starterkit
          3    UNIX for Dummies                       Person    unix








     You can use any of the following commands by pressing the first character;
        a)lias current message, n)ew alias, d)elete or u)ndelete an alias,
     m)ail to alias, or r)eturn to main menu.  To view an alias, press <return>.
                    j = move down, k = move up, ? = help
Alias: █
```

Figure 13-2:
The secret identities of your friends.

The alias you created doesn't appear right away. To update the list of aliases on the screen, press $. Elm says that it is resynchronizing your alias database. (Wow, sounds fancy!) Then your new alias appears on the screen.

You can create a small mailing list in elm — just make an alias for it. When elm asks for the e-mail address, type a list of e-mail addresses separated by spaces.

A.k.a.

The list of your aliases appears on the alias mode screen, shown in Figure 13-2. One of the aliases is highlighted, and you can move the highlight up and down either with the arrow keys or by typing the number of the alias. After you've highlighted an alias, here are the things you can do to it:

✔ Press Enter to see the e-mail address for the alias.

✔ Press **d** to delete the alias.

✔ Press **u** to undelete an alias marked for deletion (it has a *D* next to it). To highlight the alias, you have to type its number because pressing the arrow keys skips over deleted aliases.

✔ Press **m** to create a message addressed to the alias. Elm asks you for the subject of the message and to whom to send copies, and it lets you edit the text of the message as usual. The nice thing about this command is that you get to skip addressing the message.

When you are reading messages, you can make an alias for the current message. Press **a** to see the alias mode screen, and **a** again to create the alias. Elm asks you for the alias name, the person's last and first names, and a comment. This trick enables you to skip typing the person's e-mail address.

Now we return to our previous elm screen, already in progress

To leave the alias screen and go back to the elm index, press **r**. If you deleted any aliases, elm asks you whether you really, really want to delete them. Then you see the same index of messages you saw before you started fooling with aliases.

Attachments

As you probably already know, Internet e-mail is limited to text. If you want to send graphics or other nontext files, you have to use a sneaky work-around solution. Three standard sneaky work-arounds are widely used: uuencoding, MIME, and BinHex. Elm doesn't know about any of these methods, actually, but you can fool it by uuencoding a file.

It's a good idea to find out what kind of attachments your correspondent can handle before sending off a file.

Sending plain ol' text

To attach a text file to an e-mail message:

1. **Create a message as usual. Press** m.

2. **Elm asks you for the e-mail address (or addresses) to send the mail to, the subject, and the e-mail addresses to send copies of the message to. Then it runs your editor so that you can compose the message.**

3. **In the editor, use the editor's command to read in the file you want to attach.**

   In emacs, for example, press Ctrl-X I to insert a file where the cursor is.

4. **Save your message and send it as usual.**

This method of sending a text file doesn't create an official Internet e-mail *attachment;* it just sticks the text into your message. Works for us!

Sending any ol' file

To attach any file (graphics, programs, or whatever) to an e-mail message, you can use uuencoding. Your UNIX system should have a command called `uuencode` that converts any file into a uuencoded mess of characters. The `uudecode` command does the reverse, converting the scrambled bunch of characters back into a file identical to the original. Here's how to do it:

1. **In elm, press** ! **(that is,** Shift-1**) to enter a shell command.**

   You need this command so that you can run the uuencode program.

2. **Elm asks you for the shell command to execute. Type the following line:**

   ```
   uuencode file-to-send filename-to-use  >  new-file-name
   ```

   where `file-to-send` is the name of the file you want to attach to an e-mail message, `filename-to-use` is the filename you want the person receiving the file to use, and `new-file-name` is a filename to use for a temporary file containing the uuencoded version (such as `temp`).

If you want to send your file `1996-budget` to someone and have it be named `margys-budget`, for example, you type something like this:

```
uuencode 1996-budget margys-budget > temp
```

Remember that last filename (`temp`, in this example) because you need it in a minute.

Elm passes the command to the UNIX shell, which executes it. When it's finished, elm tells you to press any key to continue.

3. **Press any key.**

   You're ready to create your message.

4. **Press m.**

5. **Elm asks you for the e-mail address (or addresses) to send the mail to, the subject, and the e-mail addresses to send copies of the message to. Then it runs your editor so that you can compose the message.**

6. **In the editor, use the editor's command to read in the file you created in step 2 (we suggested calling it** `temp`**).**

   In emacs, for example, press Ctrl-X I to insert the file where the cursor is.

   In vi, press Esc to switch to command mode, press : (a colon) to get into last-line mode, type **r temp,** and then press Enter.

7. **The uuencoded file appears. Save your message and send it as usual.**

8. **Delete the uuencoded file, unless you plan to use it again. Press ! to type a shell command, and then type the following:**

```
rm filename
```

   where `filename` is the name of the temporary file you created in step 2.

After you create your uuencoded file in step 2, you can make sure that it's there by pressing **!** and typing **ls**. You can even look at it by pressing **!** and typing **more temp** (assuming that the uuencoded file is named `temp`).

Help! I got a uuencoded file!

You can tell when you get a uuencoded file because you see a line like this:

```
begin 600 budget
```

followed by a bunch of junk and a line that says `end`. Don't touch that junk! The uudecode program can turn it back into gold. Here's how:

1. **Read the message by highlighting it in the elm index and pressing Enter.**

2. **Pass the message to the uudecode program by pressing | (the vertical bar) and then typing** uudecode **and pressing Enter.**

The begin line contains the UNIX protection of the uuencoded file and the name that uudecode will give to the uudecoded file. If you can't find the file that got created in step 5, take a look at the begin line in the original message.

Making Elm Better

Like most programs, elm has options that let you control some things about the way it works. To look at your elm options, press **o** (that's the letter, not a zero). You see the Elm Options Editor, shown in Figure 13-3.

```
                      -- ELM Options Editor --
C)alendar file       : /home/abhaile/jlevine/calendar
D)isplay mail using  : more
E)ditor (primary)    : vi
F)older directory    : /home/abhaile/jlevine/Mail
S)orting criteria    : Reverse-Sent
O)utbound mail saved : =sent
P)rint mail using    : /bin/cat %s | /usr/ucb/lpr
Y)our full name      : John R Levine
V)isual Editor (~v)  : /usr/local/bin/pico -t

A)rrow cursor        : OFF
M)enu display        : ON

U)ser level          : Beginning User
N)ames only          : ON


     Select letter of option line, '>' to save, or 'i' to return to index.

Command: █
```

Figure 13-3: Things you can control about the way elm works.

To change an option, press the capital letter that appears before the closing parenthesis (this is more obvious than it sounds). Then emacs lets you choose from among the choices for that option, or it lets you type a value for the option.

Here are the options you might want to fool with (leave the rest alone):

✓ **E)ditor (primary):** This option determines which editor elm runs when you compose a message. It is usually set to vi, but we vastly prefer emacs. To each her own! To change this option, press **e**, type the command that runs your favorite editor, and press Enter.

✔ **S)orting criteria:** This option determines the order in which messages appear on the index. We prefer Reverse-Sent so that it shows us the newest messages first. To change this option, press **s**, and then press the spacebar until you see the setting you like. Press **r** to switch between forward and reverse versions of the sorting option. Then press Enter.

✔ **O)utbound mail saved:** If you want elm to save copies of mail you send, enter a folder name here (be sure that it begins with an equal sign). We use =sent. If you leave this option blank, elm doesn't keep copies of your messages. To change this option, press **o**, type the folder name, and press Enter.

✔ **Y)our full name:** This option contains the name that appears on your outgoing mail. To change it, press **y**, type your name, and press Enter.

✔ **M)enu display:** This option controls whether elm displays a little menu of commands at the bottom of the index screen. To change it, press **m**, press the spacebar until you see the setting you like (your possibilities are ON and OFF), and press Enter.

✔ **U)ser level:** This option determines which commands elm sticks into the little menu at the bottom of the index screen. Your choices are Beginning User, Intermediate User, and Expert User. (These terms could be much more judgmental — kudos to the elm people!) To change it, press **u**, press the spacebar until you see the option you want, and press Enter. Try Expert User and see what you think!

When you finish changing your elm options, press > to save the changes. Then press **i** to return to the index of messages.

Chapter 14
Pining Away

*T*he elm program is certainly a big improvement over `mail` and `rmail`, the older mail programs. But it is still tricky to use. The folks at the University of Washington in Seattle created pine, which began as a mutant version of elm, making it even easier to use than elm. Because elm is available for free, it is available on lots of UNIX-based systems, including most Internet shell providers.

Another neat thing about pine is that new mail programs can do something called *MIME,* which lets you include nontext files with your messages much more easily than in earlier systems, such as uuencoding. Neither elm nor `mail` can handle MIME.

Pine originally stood for *pine is nearly elm,* but now its authors, pumped up with self-esteem (not misplaced), proudly say that it stands for *pine is NOT elm.*

Running Pine

To run pine, just type **pine**. You see a screen like the one shown in Figure 14-1.

```
PINE 3.89   MAIN MENU                            Folder: INBOX   O Messages

        ?     HELP              -  Get help using Pine

        C     COMPOSE MESSAGE   -  Compose and send a message

        I     FOLDER INDEX      -  View messages in current folder

        L     FOLDER LIST       -  Select a folder to view

        A     ADDRESS BOOK      -  Update address book

        S     SETUP             -  Configure or update Pine

        Q     QUIT              -  Exit the Pine program



     Copyright 1989-1993.  PINE is a trademark of the University of Washington.
                        [Folder "INBOX" opened with O messages]
P Help                          P PrevCmd                    R RelNotes
O OTHER CMDS L [ListFldrs] N NextCmd                         K KBLock
```

Figure 14-1:
Pine shows
you a nice,
simple
menu.

Figure 14-1 shows you pine's *main menu,* with a list of its favorite commands.
Pine uses one-letter commands. Notice that one of the commands is highlighted — you can also choose commands by moving the highlight (pressing
the up- and down-arrow keys) and then pressing Enter. Toward the bottom of
the screen, pine tells you how many messages are in your in-box.

If you are using UNIX by way of a communications program, watch out for
which terminal you are emulating. Pine works fine if your program emulates a
VT100 terminal, but not so well if it emulates an ANSI terminal. You can usually
change which terminal your program emulates.

Leaving Pine

When you finish using pine, press **q** to quit. Pine asks whether you really, really
want to quit (it's so sure that you just pressed q accidentally). Press **y** to leave.
If you have left messages in your in-box that you have read but not deleted, pine
asks whether you want to move the messages to the read-messages folder —
press **y** or **n**. If you deleted messages, it asks whether you want them to be
expunged (really deleted) now — again, press **y** or **n**. Finally, you leave.

Sending Messages

You're in pine and you're ready to send some e-mail. No problem. To send a message, follow these steps:

1. **Press** c **to compose a new message.**

   Pine displays the screen shown in Figure 14-2, with prompts for To (the address to send the message to), Cc (addresses to send copies of the message to), Attchmnt (names of files to attach to the message), and Subject (the subject line).

   You can move from blank to blank by pressing the Tab key or the up- and down-arrow keys. You type the text of the message underneath the line that says — Message Text —.

   At the bottom of the screen is a list of the control keys you can use (the caret in front of a letter means that you press the Ctrl key with the letter — for example, ^G means that you press Ctrl-G).

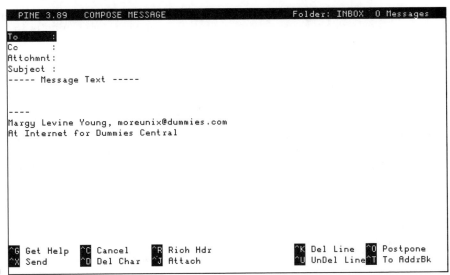

Figure 14-2: Ready to use pine to generate some junk mail.

2. **Enter the addresses and the subject line.**

   You can enter several addresses on the same line by separating them with commas.

3. **If you want to attach a file to the message, enter the filename in the** Attchmnt **(attachment) blank.**

Alternatively, you can press Ctrl-J to tell pine that you want to attach a file. It prompts you for the filename.

4. **Type the text of the message.**

5. **When you are ready to send the message, press Ctrl-X. Pine asks whether you really want to send it — just press y.**

Pine sends the message and displays the main menu again.

If you decide not to send the message after all, you can press Ctrl-C to cancel it.

This list shows you some cool things you can do while you are writing your message:

- ✔ For lots of helpful information about how to use pine, you can press Ctrl-G. Pine has complete on-line help.

- ✔ You can even check the spelling of your message — just press Ctrl-T. Pine checks all the words in your message against its dictionary and highlights each word it can't find.

- ✔ You can include text from a text file. Move your cursor where you want the text to appear, and press Ctrl-R. If you use pine on a shell Internet provider, you have to upload the file from your own computer to the provider before you can include it.

Sign here

You can make a *signature file,* a file that contains text for pine to include at the end of every message. The file must be called .signature and be in your home directory.

Use your text editor to make a signature file. Keep it short (no more than three lines long), and include your name, your e-mail address, other address information you want everyone to know, and (if there's room) a pithy or philosophical message that characterizes you.

After you've created a signature file, you don't have to type this stuff at the end of every message. To test it, send a message to yourself and see how the signature looks. The signature appears at the bottom of the message when you compose it. To omit the signature information from a message, just delete it.

Reading Your Messages

At the top of the main menu is a status line, and at the right end of it pine tells you which folder you are looking at and how many messages it has. (More on folders in a minute.) Your *inbox* folder contains incoming messages you haven't read.

To read your incoming messages:

1. **Press i to see the messages in the current folder.**

   (This step assumes that you haven't changed to another folder — you learn how to change folders later in this chapter.)

   Pine displays a list of messages (see Figure 14-3). You see one line of information per message, beginning with a + if the message was sent directly to you (not cc'd, for example). The next character is N for new messages you haven't read, D for messages you've deleted, and A for messages you have answered.

   You also see a message number, the date the message was sent, who sent it, how big it is (in characters), and the subject.

2. **To read a message, move the highlight to it.**

   You can press the up- and down-arrow keys or **p** (for preceding) and **n** (for next).

3. **When you've highlighted the message you want to read, press v to view it.**

   Pine displays the text of the message.

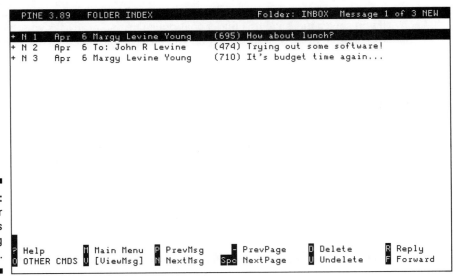

Figure 14-3:
Your messages are waiting to be read.

```
  PINE 3.89    FOLDER INDEX                      Folder: INBOX  Message 1 of 3 NEW

+ N 1     Apr   6 Margy Levine Young    (695) How about lunch?
+ N 2     Apr   6 To: John R Levine     (474) Trying out some software!
+ N 3     Apr   6 Margy Levine Young    (710) It's budget time again...




P Help          M Main Menu     P PrevMsg       - PrevPage     D Delete      R Reply
O OTHER CMDS    V [ViewMsg]     N NextMsg      Spc NextPage     U Undelete    F Forward
```

When you are looking at a message, here are some things you can do:

- Forward the message to someone else, by pressing **f**. You see the regular pine screen for composing a message, with the text of the original message included in the text of this message.

- Reply to the person who sent the message, by pressing **r**. Pine automatically addresses the message to the person who sent the original one.

- Delete the message, by pressing **d**. The message doesn't disappear right away, but it is marked with a D on the list of messages. When you exit from pine, your deleted messages really get deleted. (If you change your mind, you can undelete a message by pressing **u**.)

- Move to the next message by pressing **n**. Or move back to the preceding one by pressing **p**.

- Return to pine's main menu by pressing **m**.

- Press **?** to see pine's on-line help.

Take a look at the list of commands at the bottom of the screen. Whenever you see O OTHER CMDS, more commands are available than can fit on the menu. Press **o** to see more commands.

Saving Messages

Pine lets you create lots of folders in which to put your messages so that you can save them in an organized manner. To save a message in a folder, press **s** when you are looking at it or when it is highlighted on the list of messages.

If you save a message to a folder that doesn't exist, pine asks whether you want to create it. Press **y** to do so. When you move a message to a folder, pine automatically deletes it from your in-box. Very tidy.

Looking in a folder

After you've put messages in folders, you may want to look at them later. When you see pine's main menu, you can press **l** (the lowercase letter *L*) to choose which folder to look in. Pine automatically makes several for you, including the ones in this list:

- **INBOX:** Your incoming messages; messages remain here until you delete or move them

- **sent-mail:** Messages you've sent

- **saved-messages:** A place to save messages before you send them

Move the highlight to the one you want, and press Enter. Pine lists the messages in the folder.

You can make more folders by moving messages into them (as described in the preceding section).

Saving messages as text

If you want to use the text of a message elsewhere or download it to your own computer, save it in a text file first:

1. **View the message, or highlight it on the list of messages.**

2. **Press** e.

   Pine asks for the filename to save the message in (it puts the file in your home directory).

3. **Enter the filename and press Enter.**

That's it — pine copies the text into a file.

Printing Messages

To print a message, press **y** when you are viewing the message or when the message is highlighted on the list of messages.

What printer?

If you are dialing in to a shell Internet provider to run pine, you usually can't use the y command to print your message. The reason is that pine is running on your provider's UNIX computer and the message would print on a printer connected to that computer, which is probably nowhere near where you are.

Here is the normal way to print a message on your own computer:

1. **Save the message as a text file.**

2. **Download the file, using whichever method works with your Internet provider.**

3. **Print it from your own computer.**

What a drag — but wait! If you use Procomm or Kermit on a PC or MacKermit or VersaTerm on a Macintosh, you are in luck. These programs are so smart that pine can tell them to print directly on your computer's printer when you tell pine to display the message.

Creating Your Own Address Book

If you use pine to send messages to Internet addresses, it can certainly be annoying to type long, complicated Internet addresses. That's a good reason to let pine do it for you — set up an address book.

When you press **a** at the pine menu, you switch to *address book mode*. (It even says ADDRESS BOOK at the top of the screen.) If you have already entered some addresses, pine lists them.

When you finish fooling with your address book, press **m** to return to pine's main menu.

To create an entry in your address book when you are in address book mode:

1. **Press** a.

   Pine asks for the full name of the person.

2. **Type the person's last name, then a comma, and then the first name, and then press Enter.**

   Pine asks for a nickname (the name you type when you address mail).

3. **Type the nickname (make it short but easy to remember).**

   Finally, pine asks for the person's e-mail address.

4. **Enter it just as you would when you address a message.**

Pine stores the entry in your address-book and lists it on the address book screen.

If you make a mistake, you can edit an entry later. Just highlight it on the list of addresses, and press **e** to edit it.

You can also create an address-book entry directory from the address of a message. If you are looking at a message from someone whose address you want to save, just press **t**. Pine prompts you for the person's full name (it might even suggest it, if it's part of the message header), nickname, and e-mail address (pine suggests the address of the sender of the current message).

Attaching Files to Messages

You might want to send the following two types of files along with a message:

✔ Text files, composed entirely of ASCII text characters

✔ Other files, such as word-processing documents, spreadsheets, or graphics files

E-mail can include only ASCII characters, so if you want to send something other than text, you have to convert it into text temporarily, send it, and have the recipient unconvert it. Luckily, pine does most of this for you, using a system called MIME (*m*ultipurpose *I*nternet *m*ail *e*xtension). MIME is much more advanced than uuencoding because it remembers not only the name of the attached file but also which type of file it is.

Before sending an attached file to someone, make sure that he can decode it at the other end. Not all mail readers can understand and decode MIME attachments. Windows and Mac mail programs, such as Eudora and pine, can, but most versions of elm and plain ol' `mail` cannot. So ask your intended recipient first!

Including text in your message

If you want to send a text file to someone, you can include it as part of the text of the message. When you are composing the message, move the cursor to where you want the file to appear. Then press Ctrl-R and type the name of the file. The text appears in your message.

Attaching files

To attach one or more files to a message (by using MIME):

1. **Compose a message as usual.**

   It contains any text you want to send along with the file (or files).

2. **Press Ctrl-J to tell pine that you want to attach a file.**

3. **When pine asks for the filename, type it.**

   If the file isn't in your home directory, type the full pathname.

4. **When pine asks for an attachment comment, enter a short description of the file.**

   Depending on the mail-reading program your recipient uses, this description will show up somewhere.

   Pine displays the filename and description on the `Attchmnt` line of the screen. Pine also numbers this attachment 1 (in case you want to attach other files too).

5. **Repeat steps 2 through 4 for each file you want to attach.**

6. **Send the file as usual.**

Decoding attached messages

When you receive a message that contains MIME attachments, the message begins with a list of the attachments, like this:

```
Parts/attachments:
   1 Shown        5 lines  Text
   2   OK       478 lines  Text, "Table of contents"
   3   OK      1926 lines  Text, "Draft of Chapter 2"
```

Then comes the text that was typed in the message. Following the text are instructions for viewing each attachment, like this:

```
[Part 2, "Table of contents"  Text  478 lines]
[Not Shown. Use the "V" command to view or save this part]
```

If the attached file consists of nothing but ASCII text, pine can show it to you. To view an attachment, follow these steps:

1. **As it suggests, press** v.

   Pine asks which attachment you want to see. Actually, what it lists as attachment 1 is the text of the message. The first attached file is attachment 2.

2. **Type a number.**

   Pine asks whether you want to view the attachment or save it as a separate file.

3. **Press** v **or** s.

   If you pressed **v** to view the attachment, pine displays it on the screen.

4. **When you finish looking at it, press** e **to exit from the viewer.**

   If you pressed **s** to save the attachment as a file, pine asks for the filename to use. It suggests the name the file had when it was originally attached to the message.

If the attached file consists of other information, such as a word-processing document or a graphics file, save it, and then look at it in the appropriate program.

Pico's peek

When you compose a message by using pine, you are using a text editor called *pico*. As you have probably noticed, it's a simple, easy-to-use editor. The only command you need to know is Ctrl-X (to save and exit), and pico reminds you about it with a list of commonly used commands at the bottom of the screen.

You can also use pico on its own. To run it, type **pico *filename***, where *filename* is the name of the new file you want to create or the existing file you want to edit. Many people like pico as their regular editor because, although it is nowhere near as powerful as emacs or vi, it is considerably easier to use.

Part IV
Motif

The 5th Wave   By Rich Tennant

" WELL, I'M REALLY LOOKING FORWARD TO SEEING THIS WIRELESS E-MAIL SYSTEM OF YOURS, MUDNICK."

In this part...

Back when UNIX was written, no one had heard of graphical user interfaces (GUIs). Folks were lucky, in fact, to have a terminal with a screen rather than one that printed its messages on paper. (Can anyone here remember those bad old days?)

Now lots of UNIX systems have Motif, a zippy windowing system that looks much like Microsoft Windows. This part of the book describes how to point and click your little heart out in Motif.

Chapter 15

Lite Motif

. . . .

. . . .

Where Did Motif Come From?

The earliest UNIX systems didn't have fancy screen-oriented windowing systems. They didn't have screens at all, in fact — they used loud, rattling terminals that printed on actual paper. (The historically minded can find these types of terminals in the Computer Museum in Boston and the Smithsonian Institution in Washington, D.C. Yes, really.) As the years went on, UNIX appeared on computers that did have screens (most notably Sun workstations), and various windowing systems appeared.

One thing about the UNIX community you've probably come to appreciate by now is that you can't get everyone to agree on anything, except of course that UNIX is better than every other kind of system and that anyone who thinks otherwise is silly. So there arose, not surprisingly, a variety of incompatible windowing systems, each different from the other in various, not particularly interesting ways. Nearly all the windowing systems were *proprietary* (they belonged to one system vendor or another), and of course no vendor would dream of admitting that someone else's window system was better than theirs.

There were also a bunch of window system projects at universities. One of the more successful was the X Window project at M.I.T. (alleged to be a successor to the W Window project at Stanford — as far as we know, there wasn't a V Window project). X had many virtues, not the least of which were that it worked adequately well and that it was available for free to anyone who wanted it. So X became the window system everyone used.

X provides all the underlying mechanism that programs need to run windowing programs (indeed, a frequently voiced complaint is that X provides far too much mechanism and is huge, bloated, hard to understand, and slow), but writing programs by using the plain X facilities is still quite tedious. Several groups wrote *toolkits,* which are packages of prewritten pieces of programs that programmers can use to write their applications. The first one, the Athena Toolkit, was written mostly to test the X system, but (stop us if you've heard this before) it works adequately and is available for free, so it's popular among hobbyist and academic users. There have been a bunch of other toolkits, most notably Open Look from Sun Microsystems and AT&T. (They made a big deal of how the Open Look design had been reviewed by zillions of experts, but none of those experts must ever have used a window system, because Open Look was a pain in the neck to use.)

The Open Software Foundation, the same people who provide the OSF/1 version of UNIX, put out a toolkit called Motif, based on some work done by their members Hewlett-Packard and Digital Equipment. Unlike most other commercial toolkits, the Motif toolkit was made available by the OSF to any vendor who wanted it and was priced quite low, $1,000 for a vendor toolkit. OSF's license fees allow Motif licensees in turn to sell Motif kits to application developers for as little as $149, and they make it easy for computer vendors to bundle Motif with their UNIX systems. Motif is much more complete than the Athena Toolkit (it has a provision for handling languages other than English, for example), so it has become the primary X toolkit in use today.

How do I start Motif, anyway?

You might think that this question would be a simple one to answer, but, because UNIX is involved, it's not. The short answer is "Run mwm" (the Motif Window Manager), but that technique is not useful because you have to run mwm at the right time and place.

If you're lucky, your system manager will have set up everything for you automatically. If you're on an X terminal or a workstation running xdm (the X Display Manager), X will be running already when you sit down and will wait for you to enter your username and password, and Motif will start as soon as you log in.

The next best thing is that you're at a workstation which has been set up to run X after you log in, so X and Motif start automatically when you log in.

Failing that, you have to start them yourself after you log into UNIX. The two most common start-up commands are `startx` and `xinit`. If you're not sure which one to use, try them and see what happens. What should happen is that your screen will go kerflooie for a few seconds when it switches from old, dumb, terminal mode to new, cool, graphical X mode; a few windows will appear, running xterm (the dumb terminal emulator that runs under X); and Motif will start and draw attractive borders around all the windows.

If none of those things works, we've run out of ideas, and you will have to ask your local expert how to start X and Motif on your computer or X terminal.

TIP

How do I leave Motif, anyway?

This question is only slightly less complicated than starting Motif. As usual, we are the victim of a blizzard of options. Here are some likely possibilities:

✔ Log out by leaving the Motif Window Manager. In this case, move the mouse cursor outside of any windows, click and hold the right mouse button to display the Motif root menu, slide the cursor down to Quit, and release the button. Motif displays an incredulous little box asking whether you really want to leave mwm. Click OK.

✔ Log out by closing the main xterm window. The trick is to figure out which window is the main one. If one of them is labeled Login or

Console, that's it. Switch to that window by moving the mouse to that window and clicking the left mouse button. Then type **exit** to the shell in that window.

When X and Motif exit, the screen usually kerflooies again when it goes back to dumb terminal mode. (If your system uses the X Display Manager, it may immediately go back to the login screen, in which case you're finished.) If you end up back at a shell prompt in dumb terminal mode, you then have to exit from that as well by typing **exit** to that shell.

I'm Not Just a Server — I'm Also a Client!

X was designed from the beginning to work with computer networks. It makes a clear distinction between the *server* program, which handles the screen, keyboard, and mouse, and the *client* program, which does the actual computing. Although the two programs more often than not are running on the same computer, they don't have to be. (Readers who saw John on "The Internet Show" on public TV may recall one demonstration of an on-line subway map of Paris. That was an X application, with the X server running on a PC in the TV studio in Texas and the client program on a computer in France, connected by way of the Internet.)

X's networkability (is that a word?) is most useful in two ways. One is that you can be sitting at an X workstation attached to a local network and have windows attached to client programs running on computers all over the network, often on computers considerably more powerful than yours. The other is that there are *X terminals,* specialized computers with screens, keyboards, mice, and network connections that run only a single program, an X server. The idea of an X terminal is that it's considerably cheaper than a workstation, so you can have a few workstations or larger computers with a flock of inexpensive X terminals attached, getting nearly workstation performance for the X terminal users, but at a considerably lower price.

X terminals are probably a passing fad because these days a 486 PC that runs UNIX (including an X server program) costs about the same as an X terminal and offers more flexibility. Fortunately, X terminals and workstations running an X server look and work almost exactly the same, so we don't belabor the difference any longer.

We Don't Need No Stinkin' Policy

One area in which X is radically different from most other windowing systems is its almost complete lack of what's known as "policy." X is utterly agnostic about what windows should look like on the screen, how keystrokes and mouse clicks should be interpreted, and pretty much anything else that affects a user. This lack of policy was part of the original appeal of X because no matter which window system you were used to, you could make X look just like that system. So the good news is that X offers great flexibility. The bad news is that the word *inconsistent* barely scratches the surface of what you will run into.

How did we manage without this?

One of the ways in which X avoids having any policy built in is that it foists much of the general window-management jobs onto a program called a *window manager.* (Catchy name, huh?) The window manager handles such jobs as creating the borders around each application's main windows, controlling how you move, resize, switch among, and iconify windows, and most of the other tasks that aren't part of any particular application. It's possible to run X without any window manager, but it's rather unpleasant because, without one, there's no way to do such things as move a window.

Déjà vu déjà vu

Readers familiar with Microsoft Windows may find Motif to be strangely familiar. Its windows don't look all that much like Windows (actually, they look much like the way Windows 95 will look), but the mouse and keyboard techniques are extremely similar. That turns out to be no coincidence. Hewlett-Packard has a super-duper application environment it sells on both Windows and X, so it deliberately made its X package (from which much of Motif is derived) as similar to Windows as possible.

For users who switch back and forth between Windows and Motif (we authors, for example), this capability is a blessing because the mouse moves and keystrokes our fingers have memorized for one system work by and large in the same way in the other. This practically unprecedented level of compatibility exists between UNIX and something else, so we figure that, deep down, it must have been an oversight.

About your mouse

As an X user, you have a mouse, or a mouselike thing such as a trackball or a finger pad. Your mouse (or mouselike thing) has some buttons on it. Take a moment to count the buttons.

Finished counting? (How long could it have taken?) We hope that you found three buttons. If you found only two buttons, you have a problem because most X programs were written with three-button mice in mind and don't work well with two-button mice. It is possible in theory to reconfigure X applications to let you get to all the program's features by using only two buttons, but it's much easier to get a three-button mouse. We've found some perfectly usable ones at our local computer store for $10 or less.

Far too many window managers have been written for X, each with its own quirks and peculiarities. Motif has a window manager of its own, the Motif Window Manager, or mwm, which we describe later in this chapter.

Widgets here, widgets there

The Motif toolkit includes prewritten bits of program that programmers can use to build their applications. That wouldn't be very interesting except that the bits of program it includes are the ones that draw stuff on the screen. These *widgets* include the usual things that windowing programs use, such as menus, pushbuttons, text boxes, and scroll bars. At this point not many applications use Motif widgets, but they're becoming more popular, and we describe them later too.

A quick mouse refresher

You probably know all about how to use your mouse. But in the unlikely event that you're a little rusty on the terminology, here are a few basic terms:

Cursor: The cursor is the little doozit (a highly technical term) on the screen that shows where the mouse is pointing. The cursor often changes shape as you move it from one window to another to give you a hint of what's going on in a window. The most common cursor shapes are a black X (when you're not in any window), a little arrow (in windows with graphics), and a little, vertical hairline (in windows of text.)

Click: To click something, move the cursor to the thing to be clicked, and then press and release the mouse button. Unless otherwise directed, press the leftmost mouse button.

Drag: To drag something, move the cursor to the drag-ee, press down the mouse button, move the mouse while holding down the button, and then let go of the button when you get to where you want the drag-ee to be. Most non-Motif programs use the left button to drag stuff, and Motif programs use the middle button.

On the Border Patrol

Motif (or more particularly the Motif Window Manager) draws a border around every window on your screen, as shown in Figure 15-1. The border gives you considerable control over the window, letting you move it, hide it, change its size, and so on.

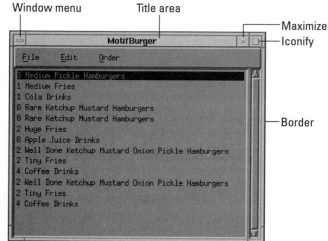

Window menu   Title area

Maximize
Iconify

Border

Figure 15-1:
A typical
Motif
window.

The borders of some windows will be missing some or all of the buttons we discuss in this section. The reason is that not all windows allow all functions. If the button's not there, you can't do what it would have done anyway.

Switching windows

In line with X's standard rule of never making up its mind about anything, you switch windows in two different ways:

- **Click-to-type, or explicit, focus:** Move the mouse cursor to the window you want to use, and click the mouse in it somewhere. The window moves to the front (that is, any overlapping windows drop behind it so that you can see the entire window.)

- **Move-to-type, or pointer, focus:** Move the mouse cursor into the window you want to use. Even though it may be partially obscured by other windows, the window becomes active. Click the window's title bar if you want to move it to the front as well.

You can tell which is the active window because the Motif Window Manager changes the color of its border to a distinctive darker color. Motif's standard window-switching rule is click-to-type.

Many (maybe most) users prefer move-to-type rather than click-to-type. Chapter 16, "Mutant Motif," tells you how to change that.

Moving a window

Moving a window around on the screen is easy. Move the cursor to the window's title bar (the part of the top border with the program name), and drag the window to where you want it to be.

Resizing a window

Changing the size of a window is nearly as easy as moving one. You simply drag the window's border to the size you want. Move the cursor to the border, at which point the cursor's shape changes to an arrow pointing at a line or a corner, and then click and drag. The top and bottom borders let you resize vertically, the left and right borders let you resize horizontally, and the corners let you resize any way you want.

While you're resizing, the window manager displays a little box that shows the size of the window. The size is normally measured in pixels (screen dots), but in programs such as xterm, it's measured in characters.

You can *maximize* a window to make it fill up the entire screen by clicking the maximize button in the top right corner of the border. Click it again to restore it to normal size. We don't find this button very useful. Unlike in Windows (from which the maximize button was inherited), Motif screens are usually big enough that it's overkill to fill the entire screen with one window.

Some programs have strong feelings about how big their windows should be. In some cases, they don't let you shrink the window to less than a minimum size. In other cases, you can't change the size at all. For these programs, attempts to resize just don't work. You can click and drag the borders all you want, but nothing moves.

Making windows go away

You can *iconify* a window, that is, make the window go away in favor of a small icon box, by clicking the iconify button in the top right corner of the window. To restore the window (get the window back), double-click the icon (click it twice quickly).

Icons normally appear in the lower left corner of your screen, but you can move them around by dragging the icon around with the mouse. After you've moved an icon, if you restore the window and then reiconify it, the icon reappears where you left it. You can lay out the icons to your taste by iconifying every window on the screen, moving the icons to tasteful positions, and then restoring the ones you want to use.

On the menu

Motif provides every window with a window menu. This menu somewhat duplicates the functions of the title bar, but it can be useful anyway.

To make the menu appear, click the menu icon in the top left corner of the border. The window menu is displayed, as shown in Figure 15-2. The Restore, Move, Size, Minimize, and Maximize choices are equivalent to the border-clicking techniques we just discussed. (Minimize is Motif-ese for "iconify.") The two remaining entries can be useful, though. Lower means to push the window behind all the rest so that it doesn't obscure any other windows. That entry is useful when you want to work on something else for a while. Close closes the window and usually also ends the program that started it. This entry can be handy for programs that get stuck or don't have any normal way to exit.

Restore	Alt+F5
Move	Alt+F7
Size	Alt+F8
Minimize	Alt+F9
Maximize	Alt+F10
Lower	Alt+F3
Close	Alt+F4

Figure 15-2: The Motif window menu.

Motif offers a set of keyboard equivalents for mouse-haters. To display the window menu, press Shift-Esc or Alt-spacebar. Then either press the cursor keys and Enter to choose one of the entries or press the underlined letter in the entry you want. For Move and Size, you press the cursor keys to move or resize the window and then press Enter when you're finished.

You can also use the Alt-key equivalents in the menu, such as Alt-F9 for minimize. If your keyboard has two Alt keys (as most PC keyboards do), you may find that the two Alt keys work differently. On our system, the left Alt key is recognized by individual programs, and the right Alt key is the one the Motif Window Manager recognizes.

More Stupid Window Manager Tricks

The window manager has a *root menu* that appears when you click the right mouse button (the right mouse button, not the left) outside any window. It looks like Figure 15-3.

Figure 15-3:
The Motif
root menu.

The contents of the root menu are infinitely configurable, as you discover in the next chapter, but Table 15-1 shows you the typical entries.

Table 15-1	**Typical Entries for the Root Menu**
Entry	*What It Does*
New Window	Starts a new xterm window
Shuffle Up	Takes the next window and moves it to the front
Shuffle Down	Takes the next window and moves it to the back
Refresh	Completely redraws the screen
Pack Icons	Moves all the icons on the window to the lower left corner
Toggle Behavior	Switches between standard and customized window manager
Restart	Restarts the window manager
Quit	Leaves the window manager

We find New Window and Refresh to be relatively useful. Shuffling windows is a waste of time because you can click the title bars of the windows you really want to see. Packing icons can be useful if you have lots of icons cluttering up your screen (which we rarely do). Toggle Behavior and Restart are useful only if you customize your window manager, so we discuss them in Chapter 16, "Mutant Motif." And Quit is handy if your system is set up so that you log out by leaving the window manager. Otherwise, it's useless too.

The Parade of Motif Widgets

Applications built with Motif use the Motif *widgets,* elements that appear in windows. This section quickly describes the most common widgets. They're all designed to be easy to use, so even without reading the instructions, it's easy to guess how they work.

Menus

Figure 15-4 shows the main window from the MotifBurger sample application that comes with Motif, with one of its pull-down menus selected. You make choices from a Motif menu in an obvious way: Click the place you want on the menu bar at the top of the application's window. If the menu has subentries (as most do), the next-level menu drops down. Click the entry you want.

Figure 15-4:
An
application
menu.

You can also drive Motif applications from the keyboard. To choose a menu entry, hold down Alt (the left Alt key if you have two), and press the underlined letter in the menu entry. If there are submenus, press the cursor up and down keys to move to the entry you want, and press Enter to select or Esc to ignore.

Occasionally you see a couple of other minor variants of menus. *Tear-off* menus are similar to pull-down menus except that they have a dotted line across the top when you pull them down. If you click the dotted line and drag the menu to a convenient place, it stays there indefinitely so that you can use it whenever you want. We don't find this feature very useful because it clutters up the screen. (Motif's old archrival Open Look had tear-off-like menus called pushpins, and Open Look proponents trumpeted them as a major advantage. Motif probably added them as much to shut up the competition as because anyone really wanted them.) Sometimes *pop-up* menus also appear when you press the right mouse button, the way the root menu appears when you click outside any window. Pop-up windows work just like pull-down windows do after they've popped up.

Too many widgets

Figure 15-5 shows a window from the MotifBurger sample application. This window is pretty awfully designed because it's full of far too many different kinds of widgets. But it was intended as a demonstration of the various kinds of widgets, which it does just fine.

Now let's look at the widget types, beginning from the left side of the figure.

Radio buttons

The Hamburgers Rare/Medium/Well Done box is called a *radio button* box because it sort of resembles the buttons on a car radio. You can click any one of the buttons to choose it, but you can choose only one radio button in a group.

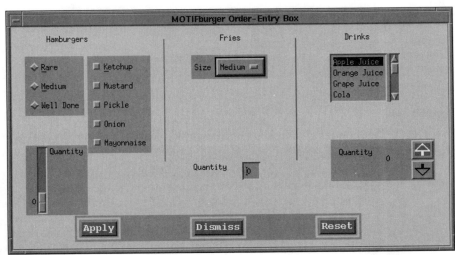

Figure 15-5:
A bunch of
widgets.

You can recognize radio buttons because they're shaped like little diamonds.

You're supposed to be able to choose radio buttons by holding down the Alt key and pressing the underlined letter, but in our experience that doesn't always work. Use your mouse to be sure.

Toggle buttons

The list of hamburger condiments, from Ketchup to Mayonnaise, are *toggle buttons*. When you click one, it turns on if it was off and turns off if it was on, sort of like a toggle switch. Unlike radio buttons, any or all of the toggle buttons in a group can be chosen.

You can recognize toggle buttons because they're little squares.

Scales or sliders

The hamburger Quantity thing is a *scale*. You can move it up or down with the mouse to control how many hamburgers to order. Although this scale looks pretty silly, in some cases it's just what you want (the volume control on a sound application, for example).

Scales can be laid out either up and down or left and right. They work the same either way.

Option menus

The fries size control is an *option menu*. When you click it, the complete set of options appears, as shown in Figure 15-6. Move the cursor to the one you want and click. It shrinks back down and displays the chosen option.

Figure 15-6:
How many
fries would
you like with
that?

Text boxes

The little quantity box under fries is a *text box*. Click the cursor there, and then type the number of orders of fries you want. The usual text-editing characters, such as arrow keys and backspace, work.

This text box is the smallest one we've ever seen. (Hey, it's just a sample application.) Most text boxes are large enough that the editing keys are useful. Many text windows also have scroll bars, which we discuss in the following section.

Scrollable lists and scroll bars

The list of drinks beginning with Apple Juice is a *scrollable list*. You can move the list up and down in its window by using the *scroll bar* to the right of the window. The little arrows move the list up and down a small, fixed amount. You can also drag the block between the arrows up and down to move the list directly.

After you've found the item you want, click it to choose and highlight it. (We've chosen apple juice here, but our favorite is grape juice because it gives us the classic cool, purple mustache.)

Pushbuttons

The last controls here are *pushbuttons*. They come in two varieties: buttons with text and buttons with drawings. The two arrows for the Drinks quantity are buttons with drawings. The Apply, Dismiss, and Reset buttons at the bottom of the window are buttons with text.

They all work in the same way. To choose the button and do whatever the button does, click it.

Chapter 16
Mutant Motif

● ●

In This Chapter

▶ How to change the way Motif works

▶ . . . if you dare

● ●

Configuring Motif: Threat or Menace?

If you've just finished reading the preceding chapter, you may have noticed that many of the ways in which Motif works are not exactly what you might like. By and large, that's tough luck, but there are a few ways in which it's reasonably possible to adjust your Motif and other X applications.

We Hope That You're Resourceful

The primary way you change the behavior of any X program, including Motif, is by changing its resources. Every X program except the simplest is built from lots and lots of little pieces of prewritten program code called *widgets*. Every item on the screen — a menu, a pushbutton, a scrollbar, you name it — is drawn by a widget. Each widget has a bunch of parameters that control its position on the screen, the colors it uses — you name it again — and these parameters are always called *resources*.

Call me Ishmael

Every resource has a name. In fact, most resources have lots of names. Consider, for example, the xclock program that most Motif folks use, which displays a clock on the screen, either digital or analog. The xclock program has a resource that controls the color of the clock's hands — it's called `xclock.clock.hands`. That is, the program is `xclock`, the widget in the program is `clock`, and the particular resource is `hands`. (This is a relatively simple name; often they go on for six or seven levels in a complex program that has widgets within widgets.)

OK, so don't call me Ishmael

Giving each resource a name is so simple and straightforward that the X crowd felt that it had to do something about it. So at each level there can be both a *class* name and an *instance* name. The theory here is that you might have a bunch of similar things of the same type; a clock program, for example, might have a bunch of different clock faces, drawn by separate clock widgets. (Imagine one clock for New York, one for Paris, and one for Tokyo, or something.) In reality, the clock program draws only one clock, but that's a boring practical detail of no interest to the X crowd.

So the clock program itself has an instance name of *xclock,* but a class name of *XClock.* The clock widget has an instance name of *clock,* but a class name of *Clock.* You get the idea. The class name is usually the instance name with the first letter capitalized, except that, if the first letter is an *X,* the second letter is capitalized too.

Is this of any use? Sometimes yes, sometimes no. In the particular case of xclock, it can indeed come in handy. When you run an X program, you can use the `-name` option to change the name of the program, which changes both the name displayed in the program's title bar and the instance name of the program. An example may clarify this. Suppose that you want to have two clocks: one showing Boston time and one showing Paris time. So you run two instances of xclock, like this:

```
$ TZ=EST5EDT xclock -name Boston&
$ TZ=WET-1CET xclock -name Paris
```

(The `TZ` stuff changes the time zone the program thinks it's in by changing the `TZ` environment variable used in the program (see Chapter 5, "The Shell Game: Using Shell Variables"). The `-name` options change the instance names to Boston and Paris. The color of the hands in the individual programs can be referred to therefore by the instance names `Boston.clock.hands` and `Paris.clock.hands`, or you can refer to all hands in all copies of xclock, regardless of time zone, by using the class name `XClock.clock.hands`.

In practice, you can usually use the class and instance names interchangeably unless you happen to be running several copies of programs you want to treat differently. We generally use instance names in the following examples. But we told you about class names because, if you fool with resources at all, you run into them.

Then how do I change a program's resources?

We were afraid you'd ask that. It's a pain. The general outline is shown here:

- ✔ Type the resources you want to change into a file.
- ✔ Tell X to read in that file.
- ✔ Persuade the programs to look at the new resources.

Let's take this one step at a time.

Resource files — yuck!

Resources generally live in a resource file, which is called (depending on the whim of the person who installed your X system) either `.Xdefaults` or `.Xresource`.

It's a plain, old text file with lines like this:

```
Boston.clock.hands:     green
Paris.clock.hands:      blue
XClock.clock.hands:     red
```

There's the name of the resource, a colon, and the value. An important and common simplification is possible: You can use an asterisk to abbreviate the middle of a resource name, like this:

```
XClock*hands:           red
```

This abbreviation turns out to be extremely handy because in most applications it's practically impossible to figure out the full name of the resources.

Within the resource file, the order of the lines doesn't matter. Instance resources override class resources, so in this case the Boston and Paris lines (which are instance names) override the Xclock line (which is a class name) for copies of the clock program that happen to be named Boston and Paris. Any other clocks get the XClock name.

X applications are extremely, totally picky about the capitalization of their resource names. And they don't give you any help if you goof — they just ignore anything that's misspelled or miscapitalized. If you load up some resources and nothing happens, that's almost always because you got the capitalization wrong.

Proving that you're resourceful

So how do you tell X about your wonderful new resources? Follow these steps:

1. **Using any text editor, type your resources into your file** .Xdefaults.

   Incidentally, the reason to call the file .Xdefaults is that, when X starts up, it automatically loads the resources in that file, so programs in future X sessions will have the benefit of them.

2. **Tell X about the new resources by using the xrdb program.**

   Type **xrdb .Xdefaults** to the shell to load them. To see which resources X thinks you have, type **xrdb -query**.

3. **Run your program and see what happens.**

   Most programs look at resources only when they start up, so existing programs aren't changed, only new ones.

Resources and Your Window Manager

The Motif Window Manager (mwm) has about a zillion resources it uses to control its operations. Fortunately, it's one of the few programs that can read resources while it's running. To tell it to do so, click the right button outside of any window and choose Restart. Then click Yes when it asks whether you really want to do that. As it restarts, it reads in any new resources you've loaded with xrdb. To change mwm's resources:

1. **Update the resources and run xrdb, as discussed earlier.**

2. **Tell mwm to restart itself.**

We don't go into all the resources (the listing in the manual takes about ten pages), but we hit some of the interesting ones.

Pointer, pointer, who's got the pointer?

The number-one resource you are likely to change is the keyboard focus policy. As we discussed in Chapter 15, "Lite Motif," there are two ways to switch from one window to another: click-to-type, or explicit focus, in which you have to click the mouse in the new window, and move-to-type, or pointer focus, in which you merely move the mouse into the window. Motif by default uses click-to-type. If you prefer move-to-type, put this line in your resource file:

```
Mwm*keyboardFocusPolicy:        pointer
```

Being decorative

Normally, mwm draws its standard border around each application's windows, something known in X-ese as window decoration. In some cases, you would rather have fewer decorations or none at all. You can control this for specific applications, as shown in this example:

```
Mwm*XClock.clientDecoration:   -title
Mwm*XEyes.clientDecoration:    none
```

This line says that, for any xclock windows, don't draw the title (but do still draw the border), and for xeyes, the program with the eyeballs that follow the mouse around, draw no decorations. The default decoration is all, to draw all the borders and buttons. The application names you use can be either instance or class names; in most cases the class name is preferable, so it affects all copies of the given program even if they're renamed.

Where's that window?

When you run a new program, mwm normally chooses a place on the screen to put the window, and if you don't like it, you have to move it later. An alternative called *interactive placement* displays an outline box you can move with the mouse and then click to put it in place. To use interactive placement, add this line to your resources:

```
Mwm*interactivePlacement:      True
```

We have mixed feelings about it; sometimes it's handy, and sometimes it's just a pain.

What's on the Menu?

It's also possible to configure the mwm root menu (that is, change the items that appear on the menu). The main use we've found for this capability is to let you start your favorite programs from the Motif Window Manager by clicking a menu item instead of typing the command to a shell.

Mwm's menus come from a file called mwmrc. The first problem is to figure out exactly where the mwmrc is. If you have a file in your home directory called .mwmrc (yes, it starts with a dot), Motif uses that. Otherwise, it finds a file called system.mwmrc somewhere in the X libraries on your computer. If you don't already have a .mwmrc of your own, you have to find the system.mwmrc one, copy that to .mwmrc in your home directory, and then modify that.

The usual place for `system.mwmrc` is in `/usr/lib/X11` or `/usr/X11/lib` or even `/usr/X11/lib/X11` (getting a little redundant here). If you can't find it, ask a local X expert where to find it. Then copy that `system.mwmrc` to your home `.mwmrc`, like this:

```
$ cp /usr/X11/lib/X11/system.mwmrc ~/.mwmrc
```

Now look at `.mwmrc` with a text editor. It has a bunch of stuff that controls what mouse clicks to what, which we suggest that you don't change. Near the front, though, should be the description of the root menu, which looks like this:

```
!! Root Menu Description
!!

Menu DefaultRootMenu
{
        "Root Menu"         f.title
        "New Window"        f.exec "xterm &"
        "Shuffle Up"        f.circle_up
        "Shuffle Down"      f.circle_down
        "Refresh"           f.refresh
        "Pack Icons"        f.pack_icons
        "Toggle Behavior..."    f.set_behavior
         no-label           f.separator
        "Restart..."        f.restart
        "Quit..."           f.quit_mwm

}
```

In this description, the menu starts with `Menu menuname` and then has the lines of the menu in curly braces. Each line has the menu line in quotes, a code saying which kind of command it is, and perhaps some other material. To add an entry that runs a particular program, add a line like this:

```
"Eyeballs"          f.exec "xeyes &"
```

The `f.exec` means to run a program, and the program to run is a quoted string that is passed to the shell.

Always be sure to put an ampersand (&) after the command but inside the quotes to tell the shell not to wait for the program to finish. Otherwise, the window manager hangs until the program finishes, which is rarely what you want.

How Many Menus Would a Menu Menu If a Menu Could Menu Menus?

Putting all your programs in one menu gets cluttered and ugly. So you can define submenus of your own. Here's how to create a new submenu for your programs:

```
!! Root Menu Description
!!

Menu DefaultRootMenu
{
        "Root Menu"            f.title
        "New Window"           f.exec "xterm &"
        "Programs"             f.menu myprograms
        "Shuffle Up"           f.circle_up
        "Shuffle Down"         f.circle_down
        "Refresh"              f.refresh
        "Pack Icons"           f.pack_icons
        "Toggle Behavior..."       f.set_behavior
         no-label              f.separator
        "Restart..."           f.restart
        "Quit..."              f.quit_mwm

}


Menu myprograms
{

        "Programs"             f.title
        "Phase of moon"        f.exec "xphoon &"
        "Graphics viewer"      f.exec "xv &"
}
```

Here in the original menu, we've inserted this line:

```
        "Programs"                 f.menu myprograms
```

It says that the line Programs should appear in the root menu. If you choose it, mwm should pop up a submenu called myprograms, which we defined immediately afterward. That menu has a title line (f.title) and a couple of programs (f.exec).

When you type this line in .mwmrc and tell mwm to restart, it uses this redefined menu, which looks like Figure 16-1.

Enthusiastic menu writers can put as many submenus as they want in the Motif menu. Sub-submenus are also possible (although also confusing) by putting f.menu items in the submenus.

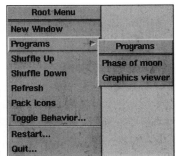

Figure 16-1:
Making your
own menu.

Toggle, Toggle

If you're wondering what your changes have done to mwm, it's possible to switch between mwm's standard behavior, ignoring all your resources and menus, and the customized one you've carefully crafted. (This feature can be a lifesaver if you've crafted yourself into the ditch.)

In the root menu, choose Toggle Behavior and click Yes when it asks whether that's what you want to do. Normally mwm uses your customized behavior. If you toggle it, it goes back to the standard one. The next toggle switches back to your custom one.

If you're not sure whether you want something like move-to-type or interactive placement, set up the resources to make it happen, try running programs the new way, toggle back to the standard behavior, try it the old way, and compare. If you find that you don't like it, take the resource out of the resource file, rerun xrdb, and restart mwm. It will come back to normal. Whew!

Part V
UNIX and the Internet

"WELL THIS HAS SURE TURNED OUT TO BE A MICKEY MOUSE SYSTEM."

In this part...

Many people are forced to use UNIX because it's the way they connect to the Internet. If you use UNIX for your Internet account, this part of the book is for you. These chapters describe how to use UNIX commands to read Usenet newsgroups, log in to other computers on the Internet, transfer files by way of FTP, explore Gopherspace, surf the World Wide Web, and waste unlimited amounts of time on the Internet Relay Chat.

Have fun, but remember: Real life is not on-line!

Chapter 17

The Wide World of the Internet

What Is the Internet?

The *Internet* — also known as the *net* — is the world's largest computer *network*. Most UNIX systems are connected to the Internet. Lots of folks (perhaps including yourself) have to learn UNIX, in fact, just so that they can use their Internet shell accounts.

The Internet isn't really a network — it's a network of networks, all freely exchanging information. The networks range from the big and formal, such as the corporate networks at AT&T, Digital Equipment Corporation, and Hewlett-Packard, to the small and informal, such as the one in our attic (with a couple of old PCs that one of us bought through the *Want Advertiser*) and everything in between. College and university networks have long been part of the Internet, and now high schools and elementary schools are joining up too. As of early 1995, more than 20,000 networks were in the Internet, with 1,000 new networks per month being added.

Am I on the Internet Already?

If you are using UNIX because you have an Internet shell account, then of course you are on the Internet. If you have a stand-alone UNIX system with no communication to any other computer, then you're not. Otherwise, there are two good ways to tell:

> ✔ Ask your system administrator. (You may well be the hundredth person to ask this question this month, so try not to be too breathless and eager.)
>
> ✔ Type this command, and see whether you get a sensible response:
>
> ```
> finger @iecc.com
> ```
>
> If your system is on the net, you should see information about the system that hosts Internet For Dummies Central (us).

Numbers for Everything

OK, so the Internet has more than a million computers attached to it. How do you find the one you want? There are two ways (nobody said that this was going to be simple). Each machine on the net is identified by a number and a name. First, let's look at the numbers and then at the names.

Each machine on the net is called a *host* in Internet-ese. A host can be a huge supercomputer or a lowly PC — it doesn't matter. If it's on the Internet, it's a host. However, PCs and Macintoshes running terminal-emulation programs or connecting through an on-line service such as America Online, are not hosts.

Each Internet host has a number assigned to identify it to other hosts, sort of like a phone number. The numbers are in four parts, such as 123.45.67.89. You should know the host number of the computer you use most, but otherwise you can forget about the numbers.

Most hosts also have names, which are much easier to remember than numbers are. The names have multiple parts separated by dots; for example, chico.iecc.com is the name of one of the computers here at Internet For Dummies Central. Some hosts have more than one name, but it doesn't matter which of them you use. This naming scheme is grandly known as the *Domain Name System,* or *DNS*.

What's in a name?

You decode an Internet name from right to left. This system may seem perverse, but it turns out in practice to be more convenient than the other way around, for the same reason we put surnames after first names. (In England, where they drive on the left side of the road, they write host names from left to right. Typical.)

The rightmost part of a name is called its *zone*. If you examine chico's full name, the rightmost part is com, which means that it is a *commercial* site as opposed to educational (edu), military (mil), governmental (gov), noncommercial organizations (org), or some other kinds of zones. If the zone is two letters long, it's the country code of the country in which the computer is located — fr for France, ca for Canada, and za for South Africa, for example.

The next part of chico's name, iecc, is the name of the company, I.E.C.C. (Yes, it's sometimes pronounced "yecch" — John should have chosen a better name.) The part to the left of the company name is the particular machine within the company. Because I.E.C.C. happens to be a rather small company with only six computers, chico's friends milton, astrud, and xuxa are known as milton.iecc.com, astrud.iecc.com, and xuxa.iecc.com.

So who am I?

Computers aren't the only ones with Internet addresses. If you use a machine that is on the Internet, you have an address too. It looks like this:

```
username@hostaddress
```

If your username is moreunix, for example, and you use the computer dummies.com, your Internet address is

```
moreunix@dummies.com
```

You use your Internet address when you send and receive electronic mail and to identify yourself when you use other Internet services. (The address moreunix@dummies.com is us, in fact — feel free to send us mail to tell us how you like the book or just to check whether your electronic mail is working. Our computer will send you an automatic response, and we authors will read the message too.)

What's It Good For?

The Internet's facilities are provided through a large set of different services. We hardly have room to provide a complete list (indeed, it would fill several books larger than this one), but some examples are shown in this section to encourage you to continue reading.

Electronic mail (e-mail)

Electronic mail is certainly the most widely used service — you can exchange e-mail with millions of people from all over the world. And people use e-mail for anything for which they might use paper mail or the telephone: gossip, recipes, rumors, love letters — you name it. (We hear that some people even use it for stuff related to work.) Electronic *mailing lists* enable you to join in group discussions and meet people over the net.

You send and receive e-mail by using the same programs you use for mail on your own UNIX system (assuming that you use a UNIX system which has users other than yourself). Chapter 13, "Climbing Elm," and Chapter 14, "Pining Away," describe how to use the popular mail programs elm and pine, respectively. Chapter 18, "Talking to the Outside World," has some general tips and tricks for using Internet mail.

On-line conversation

You can "talk" in real-time to other users anywhere on the net. Although on-line conversation is pointless for someone down the hall, it's great for quick chats with people on other continents, particularly when one party or the other isn't a native English speaker (typing is easier and clearer than talking). Chapter 18, "Talking to the Outside World," has the details.

Bulletin boards (Usenet)

A system called *Usenet* is an enormous, distributed, on-line bulletin board with about 40 million characters of messages flowing daily in more than 3,000 different topic groups. Topics range from nerdy computer stuff to hobbies such as cycling and knitting to endless political arguments to just plain silliness. The most widely read Usenet group is one that features selected jokes, most of which *are* pretty funny (see Chapter 19, "Turbocharge Your Newsreading").

File retrieval

Many computers have files of information that are free for the taking. The files range from U.S. Supreme Court decisions and library card catalogs to digitized pictures (nearly all of them suitable for family audiences) and an enormous variety of software, from games to operating systems. You can download the files to your computer by using a system called *FTP* (File-Transfer Protocol). Chapter 21, "Grabbing Files over the Net," explains how to use FTP and how to find the files that are out there on the net.

Menus and hypertext

Another form information can take is menus that can lead you to the information you want. A system called *Gopher* lets you move from menu to menu until you find what you are looking for (or give up in disgust). Chapter 23, "Gopher the Gusto," tells you how to use Gopher.

The *World Wide Web* (or just the *Web* or *WWW*) consists of pages of hypermedia. You can use various programs to read Web pages. The most common program is called Lynx. Chapter 24, "Stuck to the World Wide Web," gives you the details about the World Wide Web, Lynx, and Motif Mosaic.

Where to Go from Here

If the Internet sounds interesting and if your UNIX machine is connected to the Internet, read the rest of the chapters in this part of the book to find out how to use all these cool services.

Chapter 18
Talking to the Outside World

• •

In This Chapter

▶ Finding people's e-mail addresses

▶ E-mail addresses for folks who use on-line services

▶ Using `finger` to find people's addresses

▶ Using `whois` for finding the addresses of people at big organizations

▶ Using electronic mailing lists

▶ Using proper mail etiquette

▶ Talking to the outside world by using `talk`

• •

*E*lectronic mail is widely used on most UNIX systems. And most UNIX systems are connected to the Internet in some way that enables you to send and receive Internet mail. In addition to gossiping with folks on other Internet host systems, you can exchange mail with the users of many on-line systems, such as CompuServe and America Online.

You use the same UNIX mail programs to communicate with the Internet as you use to send mail down the hall. Chapter 18 in *UNIX For Dummies* describes how to use the standard, lousy mail program `mail` and the easier, more powerful elm. Chapter 13, "Climbing Elm," and Chapter 14, "Pining Away," in this book tell you how get the most from elm and a similar program named pine, respectively.

If you want to send a message to the authors of this book, the address for Internet For Dummies Central is `moreunix@dummies.com`. You get a reply from a mail robot (also called a *mailbot*) and possibly from a real human being.

Mail Goes Everywhere!

One of the best things about Internet mail is that it is surprisingly well connected to all sorts of other mail systems and on-line services. In most cases, the connection is seamless enough that you send mail to off-net users in exactly the same way as you send it to users directly on the net. In other cases, you have to type the address by using strange punctuation (such as ! and * and %), but in every other way you send and receive mail the same as always.

This chapter presents a short (well, *pretty* short) list of major mail and on-line systems connected to the Internet and a description of how to send mail to people on each system.

The Internet

For folks who use a real Internet host computer, their address looks like this:

```
username@hostcomputer
```

The hostcomputer part usually consists of several words connected by dots, as shown in this example:

```
moreunix@dummies.com
```

The com at the end of the host computer's name means that it's run by a commercial outfit (as opposed to gov for the government, edu for educational institutions, and so on).

America Online (AOL)

An AOL user's username is usually her full name, as many as ten letters long, or whatever cute derivative she chose. To send mail to a user named with the username AaronBurr, type this line:

```
aaronburr@aol.com
```

Note: Some AOL users have chosen mail names that are unrelated to their actual names — for them, you have to pick up the phone and call them.

Applelink

Applelink users typically use their last name as their usernames:

```
elvis@applelink.apple.com
```

AT&T Mail

AT&T Mail users have arbitrary usernames. To send mail to a user whose username is `blivet`, type this line:

```
blivet@attmail.com
```

BITNET

BITNET is a network of mostly IBM mainframes. Each system name is eight characters long or fewer. System names often contain the letters *VM,* the name of the operating system used on most BITNET sites. Usernames are arbitrary, but they are usually also eight characters or fewer. Many BITNET sites also have Internet mail domain names, so you can send mail to them in the regular Internet way.

If your Internet provider's mail program is smart, it probably has a BITNET support setup to handle BITNET systems not directly on the Internet. You can send mail to `JSMITH` at `XYZVM3`, for example, by typing this line:

```
jsmith@xyzvm3.bitnet
```

Failing that, you have to address mail directly to a BITNET gateway. Here are addresses using two gateways that tolerate outsiders' mail:

```
jsmith%xyzvm3.bitnet@mitvma.mit.edu
jsmith%xyzvm3.bitnet@cunyvm.cuny.edu
```

These two gateways are provided by M.I.T. and the City University of New York (CUNY), respectively, as a courtesy to the net community.

BIX

BIX is a commercial system formerly run by *Byte* magazine and now run by Delphi Internet. Usernames are arbitrary short strings. To mail to user NickDanger, type this line:

```
NickDanger@bix.com
```

CompuServe

CompuServe is a large on-line service. (Is there anyone who doesn't know that?) For ancient, historical reasons, CompuServe usernames are pairs of *octal* (base eight) numbers, usually beginning with the digit 7 for users in the United States and the digits 10 for users elsewhere. If a user's number is 712345,6701, the address is

```
712345.6701@compuserve.com
```

Note: The address uses a *period,* not a *comma,* because Internet addresses cannot contain commas.

Delphi

Delphi is an on-line service from the same people who run BIX, although the services are separate. (Delphi was recently sold to Rupert Murdoch, the media baron.) Delphi usernames are arbitrary strings, most often the first initial and last name of the user. To send to user joeblow, type this line:

```
joeblow@delphi.com
```

Easylink

Easylink is a mostly mail service formerly run by Western Union and now run by AT&T. Users have seven-digit numbers beginning with 62. To mail to user 6231416, type this line:

```
6231416@eln.attmail.com
```

FIDONET

FIDONET is a large, worldwide BBS network. On FIDONET, people are identified by their names, and each individual BBS (called a *node*) has a three- or four-part number in the form 1:2/3 or 1:2/3.4. To send a message to Grover Cleveland at node 1:2/3.4, type this line:

```
grover.cleveland@p4.f3.n2.z1.fidonet.org
```

If a node has a three-part name, such as 1:2/3, type this line:

```
grover.cleveland@f3.n2.z1.fidonet.org
```

GEnie

GEnie is an on-line service run by General Electric. It's the consumer end of GE's commercial on-line service, which dates back to the 1960s. Each user has a username, which is an arbitrary and totally unmemorable string, and a mail name, which is usually related to the user's name. You have to know a user's mail name, something like J.SMITH7:

```
J.SMITH7@genie.geis.com
```

MCI Mail

MCI Mail is a large, commercial e-mail system. Each user has a seven-digit user number guaranteed to be unique and a username that may or may not be unique. You can send to the number, the username, or the person's actual name, using underscores rather than spaces:

```
1234567@mcimail.com
jsmith@mcimail.com
john_smith@mcimail.com
```

If you send to a username or an actual name and the name turns out not to be unique, MCI Mail thoughtfully sends you a response listing the possible matches so that you can send your message again to the unique user number. MCI user numbers are sometimes written with a hyphen, like a phone number, but you don't have to type the hyphen in your address.

Prodigy

Prodigy is a large on-line system run by IBM and Sears. (We hear that it can have upward of 10,000 simultaneous users.) Users have arbitrary usernames such as ZZZZ99Q. Send mail to this address:

```
ZZZZ99Q@prodigy.com
```

Sprintmail (Telemail)

Sprintmail is an e-mail system provided by Sprintnet. Sprintmail used to be called Telemail because Sprintnet used to be called Telenet. (It was a technological spin-off of the original ARPANET work that led to the Internet.) Sprintmail is the major X.400 mail system in the United States. See the section "X.400: We're from the post office, and we know what you want," later in this chapter, to learn how to handle this type of address.

UUCP

UUCP is an old and cruddy mail system still used by many UNIX systems because (how did you guess?) it's free. UUCP addresses consist of a system name and a username, which are both short strings of characters.

The system here at Internet For Dummies Central, for example, has (for historical reasons) a UUCP address — iecc — in addition to its normal Internet addresses (iecc.com and dummies.com), so rather than mail us messages at moreunix@dummies.com, you can address mail to iecc! moreunix. (The !, pronounced "bang," is called a *bang path address*.)

Multihop UUCP addresses also exist: world!iecc!moreunix says to send the message first to the machine called world, which can send it to iecc, where the address is moreunix. (Think of it as e-mail's Whisper Down the Lane.) Most often, UUCP addresses are written relative to an Internet host that also talks UUCP, so you can address mail to

```
world!iecc!moreunix@uunet.uu.net
```

(although it gets here considerably faster and more reliably if you send it to moreunix@dummies.com because that avoids the UUCP nonsense). This address means that you send the message to uunet.uu.net by using regular Internet mail, and then by UUCP to world, and then another UUCP hop to iecc, and from there to the mailbox called moreunix. If you think that this method is ugly and confusing, you're not alone.

UUNET Communications is a large, nonprofit outfit that, among other things, brings e-mail to the UUCP-speaking masses, so it's the Internet system most often seen with UUCP addresses. Most UUNET customers also have regular Internet addresses that internally are turned into the ugly UUCP addresses. If you know the Internet address rather than the UUCP address, use it.

X.400: We're from the post office, and we know what you want

An X.400 address isn't just a name and a domain: It's a bunch of attributes. The official specification, written by an international standards organization in Switzerland that is dominated by government-owned post office departments, goes on for dozens, if not hundreds, of pages, but we spare you the detail (which would be fascinating if we had the space, you can be sure) and report on the minimum. The attributes that are usually of interest and the codes used to represent them are shown in this list:

- **Surname (S):** Recipient's last name

- **Given name (G):** Recipient's first name

- **Initials (I):** First or middle initial (or initials)

- **Generational qualifier (GQ or Q):** Jr., III, and so on (these folks think of everything)

- **Administration Domain Name (ADMD or A):** More or less the name of the mail system

- **Private Domain Name (PRMD or P):** More or less the name of a private system "gatewayed" into a public ADMD

- **Organization (O):** Organization with which the recipient is affiliated, which may or may not have anything to do with the ADMD or PRMD

- **Country (C):** Two-letter country code

- **Domain Defined Attribute (DD or DDA):** Any magic code that identifies the recipient, such as username or account number

You encode these attributes in an address, by using / (a slash) to separate them and writing each attribute as the code, an equal sign, and the value. Is that clear? No? (Can't imagine why.)

Here's a concrete example: Suppose that your friend uses Sprint's Sprintmail service (formerly known as Telemail, the ADMD), which has an X.400 connection to the Internet. Your friend's name is Samuel Tilden, he's in the United States, and he's with Tammany Hall. His attributes are

G: Samuel

S: Tilden

O: TammanyHall

C: US

so his address is

```
/G=Samuel/S=Tilden/O=TammanyHall/C=US/ADMD=TELEMAIL/
                @sprint.com
```

because the Internet domain for the gateway is `sprint.com`. Notice that a slash appears at the beginning of the address and just before the @. The order of the slash-separated chunks doesn't matter.

Exactly which attributes you need for a particular address varies all over the place. Some domains connect to only a single country and ADMD, so you don't use those attributes with those domains. Others (such as Sprintmail) connect to many, so you need both. It's a mess. You have to find out for each X.400 system which attributes it needs. In theory, redundant attributes shouldn't hurt, but in practice, who knows?

One minor simplification applies to the hopefully common case in which the only attribute necessary is the recipient's actual name. If the user's name is Rutherford B. Hayes, the full attribute form is

```
/G=Rutherford/I=B/S=Hayes/
```

But instead you can write

```
Rutherford.B.Hayes
```

Pretty advanced, eh? You can leave out the given name or the initial if you want. You can hope that most X.400 addresses can be written in this way, but you are probably doomed to disappointment.

In most cases, the easiest way to figure out someone's X.400 address is to have your recipient send you a message and see what the `From:` line says. Failing that, you have to experiment.

In Search of the Elusive E-Mail Address

As you've probably figured out, one teensy detail is keeping you from sending e-mail to all your friends out there on the Internet: You don't know their addresses. In the rest of this chapter, you learn several ways to look for addresses. But we save you the trouble of reading the rest of this chapter by starting out with the easiest, most reliable way to find out people's e-mail addresses:

> Call them on the phone and ask them.

Pretty low-tech, huh? For some reason, this seems to be the absolute last thing people want to do. But try it first. If you know or can find out the phone number, it's much easier than any of the other methods.

Fun with fingers

If you know the name of the computer your friend uses, you might be able to use the `finger` command to find her username. Then you can guess the address (it's in the format `username@computername`).

Most UNIX systems (and all UNIX systems connected to the Internet) have a `finger` program. You can use it to find information about a host computer or about an individual. The `finger` command is described in detail in Chapter 17 of *UNIX For Dummies*. The key point is this: Just type **finger** and the username you want more information about. If you don't know the person's username, you can type **finger** @ followed by the name of the computer the person uses, like this:

```
finger @iecc.com
```

Whaddaya mean you don't know your own address?

It happens frequently—usually because a friend is using a proprietary e-mail system which has a gateway to the outside world that provides instructions for how to send messages to the outside but no hint for how outsiders send stuff in. Fortunately, the solution is usually easy: Tell your friend to send you a message. All messages have return addresses, and all but the absolute cruddiest of mail gateways put on a usable return address. Don't be surprised if the address has a great deal of strange punctuation. After a few gateways, you always seem to end up with things like this:

```
"blurch::John.C.Calhoun"%farp@slimemail.com
```

But usually if you type the strange address again, it works, so don't worry about it. Better yet, use the address book or alias feature of your mail program to save the funky address in your address book.

Project that plan! (Or is it plan that project?)

If your friend uses a UNIX system, the response to the `finger` command comes back with a *project* and a *plan*. You too can have a project and a plan so that you look like a well-informed, seasoned network user (appearances are everything).

Your project is a file called `.project` (yes, it begins with a dot), and your plan is a file called `.plan` (it begins with a dot too). Using a text editor, create these files in your home directory. You can put anything you want in these files , as long as it's text. The `finger` command shows

only the first line of the project but all of the plan. Try not to go overboard. Ten lines or so is all people are willing to see, and even that's stretching it if it's not really, *really* clever.

Because their filenames begin with dots, the `.project` and `.plan` files are *hidden files* and don't appear in normal `ls` listings. To see a listing of all your files, including the hidden ones, type this command:

```
ls -a
```

The big finger

Some places, universities in particular, have attached their finger programs to organizational directories. If you finger `bu.edu` (Boston University), for example, you get the following response:

```
[bu.edu]
Boston University Electronic Directory (finger access)
This directory contains listings for Students, Faculty, Staff
          and University Departments. At present, most
          information about students is not accessible off-
          campus or via finger on bu.edu. The primary di-
          rectory interface is ph; if this is not avail-
          able, finger accepts <user>@bu.edu where <user>
          can be a login name or FirstName-LastName (note
          dash '-' not space). Also note that <user> can
          include standard UNIX shell patterns.  ...
```

So you can try fingering user `Jane-Smith` at host `bu.edu` to find the address. Other universities with similar directories include M.I.T. and Yale. It's worth a try — the worst that can happen is that it will say "not found."

Hey, Ms. Postmaster

Sometimes you have a good idea which machine someone uses, but you don't know the name. In that case, you can try writing to the postmaster. Every *domain,* the part of the address after the at-sign (@), that can receive Internet mail has the e-mail address `postmaster`, which contacts someone responsible for that machine. So if you're relatively sure that your friend uses `moby.ntw.org`, you might try asking (politely, of course) `postmaster@moby.ntw.org` for the address. (We assume that, for some rea-

son, you can't just call your friend and ask for the e-mail address.)

Most postmasters are overworked system administrators who don't mind an occasional polite question, but you shouldn't expect any big favors. Keep in mind that the larger the mail domain, the less likely it is that the postmaster knows all the users personally. Don't write to `postmaster@ibm.com` to try to find someone's e-mail address at IBM.

Whois Out There on the Net?

A long time ago (at least, a long time ago in the *network* frame of mind — 15 or 20 years), some network managers began keeping directories of network people. The system that lets you look up people in these directories is called *Whois.* Most UNIX systems have a `whois` command to perform the lookup.

In practice, however, it isn't that simple. For one thing, around the end of 1992, the main system that keeps the Internet Whois database moved, and some `whois` commands haven't been updated to reflect that move. The standard computer that most Whois programs used to contact now holds only the names of people who work for the U.S. Department of Defense.

Fortunately, you can tell the Whois system to use a particular server — the civilian Internet service is now at `whois.internic.net`. It may be busy, so you may have to try several times.

To try the `whois` command, type something like this:

```
whois Young
```

It should contact the Whois database and tell you about all the people named Young. If you don't find the person you want, you can tell whois to use a different Whois database, like this:

```
finger -h whois.internic.net Smith
```

because the civilian Internet service is now at whois.internic.net. The -h stands for *host,* as in the host where the server is.

Many universities and large companies have their own whois servers, so you can also try, for example, whois.stanford.edu for people at Stanford University.

For systems that don't have the whois command, you can usually use telnet (see Chapter 20, "Telnetting Around the Net") instead. You can telnet to whois.internic.net; then, at the prompt, type **whois *whoever*.** For European net people, try typing **whois.ripe.net**. A large list of Whois servers is in a file you can FTP (see Chapter 21, "Grabbing Files over the Net") from sipb.mit.edu, in the file /pub/whois/whois-servers.list.

But don't be surprised if you don't find the person you are looking for — only one of us world-famous authors here at Internet For Dummies Central (the one who runs the computers) is listed! You can also try entering just the person's first name or nickname.

TIP

Know what?

One more address-finding system worth trying is *Knowbot.* You telnet (see Chapter 20, "Telnetting Around the Net") to this address:

info.cari.reston.va.us 185

(The 185 means that you want to log in to the Knowbot server rather than to the usual login prompt.) It then displays a prompt. Just type the person's name and wait, sometimes for as long as several minutes, as it looks through a bunch of directories and tells you what it finds. Knowbot has access to some directories that are not otherwise easily accessible, including the one for MCI Mail, so it's worth checking. In our experience, though, it sometimes misses things — we have MCI Mail accounts, for example, but for some reason Knowbot can't find us there.

A New Way to Get Junk Mail: Electronic Mailing Lists

Now that you know all about how to send and receive mail, only one thing stands between you and a rich, fulfilling, mail-blessed life: You don't know many people with whom you can exchange mail. Fortunately, you can get yourself on lots of mailing lists, which ensures that you arrive every morning to a mailbox with 400 new messages. (Maybe you should start out with one or two lists.)

The point of a mailing list is simple. The list itself has a mail address, and anything (more or less) that someone sends to that address is sent to all the people on the list, who often respond to the messages. The result is a running conversation. Different lists have different styles. Some are relatively formal and hew closely to the official topic of the list. Others tend to go flying off into outer space, topicwise. You have to read them awhile to be able to tell which list works in which way.

Usenet news is another way to have running e-mail-like conversations, and the distinction between the two is blurry. (Some topics are available both as mailing lists and on Usenet, so people with and without access to news can participate.) Chapter 19, "Turbocharge Your Newsreading," discusses Usenet.

Getting on and off lists

The way in which you get on or off a mailing list is simple: You send a mail message. Two general schools of mailing-list management exist: *manual* and *automatic.* Manual management is the more traditional way: Your message is read by a human being who updates the files to put people on or take them off the list. The advantage to manual management is that you get personal service; the disadvantage is that the list *maintainer* may not get around to servicing you for quite a while if more pressing business (such as her real job) intervenes.

These days it's more common to have lists maintained automatically, which saves human attention for times when things are fouled up. The most widely used automatic mailing managers are know as *LISTSERV* and *Majordomo.*

Joining manual lists

For manual lists, there is a widely observed convention regarding list and maintainer addresses. Suppose that you want to join a list for fans of James Buchanan (the 15th President of the United States, the only one who never married, in case you slept through that part of history class) and that the list's name is buchanan-lovers@woofity.com.   The manager's address is almost certainly buchanan-lovers-request@woofity.com. In other words, just add -request to the list's address to get the manager's address. Because the list is maintained by hand, your request to be added or dropped doesn't have to take any particular form, as long as it's polite. "Please add me to the buchanan-lovers list" works well. When you decide that you've had all the Buchanan you can stand, another message saying "Please remove me from the buchanan-lovers list" works equally well.

Messages to -request addresses are read and handled by human beings who sometimes eat, sleep, and work regular jobs as well as maintain mailing lists. For this reason, they don't necessarily read your request the moment it arrives. It can take a day or so to be added to or removed from a list, and after you ask to be removed, you usually get a few more messages before they remove you. If it takes longer than you want, be patient. And *don't* send cranky follow-ups — they just cheese off the list maintainer.

Joining LISTSERV lists

You put yourself on and off a LISTSERV mailing list by sending mail to LISTSERV@some.machine.or.other, where some.machine.or.other is the name of the particular machine on which the mailing list *lives*. Because LISTSERV list managers are computer programs, they're pretty simpleminded, so you have to speak to them clearly and distinctly.

Suppose that you want to join a list called SNUFLE-L (LISTSERV mailing lists usually end with -L), which lives at ntw.org. To join, send to LISTSERV@ntw.org a message that contains this line:

```
SUB SNUFLE-L Roger Sherman
```

You don't have to add a subject line or anything else to this message. SUB is short for subscribe, SNUFLE-L is the name of the list, and anything after that is supposed to be your real name. (You can put whatever you want there, but keep in mind that it shows up in the return address of anything you send to the list.) Shortly afterward, you should get two messages in return:

- ✔ A chatty, machine-generated welcoming message, telling you that you've joined the list, along with a description of some commands you can use to fiddle with your mailing-list membership.

- ✔ An incredibly boring message, telling you that the IBM mainframe ran a program to handle your request and reporting the exact number of milliseconds of computer time and number of disk operations the request made necessary. *Whoopee.* (It is sobering to think that somewhere people find these messages interesting.)

To send a message to this list, mail to the list name at the same machine — in this case, `SNUFLE-L@ntw.org`. Be sure to provide a descriptive `Subject:` for the multitudes who will benefit from your pearls of wisdom. Within a matter of minutes, people from all over the world will read your message.

To get off a list, you write again to `LISTSERV@some.machine.or.other` and this time send this message:

```
SIGNOFF SNUFLE-L
```

or whatever the list's name is. You don't have to give your name again because, after you're off the list, LISTSERV has no additional interest in you and forgets that you ever existed.

Joining Majordomo lists

Majordomo works much like LISTSERV does (and it's not a coincidence either). To subscribe to a list maintained by Majordomo, send a message to `majordomo@computername` (that is, the computer on which the list lives). The message should contain in the body of the message (not in the subject line) a line like this one:

```
subscribe unicycle-lovers
```

Substitute the name of the mailing list in place of `unicycle-lovers`. Unlike LISTSERV, you *don't* put your real name after the mailing-list name.

To get off the list, send a message like this one:

```
unsubscribe unicycle-lovers
```

Now what?

After you join a mailing list, you should get in response a message with instructions about how the list works. LISTSERV and Majordomo lists send back instructions about how to use LISTSERV and Majordomo commands to control your subscription to the list. Be sure to read these instructions so that you can find out how to post messages to the list.

Before posting anything, however, by all means read the mailing list for at least a week. Don't jump in with both feet until you have taken a look at what folks are talking about. Make sure that you are reading the right list and that people haven't already answered the question you are about to ask. If possible, wait until the FAQ (list of answers to Frequently Asked Questions) comes by, which is usually once a month.

Etiquette Counts

Sadly, the great Etiquette Ladies, such as Emily Post and Amy Vanderbilt, died before the invention of e-mail. But this section tells you what they might have suggested about what to say and, more important, what *not* to say in electronic mail.

E-mail is a funny hybrid, something between a phone call (or voice mail) and a letter. On one hand, it's quick and usually informal; on the other hand, it's written rather than spoken, so you don't see any facial expressions or hear tones of voice.

Bursting into flame

Pointless and excessive outrage in electronic mail is so common that it has a name of its own: *flaming*. Don't flame. It makes you look like a jerk.

When you get a message so offensive that you just *have* to reply, stick it back in your electronic in-box for a while and wait until after lunch. Then, don't flame back. The sender probably didn't realize how the message would look. In about 20 years of using electronic mail, we can testify that we've never, never, regretted *not* sending an angry message. (But we *have* regretted sending a few. Ouch.)

When you're sending mail, keep in mind that someone reading it will have no idea of what you *intended* to say — just what you *did* say. Subtle sarcasm and irony are almost impossible to use in e-mail and usually come across as annoying or dumb instead. (If you are a truly superb writer, you can disregard this advice, but don't say that you weren't warned.)

E-mail always seems ruder than it's supposed to

Here's what we mean:

- When you send a message, watch your tone of voice.

- Feel free to stick in little "smiley" faces to show when you are joking, like this: :-) Sarcasm and irony are hard to communicate and often just come across as annoying with the humor lost.

- If someone sends you an incredibly obnoxious and offensive message, as likely as not it is a mistake or a joke gone awry. In particular, be on the lookout for failed sarcasm.

Sometimes it helps to put in a :-), or *smiley,* so that people know that you are joking. In some communities, notably CompuServe, <g> or <grin> serves the same purpose. Here's a typical example:

```
People who don't believe that we are all part of a warm,
          caring community who love and support each other
          are no better than rabid dogs and should be
          hunted down and shot. :-)
```

Smileys sometimes help, but if a joke needs a smiley, maybe it wasn't worth making. It may sound as though all your e-mail is supposed to be totally humorless. It's not that bad, but until you have the hang of it, limit the humor. You'll be glad that you did.

TIP

Chain letters: Arrrrrggghhh!

One of the most obnoxious things you can do with e-mail is to pass around chain letters. Because all mail programs have forwarding commands, with only a few keystrokes you can send a chain letter along to hundreds of other people. Don't do it. Chain letters are cute for about two seconds, and then they're just annoying.

A few chain letters just keep coming around and around, despite our best efforts to stamp them out. Learn to recognize them now and avoid embarrassment later. Here are some of the hangers-on:

Dying boy wants greeting cards: (Sometimes it's business cards.) Not anymore, he doesn't. Several years ago, an English boy named Craig Shergold was hospitalized with what was thought to be an inoperable brain tumor. Craig wanted to set the world record for most greeting cards. Word got out, and Craig received millions and millions of cards and eventually got into the *Guinness Book of World Records.* When it turned out that maybe the tumor *wasn't* inoperable, U.S. TV billionaire John Kluge paid for Craig to fly to the United States for an operation, which was successful. So Craig is OK now and definitely doesn't want any more cards. (You can read all about this story on page 24 of the July 29, 1990, edition of the *New York Times.*) Guinness is so sick and tired of the whole business that it closed the category — no more records for the most cards are accepted. If you want to help dying children, give the two dollars that a card and stamp would have cost to a children's welfare organization, such as UNICEF.

The modem-tax rumor: In 1987 the Federal Communications Commission (FCC) briefly floated a proposal for a technical change to the rules governing the way on-line services, such as CompuServe and GEnie, are billed for their phone connections. Implementing the proposal would have had the effect of raising the prices these services charge. Customers of on-line services made their opposition clear immediately and loudly, members of Congress made concerned inquiries, and the proposal was dropped — permanently. Unfortunately, undated alarmist notices about the proposal have circulated around bulletin boards ever since. If you see yet another modem-tax scare, demand the FCC's current docket number because the FCC — as a government bureaucracy — can't blow its nose without making announcements, accepting comments, and so on. So no docket means no action, which means that it's the same old rumor you should ignore.

(continued)

(continued)

Make big bucks with a chain letter: Usually these letters, signed by "Dave Rhodes," contain lots of testimonials from people who are now rolling in dough and tell you to send $5 or so to the name at the top of the list, put your name at the bottom, and send the message to a zillion other suckers. Some even say "This isn't a chain letter" (you're supposedly helping to compile a mailing list or something, which is your 100 percent guaranteed tipoff that it *is* a chain letter). Don't even think about it. These chain letters are extremely illegal, and, besides, they don't even work. (Why send any money? Why not just add your name and send it on?) Think of them as highly contagious gullibility viruses. Just ignore them, or perhaps send a polite note to the sender's postmaster to encourage her to tell users not to send any more chain letters.

The "two-fifty" cookie recipe: According to this one, someone was eating cookies somewhere (Mrs. Fields and Neiman-Marcus are frequently cited) and asked whether she (it was always a she) could have the recipe. "Sure," came the answer, "that'll be two-fifty, charged to your credit card." "OK." When the credit-card statement came, it turned out to be two-hundred-and-fifty *dollars,* not two dollars and fifty cents. So in retribution, the message concludes with the putative Mrs. Fields or Neiman-Marcus recipe, sent to you for free. The story is pure hooey: Mrs. Fields doesn't give out her recipes, for money or otherwise; Neiman's has never even served chocolate-chip cookies. The recipe, which varies somewhat from one version to the next, makes perfectly OK cookies, but we don't think that it's any better than the one on the back of the bag of chips. This same story, by the way, circulated hand-to-hand in the 1940s and 1950s, except that the recipe was for a red-velvet cake served at the restaurant in one of the big New York department stores. It wasn't true then either.

How private is e-mail?

Relatively, but not totally. Any recipient of your mail might forward it to other people. Some mail addresses are really mailing lists that redistribute messages to many other people. In one famous case, a mistaken mail address sent a message to tens of thousands of readers. It began, "Darling, at last we have a way to send messages that is completely private."

The usual rule of thumb is to not send anything you wouldn't want to see posted next to the water cooler or perhaps scribbled next to a pay phone. The latest e-mail systems are starting to include encryption features that make the privacy situation somewhat better so that no one who doesn't know the keyword that was used to scramble a message can decode it. No standard exists yet for encrypted mail, so you have to ask the folks with whom you exchange sensitive mail whether they use any e-mail encryption.

Another possibility to keep in the back of your mind is that it is technically not difficult to forge e-mail return addresses, so if you get a totally off-the-wall message from someone that seems out of character for that person, someone else may have forged it as a prank.

Live Talk Networking

In Chapter 17 of *UNIX For Dummies,* we describe the `talk` command, which lets you talk to other folks on your own UNIX system or on other parts of the Internet. Type a command like this:

```
talk president@whitehouse.gov
```

While `talk` is running, you see what you type in the top half of the screen and what the other person types in the bottom half.

If someone wants to talk to you, you see a message about it. If you want to talk back, type the `talk` command the message suggests.

To talk to lots of people at the same time, see Chapter 25, "Dealing with Excess Free Time: Internet Relay Chat."

The 5th Wave — By Rich Tennant

"ONE OF THEIR BLIMPS BROKE ITS MOORING AND FLOATED IN HERE ABOUT TWO HOURS AGO. THEY HAVEN'T BEEN ABLE TO LOCATE IT YET."

Chapter 19
Turbocharge Your Newsreading

• •

• •

What Is Usenet?

Mailing lists are an OK way to send messages to a small number of people, but they're a lousy way to send messages to a large number of people. For one thing, just maintaining a big list with thousands of people is a great deal of work, even if you automate most of it with something like LISTSERV, which was discussed in Chapter 18, "Talking to the Outside World." (On a large list, every day a few of the addresses go bad as people move around and system managers reconfigure addresses.) For another thing, just shipping the contents of messages to thousands and thousands of addresses puts a huge load on the system that sends them out.

Usenet news (also known as *net news*) solves that problem and creates a host of others. Usenet is a large, distributed *BBS (bulletin board system)*. The principle is quite simple: Every Usenet site ships a copy of all *articles* (news-speak for messages) it has received to all its neighbors several times a day. (To avoid wasted effort, each article contains a list of sites to which it has already been sent.) It's sort of a global game of Whisper Down the Lane, although computers don't scramble the messages at each stage, like people do. Different host-to-host connections run at different speeds, but for the most part news articles slosh around to nearly every directly connected Usenet site within a day or two of being sent. (If your machine is directly on the Internet rather than connected over the phone, most news arrives within a few hours.) The amount of news that flows around the world is truly staggering. One of our local commercial Internet providers reports that he's now receiving upward of 200 megabytes of new news every day.

You have to learn three Important News Skills:

✔ How to read the news that interests you

✔ How not to read the news that doesn't interest you, because far more news is sent every day than any single human could ever read

✔ How to post articles of your own (definitely optional)

Not every UNIX system gets Usenet newsgroups. Some employers have the benighted idea that spending hours every day reading `alt.fan.power.rangers` and `rec.sports.baseball.ny-mets` might not be the absolute best use of your time. If none of the newsreaders in the chapter works on your system, come up with some plausible reason to read newsgroups, and talk to your system administrator or Internet provider. ("Gee, I really need up-to-date information about widgets, so I have to be able to read the `comp.gizmos.widgets` newsgroup every day.")

How Do I Read It?

Most UNIX systems have at least one program for reading Usenet newsgroups — these programs are called *newsreaders.* The most basic is rn; more powerful versions are called such things as trn and nn and tin. This chapter describes trn in detail, because it's our favorite, and describes nn and tin a little too. Many systems provide at least one of these programs for reading Usenet newsgroups.

For general information about Usenet newsgroups, see Chapter 11, "Using Network News," and Chapter 12, "A Sampler of Network News Resources," in *The Internet For Dummies,* by John R. Levine and Carol Baroudi (IDG Books).

Editor swamp alert

If you decide to respond to articles, either by e-mail or by posting a follow-up article, your newsreader will run a text-editing program. We can't predict which one it will be, because it depends on the way the system is set up. It will probably be either vi or emacs, neither or which is particularly easy to use (see Chapter 11, "Oy, Vi!" and Chapter 12, "Have a Big Emacs").

Running Trn

Trn is a major improvement over rn, on which it is based, because it is *threaded* (in fact, its name stands for *t*hreaded *r*ead*news*). In newsgroup lingo, a *thread* is an article along with all its follow-up articles, including follow-ups to follow-ups and so on. Trn can organize all the articles in a newsgroup into threads, list them, and enable you to choose the topics that look interesting. This ability makes it easy to find the wheat from among the chaff (the articles of interest amid all the surrounding dreck).

To run trn, just type **trn** — simple enough. If your system doesn't have it, tough luck. Skip ahead for information about nn or tin, or refer to Chapter 11, "Using Network News," in *The Internet For Dummies* to learn how to use rn.

If you find that trn can't perform all the commands we tell you about in this chapter, you may have to tell it specifically that you plan to use all of its features. To do this, type **trn -x -X** to run it. If it's annoying to type this command every time, make a shell script that contains this command (refer to Chapter 4, "An Introduction to Scripts").

Remember your first time?

The first time you run trn, it checks in your home directory to see whether you have a file named .newsrc. (Yes, the filename begins with a period.) You may not have noticed the file because the period at the beginning of the filename makes it hidden in normal file listings. The .newsrc file stores information about which newsgroups you subscribe to and which messages you've already read in each one. (For the gory details about .newsrc, see the section "Preventing Alzheimer's," later in this chapter.)

If you've ever run trn or other newsreaders, such as rn and nn, they created this file. If not, trn doesn't find it the first time it runs.

Not a problem! Trn just makes you a brand-new one, in your home directory. It also figures that you must be a newbie, so it displays some (allegedly) helpful messages. Press the spacebar to make them go away.

This new .newsrc file is a list of every blessed newsgroup your system carries, and the list can be long. This first time you run trn, you have to go through them and unsubscribe to the groups you don't plan to read. Don't worry — you can change your mind later and subscribe again. For each newsgroup in the list, it asks whether you want to read it, to which you reply **y** or **n**. If you get tired of answering questions, press **N** to tell it not to subscribe to any more groups. (You can go back later and pick up ones you might have missed.)

After the first time

After you've run trn once, it remembers which newsgroups you are interested in and asks you about only those you subscribe to.

When new newsgroups are created, which happens every day now that Usenet is getting to be so popular, trn asks whether you want to add them to your .newsrc file. You see the following message:

```
Newsgroup alt.binaries.sounds.utilities not in .newsrc —
            subscribe? [ynYN]
```

To subscribe to the newsgroup and begin reading it now, press **y** (that's a small *y*). To skip it forever, press **n** (again, a small one). To add all the new newsgroups, press **Y**. To tell trn not to ask you about any of the new groups, press **N**.

If you choose to subscribe to a newsgroup, trn asks:

```
Put newsgroup where? [$^.Lq]
```

The various potions in the square brackets control exactly where in your .newsrc file you want to put this newsgroup. To put it at the end, just press the spacebar.

Trn thoughtfully lets you know whether you have e-mail waiting. If so, it says (Mail) at the beginning of some prompts.

Choosing Newsgroups to Read

For each newsgroup in your `.newsrc` list, trn suggests that you read its articles. If this is your first time, the newsgroup is probably `news.announce.newusers`, the newsgroup for folks who are new to newsgroups. It's not a bad idea to peruse these articles, but we get to that topic later. The way trn suggests a newsgroup is with this message:

```
67 unread articles in news.announce.newusers — read now? [+ynq]
```

(The number of messages varies.) The `[+ynq]` tells you possible responses:

- ✔ Press **+** to see the list of threads for this newsgroup so that you can select which threads to read. (If you choose this option, skip down to the section "Picking Up the Threads.")

- ✔ Press **y** to go ahead and look at the newsgroup article by article. (If you choose this one, skip down to the section "Reading the News.")

- ✔ Press **n** to not read this newsgroup, at least not now. Trn suggests the next newsgroup on its list.

- ✔ Press **q** to quit trn altogether.

You can also press **u** (small, not capital) to unsubscribe from the newsgroup so that you will never be bothered by it again.

If you always like to look at the thread selector for a newsgroup, you can tell trn to make + (go to the thread selector first) the default for the newsgroup rather than y (go directly to reading articles). When trn asks whether you want to read the newsgroup, press **t** (a small *t*). This choice turns thread selection on for this newsgroup, assuming that it was off. (If it was already on, it turns it off.) For each newsgroup, trn remembers whether you like to select threads first and presents the appropriate default so that, if you press the spacebar, you get what you want. We invariably prefer to see the thread selector unless the group has so few messages that it's easier to look at all of them.

Commanding trn

When trn gives you a list of possible commands in square brackets (such as `[+ynq]`), you generally can press any of the options that are listed. Don't press Enter — trn moves along right away as soon as you press a key. Also, you can press the spacebar to choose the first option in the square brackets (this one is the default option).

Occasionally commands are more than one letter long, usually because they enable you to specify extra information, such as a filename in which to save a message. Commands that are longer than one letter must be followed by pressing Enter so that trn knows when you are finished typing.

Trn cares about capital versus small letters — it has so many commands that a capital letter frequently does something different from its small counterpart. Be careful to capitalize commands the same way we do.

Trn is always doing one of four things:

- ✔ Offering a newsgroup to read
- ✔ Displaying a list of threads to choose among
- ✔ Offering an article to display
- ✔ Pausing while it displays an article that is too long to fit on the screen

Confusingly, different commands work in these four situations. Luckily, you don't have to use many commands very often, and trn suggests the most likely options.

You can press **h** at any time to see trn's on-line help. It's rather concise but can certainly be helpful, especially as a reminder.

Picking Up the Threads

It's about time to read some news! When trn asks whether you want to read a newsgroup and offers the options [+ynq], press + to see the list of threads for the newsgroup. You see a list of threads like the one shown in Figure 19-1.

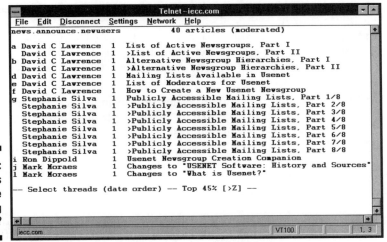

```
┌─────────────────────────────────────────────────────────────────────┐
│ ─                    Telnet - iecc.com                         ▼ ▲   │
│ File  Edit  Disconnect  Settings  Network  Help                      │
├─────────────────────────────────────────────────────────────────────┤
│news.announce.newusers          40 articles (moderated)            ▲  │
│                                                                      │
│a David C Lawrence   1  List of Active Newsgroups, Part I             │
│  David C Lawrence   1  >List of Active Newsgroups, Part II           │
│b David C Lawrence   1  Alternative Newsgroup Hierarchies, Part I     │
│  David C Lawrence   1  >Alternative Newsgroup Hierarchies, Part II   │
│d David C Lawrence   1  Mailing Lists Available in Usenet             │
│e David C Lawrence   1  List of Moderators for Usenet                 │
│f David C Lawrence   1  How to Create a New Usenet Newsgroup          │
│g Stephanie Silva    1  Publicly Accessible Mailing Lists, Part 1/8   │
│  Stephanie Silva    1  >Publicly Accessible Mailing Lists, Part 2/8  │
│  Stephanie Silva    1  >Publicly Accessible Mailing Lists, Part 3/8  │
│  Stephanie Silva    1  >Publicly Accessible Mailing Lists, Part 4/8  │
│  Stephanie Silva    1  >Publicly Accessible Mailing Lists, Part 5/8  │
│  Stephanie Silva    1  >Publicly Accessible Mailing Lists, Part 6/8  │
│  Stephanie Silva    1  >Publicly Accessible Mailing Lists, Part 7/8  │
│  Stephanie Silva    1  >Publicly Accessible Mailing Lists, Part 8/8  │
│i Ron Dippold        1  Usenet Newsgroup Creation Companion           │
│j Mark Moraes        1  Changes to "USENET Software: History and Sources"│
│l Mark Moraes        1  Changes to "What is Usenet?"                  │
│── Select threads (date order) ── Top 45% [>Z] ──                  ▼  │
│                                                                      │
│◄│                                                                ►│  │
│ iecc.com                                    │VT100│        │1, 3│    │
└─────────────────────────────────────────────────────────────────────┘
```

Figure 19-1:
What topics
are we
talking
about?

The top line of the screen shows the name of the newsgroup (in this example, it's news.announce.newusers), along with the number of articles waiting to be read and whether it is moderated. (Moderated newsgroups have editors who control which messages get posted.)

Underneath that is a list of articles, organized into threads. Each thread is assigned a letter, down the left edge of the screen. (Trn skips some letters, which are used for commands.) For each article, you see the author and the subject line.

The bottom line of the display tells you to choose some threads and tells you whether there are more articles than will fit on the screen (there usually are). For example, Figure 19-1 contains the top 45 percent of the articles in the newsgroup.

If you want to read the articles in a thread, press the letter assigned to the thread. A plus sign appears next to the thread letter, showing that this thread has been chosen. (If you change your mind, press the thread's letter again to deselect it.)

To see more threads, press >. You can tell when you get to the end of the list of threads when you see Bot on the bottom line of text.

To back up and see previous pages of threads, press <. To begin at the beginning again, press ^, or to go to the end, press $.

When you've chosen the threads you want, use one of these commands:

- Press **X** (that's a capital *X*) to mark all the articles in all the threads you *didn't* choose as having been read already so that trn doesn't ask you about them again. Then begin reading the articles in the threads you *did* pick.

- Press **N** to forget all about this newsgroup and look at the next one on your .newsrc list. Or press **P** to move to the preceding newsgroup. (Be sure to capitalize most of these commands.)

Reading the News

If you pressed X after choosing the threads you wanted, or if you pressed y when trn first asked about the newsgroup, trn begins showing you the articles one at a time. First, it shows you the article's headers, as shown in Figure 19-2.

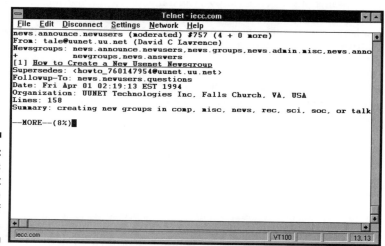

Figure 19-2:
Cryptic
headers at
the
beginning of
an article.

You have several options:

- To see the rest of the article (or at least the next screenful), press the spacebar. You see the next page of text. If the article is several pages long, you see a MORE prompt at the end of each page, until you get to the end of the article.

  You can get a sense of how long the article is by looking at how much you've read. The MORE prompt tells you what percentage of the article you've seen so that you can tell how far you have to go.

✔ If the article doesn't interest you, press **j** (a small *j*) to "junk" the article. This choice tells trn to mark the article as read (so that it doesn't offer it to you again later) and go to the end of the article.

✔ If the entire topic is boring and you don't want to see any more articles that have the same subject line, press **k** (a small *k*) to kill the topic. Trn skips any articles in this thread (or any other thread) that have the same text in the subject line.

✔ To bag the entire thread, including articles with a different subject line, press **J** (that's a capital *J*). Trn forgets about any response to this article or responses to those responses or responses to the article that this one is a response to (you get the idea), regardless of whether they have the same subject line as this article. That is, they are marked as read.

✔ To quit looking at this newsgroup (for now, anyway), press **q**. Trn asks you about the next newsgroup in your list.

At the end of the article, trn asks:

```
End of article 757 (of 818) — what next? [npq]
```

Again, you have lots of options:

✔ To see the next article you haven't read yet, press **n** or the spacebar.

✔ To see the preceding unread article, press **p**. (If you've already read all the previous articles, nothing happens.)

✔ To see the last article trn displayed before the current one, press **P**. This choice displays the preceding article even though you read it already.

✔ To see the same article again, press Ctrl-R.

✔ To quit reading this newsgroup, press **q**. Trn asks whether you want to read the next newsgroup in your list.

✔ To kill (mark as read) all articles that have this subject line, press **k** (a small *k*).

✔ To kill the entire thread, including articles with a different subject line, press **J** (that's a capital *J*).

✔ If you are way behind on reading this newsgroup and you want to give up the idea of ever catching up, press **c** (that's a small *c*). Trn marks all the unread articles in the newsgroup as read. The next time you read this group, you see only the new articles.

✔ If you have totally lost interest in this newsgroup, press **u** (a small *u*) to unsubscribe from it.

Rot what?

Usenet has a system for protecting you from gross, disgusting, obscene, or otherwise offensive articles. Offensive articles can be posted by using a simple code called *Rot 13*. If you try to read an article and it appears as gibberish, you can press Ctrl-X to start the article over and decode it as it goes. But don't complain to us (or anyone else) if it offends you! Incidentally, if you press Ctrl-X by mistake and want to read the article *au naturel*, press Ctrl-R to redraw it normally.

File It, Please

You can save the text of an article in a file if you want to transfer it to another machine, include it in a word-processing document, or just plain keep it:

1. **When you are at the end of an article you want to save, type this command:**

```
s filename
```

Replace `filename` with the name you want to give to the file that contains the article.

If the file already exists, trn sticks the article at the end of it. (This is nice if you want to save an entire series of articles together in a file — as you save each article, trn adds it to the end of the file.)

Searching for something

You can use trn's search command to find articles that contain a particular word or set of characters in the subject line, anywhere in the header, or anywhere in the article. To search for articles that contain *text* in the subject line, type this command:

```
/text
```

If you want to look for articles that contain *text* anywhere in the header, type this command:

```
/text/h
```

For articles that contain *text* anywhere in the text of the articles themselves, as well as in the headers, type this command:

```
/text/a
```

To search backward through previous articles, type ? rather than / in any of these commands.

If the file doesn't exist, trn asks what kind of file to make:

```
File /usr/margy/News/save.it doesn't exist—
        use mailbox format? [ynq]
```

2. **To save it in a regular text file, press n. To save it in the kind of file in which mail programs store e-mail messages, press y.**

If you don't tell trn otherwise, it saves files in a directory named News in your home directory. You can enter a pathname if you want to put the file elsewhere. Use a tilde (~) to tell trn to put a file in your home directory, like this:

```
s ~/article.about.cats
```

We find it most convenient to save messages in mailbox format because then we can use a mail program such as pine or elm to handle files of saved articles. (The only difference between a mailbox file and a nonmailbox file is that a mailbox has a separator line before each message.)

When Is an Article Not Really an Article?

Sometimes a news article contains not plain text, but rather a coded version of a binary file or group of files. There are two common ways to sneak files into articles: uuencoding and shar files.

In a *uuencoded* message, a single binary file is turned into a bunch of ugly-looking text, like this:

```
begin 644 sample
M5V]W(2!)9B!Y;W4@86-T-T=6%L;;'D@='EP960@:6X@=&AI<R!W:&]L92!F:6QE
M(&%N9"!U=61E88V]D960@:70@:70@<W5C8W5S<5;9U;&QY+"!T*>6]U)W9E(&&$@<F5A
M;&QY(&1E9&E&8871E9"E"R96%D%97(N("!!$<F5(&&$;'5S92!F]T92!A="!M;;W)E
M=6I>$!I96-C++F+O;2!A;F0F-"UE;&(#V" +"+$:6;G&;1IL>(;&OH);+&/Q-(+&/(&LV+(+:(+@T*
"#OH*
'
end
```

Usually uuencoded files are much longer than this one, but they're all equally ugly. Really long ones are often split across several news messages to keep each individual article to a reasonable size. Uuencoded files are most often found in groups such as comp.binaries.ms-windows, in which case they're runnable programs, or in groups such as alt.binaries.pictures.erotica, in which case they're digitized pictures of, er, various stuff.

A *shar file* (short for *shell archive*) contains a group of files. Most often they contain program source code, but they can contain any text files. Here's a short example:

```
#!/bin/sh
# This is a shell archive (produced by shar 3.49)
# To extract the files from this archive, save it to a file,
        remove
# everything above the "!/bin/sh" line above, and type "sh
        file_name".
#
# made 05/25/1994 01:43 UTC by johnl@iecc
# Source directory /usr/johnl
#
# existing files will NOT be overwritten unless -c is speci-
        fied
#
# This shar contains:
# length  mode          name
# ——— ——— ————————————
#    112 -rw-rw-r— poem
#
# ============= poem ==============
if test -f 'poem' -a X"$1" != X"-c"; then
      echo 'x - skipping poem (File already exists)'
else
echo 'x - extracting poem (Text)'
sed 's/^X//' << 'SHAR_EOF' > 'poem' &&
I eat my peas with honey
I've done it all my life
It makes them taste real funny
But it keeps them on my knife.
SHAR_EOF
chmod 0664 poem ||
echo 'restore of poem failed'
Wc_c="'wc -c < 'poem''"
test 112 -eq "$Wc_c" ||
      echo 'poem: original size 112, current size' "$Wc_c"
fi
exit 0
```

Trn makes it easy to extract the useful bits from uuencoded or shar files. When you see this type of message, you can extract its contents by pressing **e** followed by typing the name of the directory in which to extract it. (If you just press e and then Enter, trn uses your News directory.) Multipart uuencoded files are also handled more or less automatically. After you extract the contents of the first part of a uuencoded message, trn says (continued), and it's up to you to find the next part and press e again. After the last part, it says Done. Shar files are extracted in the same way as uuencoded files, except that there's no such thing as a multipart shar file. (Large programs may be multipart messages, but each one is a separate shar file.)

Shar and uuencode files present some enormous potential security holes. Shar files are really no more than lists of commands for the UNIX shell that create the files to be extracted. This setup offers considerable flexibility, but it also means that a prankster can stick in some commands you would just as soon not execute, such as ones that delete all your files. Shar files from moderated groups (that is, groups in which all the messages are examined and approved by a third party before being sent out) are generally OK, but the files in other groups are only as reliable as the people sending them. Shar scanning programs are available that scan shar files for untoward commands. Check with your system manager to see whether any of these programs is available on your system.

Uuencoded files of pictures are unlikely to cause any trouble, other than the hair on your palms you may get from looking at some of them. Uuencoded binary programs should be treated with the same skepticism as any other binary programs. Again, the ones that come from moderated groups are pretty safe; others are less so. A scan with a virus checker is always appropriate.

Dealing with Articles That Demand a Response

If you read an article that demands a response, you have two options: You can respond privately by sending e-mail to the person who wrote it, or you can post a follow-up article to the newsgroup. This list shows you how to decide which way to go:

- ✔ If your response will be of interest to only the person who wrote the article, send e-mail.

- ✔ If you are really mad, take a walk before doing anything. If you're still mad and you just *have* to reply, send e-mail.

- ✔ If the original article contains errors that everyone reading it should know about, post a follow-up article, but only after checking that 12 other people haven't already done the same thing.

- ✔ If you have additional information about the subject that will be of universal interest to those reading the original article, post a follow-up article.

Responding privately by e-mail

When you are at the end of an article to which you want to respond privately, these steps show you what to do:

1. **Decide whether you want to quote parts of the article in your e-mail. If you do, press R. Otherwise, press r.**

   Trn displays a bunch of confusing messages, followed by a question about including a prepared file.

2. **Assuming that you have not prepared a text file in advance that you now want to include in your e-mail, press Enter to tell trn not to include any file.**

   Trn asks which editor you want to use.

3. **If you don't like the editor it suggests, type the command you use to start your editor. Otherwise, just press Enter.**

   Trn runs the editor. If you chose to include the text of the original article, it is already sitting on-screen, indented to show that you are quoting it. The headers for the e-mail are at the top of the screen too.

4. **Delete unnecessary text.**

   Be sure to delete the boring header lines from the original article (not the ones that address your e-mail message, at the top of the screen — the ones that are quoted from the original article). Also delete parts of the article that you don't plan to discuss in your e-mail message. Pare the quoted text to the bare minimum, just enough to remind the person which article it is you just read and are responding to.

5. **Type your reply. Be clear, polite, and reasonable.**

6. **Save your message and exit from the editor, using whatever commands work in your editor.**

   Trn asks:

   ```
   Check spelling, Send, Abort, Edit, or List?
   ```

7. **To run a spell checker, press C. To forget all about sending this e-mail, press A. To return to the editor to make one more little change, press E. And to send the message, press S. Then press Enter.**

   Trn asks whether you want it to stick your signature file at the end of the message. (A signature file is a file called .signature in your home directory, containing your name, return address, and other info.)

8. **Press y or n and press Enter.**

   Trn returns you to where you left off — right at the end of the article you just responded to.

Actually, you can press r to send an e-mail message to anyone, not just to the person who wrote the article you just read. If you suddenly get the urge to write a note to your mom, press r and follow the steps to enter the editor. After you are editing your response, you can change the To: line to any address you want rather than to the article's author, and the Subject: line to any subject.

Possibly making a fool of yourself

OK, you've decided to take the plunge. You have something so interesting to say that you want to post it publicly, where it can be read, appreciated, savored, misconstrued, or laughed at. Here's how:

1. **Press F to tell trn that you want to post a follow-up article, and include some or all of the original article.**

   Trn gives you a warning, like this:

   ```
   This program posts news to thousands of machines through-
           out the entire civilized world. Your message will
           cost the net hundreds if not thousands of dollars
           to send everywhere. Please be sure you know what
           you are doing.

   Are you absolutely sure that you want to do this? [ny]
   ```

2. **If you have thought better of it, press n or the spacebar. You can always send an e-mail message to the article's author and then decide to go public later. If you still want to post an article, press y. Then press Enter.**

   Trn asks whether you want to include a prepared file.

3. **Assuming that you have not prepared a text file in advance that you now want to include in your article, press Enter to tell trn not to include any file.**

   Trn asks which editor you want to use.

4. **If you don't like the editor it suggests, type the command you use to start your editor. Otherwise, just press Enter.**

   Trn runs the editor. If you chose to include the text of the original article, it is already sitting on the screen, indented to show that you are quoting it. The headers for your follow-up article are at the top of the screen too.

   Take a look at the Newsgroups: line at the top of the message. It lists the newsgroups to which this article will be posted.

5. **Delete any newsgroups that wouldn't be interested in your article.**

6. **Move down to the beginning of the text of the article you are replying to, and delete unnecessary text.**

   Be sure to delete the boring header lines along with any parts of the article you don't plan to refer to. Pare the quoted text to the minimum, just enough to remind newsgroup readers what exactly you are responding to.

7. **Type your reply. Be clear, polite, and reasonable.**

8. **Save your message and exit from the editor, using whatever commands work in your editor.**

   Lines in Usenet articles are usually limited to 70 characters. If any of the lines in your article is longer than that, trn warns you about it so that you can go back and fix it. Then it gives you this choice

   ```
   Check spelling, Send, Abort, Edit, or List?
   ```

9. **To run a spell checker, press** C. **To forget all about posting this article, press** A. **To return to the editor to make one more little change, press** E. **And to send the message, press** S. **Then press Enter.**

   Trn sends your article out into the universe and displays a message confirming this. Then you are back at the end of the article to which you responded.

When you post an article to an unmoderated newsgroup, the article is distributed directly all over the Internet. When you post to a moderated newsgroup, the article is e-mailed to the person (or group) who moderates the newsgroup. The moderator decides whether the article is appropriate to post. You generally get an automated response from the moderator's computer, and sometimes follow-up mail from the moderator.

Being Original

You can post an article that isn't a follow-up to any other message. That is, you can launch a brand-new thread on a brand-new topic, if you like.

To do so, press f when you are reading the newsgroup to which you want to post the article. Trn asks whether you want to respond to the article you just read or start a new topic. Choose to start a new thread.

Fiddling with Your Newsgroups

When trn offers a newsgroup for you to read, there are actually dozens of commands you can give. In addition to the four commands listed earlier in this chapter (+, y, n, and q), you can also use these commands to add or delete newsgroups from your list:

✔ To delete a newsgroup from your list (that is, to unsubscribe to it), press u (that's a small *u*).

✔ To add a newsgroup that's not on your .newsrc list, type

```
g newsgroupname
```

Replace newsgroupname with the exact name of the newsgroup. For example, if you are interested in naturist activities, type

```
g rec.nude
```

✔ If you are not sure of the exact name of the newsgroup you are looking for, type

```
a text
```

Replace text with a word or part of a word. For example, if you are interested in gardening, type

```
a garden
```

If trn finds any newsgroups with names that contain those characters, it asks whether you want to subscribe to each one. Press y or n to subscribe or not. When trn asks where to put the newsgroup, just press the spacebar.

Preventing Alzheimer's

All newsreading programs store information about your particular preferences and situation, including what newsgroups you subscribe to and which messages you've already read. (Messages in each newsgroup are numbered, so it can just remember the range of message numbers you've seen.) The information is stored in a file named .newsrc. Whether you use rn, trn, or nn to read the news, they all share the information in the .newsrc file. This file is the way that most newsreading programs don't forget all about what you've subscribed to and what you've already read.

To look at your `.newsrc` file, when trn asks whether you want to look at a newsgroup, press L (be sure it's capitalized). You see a listing like this:

```
#  Status    Newsgroup
 0  (READ)    local.risks! 1-5548,5551-5556
 1  (UNSUB)   local.pcdigest! 1-7197
 2  (UNSUB)   comp.binaries.ibm.pc.d! 1-17823
 3  (UNSUB)   comp.sys.ibm.pc.digest! 1-580
 4  (UNSUB)   comp.text.desktop! 1-2558
 5  (UNSUB)   rec.food.veg! 1-36863,37791,37958
 6      37    rec.humor.funny! 1-3424
 7  (UNSUB)   rec.humor! 1-105750,106727,107119
 8     152    rec.arts.startrek.info! 1-1942
 9  (UNSUB)   news.lists.ps-maps! 1-1111
10  (UNSUB)   comp.sys.ibm.pc.programmer! 1-5748
11  (UNSUB)   comp.specification! 1-1337
12  (UNSUB)   comp.text.tex! 1-35685
```

The first column of the listing just numbers the groups for your reference. The second column says:

- a number, meaning that you subscribe to the group and that's how many unread articles are waiting for you
- READ, meaning that you subscribe to the group and have read all its articles
- UNSUB, meaning that you once subscribed to it but unsubscribed in disgust
- BOGUS, meaning that it's not in the official list of real newsgroups
- JUNK, meaning nothing (trn ignores lines that say *JUNK* here)

A colon after a newsgroup name means that you're subscribed to the group, and an exclamation point means that you're not. The number ranges are the article numbers of the articles that are marked as having been read.

Reading the best ones first

Trn goes down the list of newsgroups in your `.newsrc` file, asking you about each one in order. If your `.newsrc` file has many newsgroups in it, it's a good idea to put first the ones you read most often. This avoids having to skip over the less interesting ones each time.

When trn asks whether you want to read a newsgroup and you want to move this newsgroup, press m and Enter. Then press one of the following:

- ✔ Press ^ to put it first.
- ✔ Press $ to put it last.
- ✔ Type a number to tell trn what line number to put in your .newsrc file.
- ✔ Press + and the name of another newsgroup to put it after that newsgroup.
- ✔ Press q to forget the whole thing.

Killing Articles That Displease You

We abhor violence as much as you do, but sometimes you gotta do what you gotta do. An ugly fact of Usenet life is that a great deal of garbage appears in newsgroups, mixed in with the good stuff. One powerful method of avoiding it is to use trn's thread selector, described earlier in this chapter. A more permanent method is the *kill file*.

What's a kill file?

Trn has two kinds of kill files: your global kill file, which applies to all your newsgroups, and kill files for each newsgroup. Both types of kill files contain information about which types of Usenet messages you never, never want to see. Messages described in your kill files are simply skipped over by trn, so they never bother you.

For example, what if some idiot decides that it is very funny to send gross and useless messages to a newsgroup that you like to read? You can skip over them, true, but wouldn't it be nice to just tell trn, "Look, if you get any messages from that idiot, ignore them! I don't want to see them!" With kill files, you can.

Alternatively, if you are interested in only a small subject of the articles in a newsgroup, you can tell trn, "In this newsgroup, I want to see only articles that contain thus-and-such in the subject." Rather than kill a group of articles, you can kill all but a group of articles. You can use kill files to select articles, too.

The global kill file contains a list of commands that trn executes every time you begin reading a newsgroup. Newsgroup kill files contain the commands that trn executes when you enter that particular newsgroup. The commands usually tell trn which articles to kill (that is, ignore and never show you) or select (that is, ignore all the *other* articles). Your global kill file is stored in your News directory and is named KILL.

The kill files for each newsgroup are stored in subdirectories of your News directory. For example, your kill file for the rec.humor.funny newsgroup is stored in News/rec/humor/funny/KILL.

It's usually better to use newsgroup kill files rather than the global kill files because the types of articles you want to kill or to select tend to differ widely from newsgroup to newsgroup. It can slow down your newsreading if trn has to execute a bunch of unnecessary commands at the beginning of each newsgroup. On the other hand, an unfortunate spate of advertisements has recently been posted to every newsgroup in the known universe (a practice known as *spamming*, which is an insult to the Spam brand meat-type product), for which a global kill file is the best response.

License to kill

You can add commands to your newsgroup kill file when you are choosing the threads to read, but the best time is when you are reading articles. When you are looking at a particularly obnoxious article, here's how to draw some blood:

1. **Press** A **(be sure to capitalize it).**

   This step adds a command to the newsgroup kill file, telling trn what to do with all articles that have the same subject as this article, both now and in the future, forever.

   Trn then asks [+j.,] (surely one of the most inspired prompts of all time). This is its way of asking what exactly you want to do with these articles.

2. **To kill (skip) all the articles, press** j. **To kill all the articles as well as any replies to them, press** , **(a comma).**

A faster way of killing articles on the same subject as the current articles is by pressing K (capitalized). This is the same as typing Aj.

Narrowing your view

Alternatively, you may want to tell trn that you are interested in articles *only* on a certain subject, now and forever. When you are looking at an article on that subject, press A (capitalized). Then press + to look at only articles on that subject. Or press . (period) to look at only those articles and replies to them.

Editing the kill file

You can use a text editor to look at what's in your kill file and make some changes. To edit your global kill file, wait until trn is asking you whether you want to read a newsgroup. Instead of answering, press Ctrl-K. To edit a newsgroup kill file, when you are reading that newsgroup, press Ctrl-K. Either way, trn runs a text editor and loads up the appropriate kill file.

Each line in a kill file contains one command, telling trn to either skip all articles that fit a certain description or to look only at articles that fit a description. The first line in a kill file tells trn the message number of the latest message that trn has looked at, like this:

```
THRU 13567
```

Commands look like this:

```
/Buzz off, buddy!/:j
```

The text between the slashes tells trn what text to look for in the subjects of articles. The character after the colon (a *j*, in this example) tells trn what to do with the articles: *j* to junk them, a comma to junk them and their replies, a + to select only them, and a period to select only them and their replies. Not exactly easy to remember!

Here's another example: Suppose that you read the newsgroup news.groups, which is where discussions about new newsgroups take place. However, there can be several hundred messages a day. You are interested only in articles that have anything to do with cats. To see only those articles, you can add this line to the kill file for the news.groups kill file:

```
/cat/:+
```

This command selects all articles with a subject line that contains the word *cat*.

Undoing death

If you add a command to a kill file and then you change your mind, the only way to get rid of it is to edit the kill file. When you are in the newsgroup, press Ctrl-K to edit the file. Look for the command (if it's the last one you created, it's at the end of the file). Using your editor's commands, delete the entire line, or modify it until it does what you want.

Using Nn

Nn is yet another newsreader, written by Kim F. Storm in Denmark. It's supposed to be easier to use because it displays a bunch of menus. Here's a quick introduction to nn.

To run nn, type nn.

In nn, whenever you want help, just press ?. You see a terse but helpful list of commands.

Get me out of here

To exit from nn, press Q (be sure it's capitalized or else it won't work).

Choosing newsgroups

When you start nn, it asks whether you want to read a newsgroup, whichever newsgroup happens to be first in nn's huge list of available groups. Until you have unsubscribed to the vast list of newsgroups, this is kind of annoying. Here's how to find the newsgroup you want:

1. **Quit from the newsgroup you are reading, if any, so that nn asks about a newsgroup, like this:**

   ```
   Enter rec.humor.funny (18 unread)?
   ```

   At this point, nn accepts only two answers: Y and N.

2. **Go ahead, lie, and press Y.**

   You see a list of the articles in this newsgroup (more on this list in a minute).

3. **To go to the newsgroup you actually want to read, press G (make sure to capitalize it).**

   You see the Group or Folder prompt.

4. **Type the name of the newsgroup you want to read, and press Enter.**

   You see a prompt entitled Number of articles.

5. **Press j to tell nn that you don't particularly want to return to that first newsgroup — you want it to jump to this new one.**

Choosing articles

After you have found the newsgroup you want, nn shows you a list of its articles (or at least as many as it can fit on your screen), as shown in Figure 19-3. Each article has a letter by it, and you can see who wrote it and what its subject line is. If an article has > or >> or something like that as the subject, it means that it has more or less the same subject line as the preceding article.

The prompt at the bottom of the screen tells you that this is only the top 1 percent of the articles in this newsgroup. Yikes!

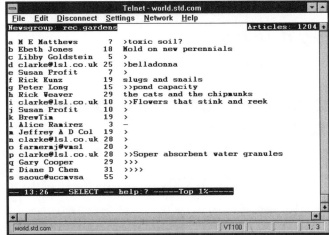

Figure 19-3:
A menu of articles in your favorite newsgroup.

Here's how to read some articles:

1. **Tell nn which articles interest you, by pressing their letters.**

   If you want to read a range of articles, you can use a dash. If you want to read articles *b* through *j*, for example, you can type b-j. If you want to tell nn to select an article and all the other articles with the same subject, type a * after the letter.

2. **When you have selected the articles on this page, you can move to the next page of the list by pressing >. To move back a page, press <.**

   Pressing the spacebar also moves to the next page, at least until you get to the last page. (When you get to the last page, you see Bot on the bottom line rather than a percentage.)

3. When you get to the last page of the list or you feel that you've marked enough articles for the time being, press X **(capitalized).**

A bunch of commands are available at this point, but this one marks the articles that you didn't select as read, at least on the pages of the list that you saw, and begins showing you the articles you selected. That's usually what we want to do.

If you didn't make it all the way to the end of this newsgroup and you might want to come back to select some more articles, press Z instead of X (but still capitalized).

Now you begin to see some news.

Reading articles

Nn shows you articles like the one in Figure 19-4.

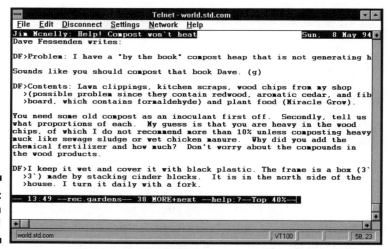

Figure 19-4:
At last — an article!

If the article is longer than can fit on the page, the prompt line at the bottom tells you how far through it you've gotten (as a percentage). Press the spacebar to see more. When you get to the end of the article, press the spacebar to see the next article.

When you are looking at an article, here are other things you can do:

✔ Press ^ or $ to get to the first or last page of a long article.

✔ Press D (capitalized) to decode an article that is encoded using rot-13 encoding. (This code is used for offensive articles that might gross you out. Use this command with care.)

✔ Press n (small letter) to skip the rest of the article and move on to the next one.

✔ Press k to kill this article and all other articles with the same subject. If you want to store this command in a kill file (as described earlier in this chapter), press K.

✔ Press * to see the next article that has the same subject this one has. Nn shows you articles that match even if you didn't select them earlier.

✔ To go back to selecting articles, press =.

✔ Press S to save the article in a text file. Better yet, press O to save it with abbreviated headers (the headers are always boring), or press W to save it with no headers at all. (Amazingly, you can use *either* capital or small letters to give these commands. Phenomenal user-friendliness.)

✔ When you are sick of reading this newsgroup, press N (that's a capital letter) to move on to the next one in the list. This command leaves the articles that you didn't read marked as unread, so you have another shot at them.

If you don't think that you'll want to read the rest of the articles in this newsgroup, press X instead of N (and capitalize it). This marks all the articles in the newsgroup as read and moves on to the next one.

Mouthing off privately

If you want to respond to an article after reading it, these steps show you how to send an e-mail message to the person who posted the article:

1. **Press** R **(capitalized).**

   Nn asks whether you want to include the original article.

2. **Press** y **or** n.

   Nn runs an editor to allow you to write your response. When you have saved your message and exited from the editor, you see this prompt:

   ```
   a)bort e)dit h)old m)ail r)eedit s)end v)iew w)rite
   Action: (send letter)
   ```

3. **To send the letter, press** s. **If you've changed your mind, press** a.

Mouthing off publicly

If you want to respond to an article by posting a follow-up article:

1. **Think about whether what you have to say is actually going to be of general interest to the thousands of people who read this newsgroup.**

   If not, respond privately (see the preceding section).

2. **Press F to create a follow-up article.**

   Nn asks whether you want to include the original article.

3. **Press y or n.**

   Nn runs an editor, creates the appropriate headers for the article, and includes the original article if you requested it.

4. **If you included the original article, delete the boring parts of the original article, along with the parts you don't plan to talk about, the signature at the end, and so on.**

5. **Type the text of your response.**

   Check it for spelling, grammar, good taste, charm, and factual accuracy. You're going to be taking a minute or two of thousands of people's time, so use it wisely. (We book authors should take our own advice!)

6. **Save the article and exit from the editor.**

   When you have saved the article and exited from the editor, you see this prompt:

```
a)bort c)c e)dit h)old m)ail r)eedit s)end v)iew w)rite
Action: (post article)
```

7. **To post the article, press s. If you have thought better of it, press a. If you want to send it as mail instead, press m.**

Using Tin

The last newsreader we'll look at, briefly again, is tin, written by Iain Lea, at Siemens in Germany. Tin makes better use of a terminal screen than do the other newsreaders, so many users prefer it to the other leading brands.

Start tin by typing **tin** (tricky, eh?) You see a screen like the one in Figure 19-5.

```
┌──────────────────────────────────────────────────────────────────────┐
│ ▬                                                              ▼  ▲    │
├──────────────────────────────────────────────────────────────────────┤
│  File   Edit   Disconnect   Settings   Script   Network   Help         │
│                      Group Selection (125)            Type 'h' for help│
│                                                                        │
│ ->      21   news.groups                       13                      │
│         22   news.groups.reviews               1                       │
│         23   news.lists                                                │
│         24   news.lists.ps-maps                                        │
│         25   comp.arch                                                 │
│         26   comp.archives                      148                    │
│         27   comp.compilers                                            │
│         28   comp.compression                                          │
│         29   comp.compression.research                                 │
│         30   comp.dcom.lans.ethernet                                   │
│         31   comp.dcom.telecom                 19                      │
│         32   comp.dcom.telecom.tech            2                       │
│         33   local.telecom                                             │
│         34   alt.dcom.telecom                  1                       │
│         35   alt.snail-mail                                            │
│         36   local.teletech                    2                       │
│         37   comp.society.privacy              1                       │
│         38   comp.doc                                                  │
│         39   comp.doc.techreports                                      │
│         40   comp.internet.library                                     │
│                                                                        │
│ ▏Ready                                          ▕VT100▏        ▏24, 1▏  │
└──────────────────────────────────────────────────────────────────────┘
```

Figure 19-5:
Tin shows
you some
newsgroups.

Choosing newsgroups

Your subscribed groups are listed with a line number at the left and the number of unread articles at the right. You can move up and down by pressing the cursor keys and PgUp and PgDn or by typing the line number. To look at the articles in a group, move the cursor to that group's line and press Enter.

Tin updates the index files it keeps for the group (which can take a while for a busy group) and then displays a list of articles (see Figure 19-6).

```
┌─────────────────────────────────────────────────────────────────────────┐
│ ─                                                                   ▼ ▲  │
│ File   Edit  Disconnect  Settings  Script  Network  Help                 │
│ ┌───────────────────────────────────────────────────────────────────────┤
│                  comp.dcom.telecom (212 329)          Type 'h' for help  │
│ ─> 41          SRI Ends Two Bobs' MGR              Will Martin <wmartin@STL-│
│    42          SRI Ends Two Bobs                   The Tibetian Traveller <G│
│    43     1    SONET Management Standards?         Don Berryman <don@adc.com│
│    44          Ruling on 800 Numbers From Payphones Stephen Goodman <00039456│
│    45          Replace POST-MAIL by FAX            herb@halcyon.com (Herb Ef│
│    46          Remote Telephone Access Information Wa Warren Birnbaum <wjb@cheo│
│    47     1    Reach Out and Pay Someone           Peter M. Weiss <PMW1@PSUV│
│    48          Radio by Phone                      Paul Robinson <PAUL@TDR.C│
│    49     1    Radio Frequency Interference on Reside bill@noller.com (Bill Tig│
│    50          Radio Frequency Interference on Reside drw@severi.mit.edu (Dale│
│    51          Query re: Voice Dictation          Mike McCrohan <mccrohan@i│
│    52          Proposed Upgrading of Canada Direct Se Dave.Leibold@f730.n250.z1│
│    53   + 6    Problems With Call Return           Ed Ellers <edellers@delph│
│    54          Phone Line in Use Indicator From Radio 1JCR7732@ibm.mtsac.edu@cc│
│    55     3    Palestinian Country Code            goudreau@dg-rtp.dg.com (B│
│    56   + 3    Pac-Tel (PC) Communication Software przebien@news.delphi.com│
│    57          PCBX Systems                        paulb@iconz.co.nz (Paul B│
│    58          Ontario Computing Strategy          TELECOM Moderator <teleco│
│    59   +      No 911 Available as Tot Drowns      Dave.Leibold@f730.n250.z1│
│    60   +      New Long Distance Company is Advertisi Carl Moore <cmoore@brl.mi│
│ ┌───────────────────────────────────────────────────────────────────────┤
│  Ready                                            VT100          24, 1    │
└─────────────────────────────────────────────────────────────────────────┘
```

Figure 19-6:
A list of
articles for
telephone-
oriented
propeller-
heads.

Choosing and reading articles

For each topic, there's a line number, a plus sign if there are unread articles
with that topic, the number of follow-ups to the article, the title, and the author.

To read a particular article, move to the article by pressing the cursor keys or
by typing the line number, and then press Enter. It's usually more convenient to
press Tab to go to the next unread article.

In an article, you can use these keys:

 ✔ Press Tab to go to the next page of the article or on the last page to the
   next unread article. On the last page of the last unread article, it goes to
   the next group with unread news. (Perhaps we should offer a "tin convenience keyboard" that has only a giant Tab key.)

 ✔ If you want to skip to the next article without reading the rest of the
   current one, press n to move to the next article or N to move to the next
   unread article.

 ✔ Press i to go back to the article index (the list of article names) and i
   again to return to the index of newsgroups.

✔ Most other commands are similar to trn and nn: r or R to reply to the author of an article, f or F to post a follow-up, c to catch up a group (pretend that you've read it all), and so forth.

✔ Press h at any point for a surprisingly readable help screen.

Getting uuencoded and shar files out of articles

One thing that tin does quite differently is extract uuencoded or shar files. It's not hard, but it's not obvious:

1. **Display the article index for the group with the articles you want to extract.**

2. **Move to each article to be extracted (just one for a shar file, and one or more for a multipart uuencoded file), and tag each one by pressing T.**

   Tin displays sequential numbers for each article tagged.

3. **Tell tin to save the tagged articles in a temporary file by pressing s.**

4. **When tin asks for a filename, give it one.**

   A traditional temporary file name is foo.

   After tin saves the articles, it asks what to do with them.

5. **Press s to extract a shar file or press u for a uuencoded one.**

   Tin thoughtfully deletes the temporary file if the extract worked.

6. **Press U to untag the articles you just saved and extracted.**

Leaving tin

Press q for quit. (You probably guessed that.) Tin asks whether it should catch up all the groups you looked at (that is, mark all unread articles as read). Press n, and you're done.

Chapter 20

Telnetting Around the Net

● ●

In This Chapter

▶ The next best thing to being there

▶ Reach out and log in

▶ A few words from IBM

▶ Telnetting around the world

▶ More libraries, databases, and on-line services than any sane person would want

● ●

*I*n Chapter 20 of *UNIX For Dummies,* we described (among other things) how to use the telnet program to log in to computers other than your own. If your UNIX system is connected to the Internet, there are lots of computers you can log in to in this way — even some computers on which you don't have an account. Here's how!

How Can You Be in Two Places at Once When You're Not Anywhere at All?

What telnet does is simple: You log in to a remote *host* (telnet-ese for a computer) as though your *terminal* (workstation, PC, whatever) were attached directly to that host. Because all hosts on the Internet are officially equal, you can log in to a host on the other side of the world as easily as you can log in to one down the hall, with the only difference that the connection to the distant host may be a little slower.

Although *telnet* (the most commonly used remote login program) is in principle simplicity itself, because computers are involved, simplicity just isn't what it used to be. To run telnet, you type the telnet command followed by the name of the host you want to use. If everything goes well, you are then connected to that host.

Here's how to use telnet to log on to another computer:

1. **Type** telnet **and the host name of the computer you want to use. For example, type this line:**

```
% telnet xuxa.iecc.com
```

You see a message like this:

```
Trying 140.186.81.47 ... Connected to xuxa.iecc.com.
Escape character is '^]'.

System V UNIX (xuxa)
login:
```

2. **Type the login name (username) and password you have on that system when you are prompted, just like you log in to your ol' familiar UNIX system.**

3. **After you log in, you may see messages to greet you, like this:**

```
Terminal type (default VT100):
```

Notice a couple of points here:

✔ Some versions of telnet report the numeric addresses of the hosts they contact. If your version does this, note that number in case of later trouble with the network connection.

✔ The thing that's absolutely essential to note is the *escape character,* which is your secret key to unhooking yourself from the remote host if it ever becomes recalcitrant and stops doing anything useful.

✔ The escape character in the preceding example (the most common one on UNIX systems) is ^], which means that you hold down the Ctrl key and press] (the right-bracket character on your keyboard).

✔ If you use a program on the remote system that needs to use that escape character for its own purposes, you can choose another escape character. See the section "Whipping Telnet into Shape," later in this chapter.

After you're logged in, you can work pretty much as though you were indeed directly logged in to the remote host. The main difference is that characters take a little longer to appear on-screen — as long as a full second or more. In most cases, you can keep typing even when what you typed hasn't yet appeared; the remote host eventually catches up.

Most systems on the Internet do *not* provide any public logins. (There's no equivalent of anonymous FTP, which is described in Chapter 21, "Grabbing Files over the Net.") Hence, there's not much point in telnetting to a system unless either you have an account on that system or its owner explicitly offers a public login. In particular, it's particularly poor form to telnet to a remote system and try to guess a login and a password. (It's also not very difficult for the remote system's manager to figure out who's doing that and to ask your administrator to tell you to cut it out.)

If you were wondering what the point is of having a telnet server with no public logins, it's so that the system's authorized users can log in over the net when they're not physically nearby.

Terminal Type Tedium

If you use a full-screen program, such as the UNIX text editors emacs and vi or the mail programs elm and pine, you have to set your *terminal type*. This problem shouldn't exist in the first place. But it does, so you have to deal with it.

The problem is that about a dozen different conventions exist for screen controls such as *clear screen* and *move to position (x,y)*. The program you're using on the remote host has to use the same convention your terminal does (if you're using a terminal) or that your local terminal program does (if you're on a PC or a workstation).

If the conventions are not the same, you get *garbage* (funky-looking characters) on-screen when you try to use a full-screen program. In most cases, the remote system asks you what terminal type to use. The trick is knowing the right answer.

✔ If you're using the X Window system, with or without Motif, the answer is more likely to be *VT-100,* a popular terminal from the 1970s that became a de facto standard. You might also try *xterm,* the name of the standard X program that does terminal emulation.

✔ If you're using a PC and an emulation program, the best answer is usually *ANSI* because most PC terminal programs use ANSI terminal conventions. (*ANSI* stands for the *American National Standards Institute.* One of its several thousand standards defines a set of terminal control conventions that MS-DOS PCs — which otherwise wouldn't know an ANSI standard if they tripped over one — invariably use.)

✔ In places where a great deal of IBM equipment is used, the terminal type may be *3101,* an early IBM terminal that was also popular.

The ANSI and VT-100 conventions are not much different from each other, so if you use one and your screen is only somewhat screwed up, try the other.

TECHNICAL STUFF

Who cares about terminal types?

Back in the good old days — like about 1968 — most computer systems used only one kind of terminal: a genuine Teletype brand *Teletype*. Teletype machines, direct descendants of the news Teletypes (familiar from old movie footage of newspaper production), were simple beasts. That is, they were simple conceptually — physically, they had an incredible number of moving parts. The only things these machines did other than type text was return the carriage and ring the bell.

Then people realized that you could combine a keyboard with a slightly modified television screen and build a video terminal. Dozens of manufacturers appeared, most now long forgotten, and they all noticed that you could do a great deal more with a screen than you could with an old Teletype. For example, you could clear the screen, draw text in specific places, shift text up and down — all sorts of handy stuff. So each manufacturer assigned otherwise unused character codes as *control characters* to handle these special functions. Naturally, no two terminals used the same assignment.

Meanwhile, on a small planet far, far away — oops, sorry, wrong book. Meanwhile, in Berkeley, California, in the late 1970s, what is now known as Berkeley UNIX was taking shape. People at Berkeley had amassed large and completely miscellaneous collections of incompatible terminals. Which terminals would Berkeley UNIX support? Here's a hint: Terminals had to be bought from outside and cost real money, whereas software was written by students and was free. Naturally,

Berkeley UNIX supported every single terminal type on the campus, using a large database of hundreds of terminal types with the particular control sequences needed for each terminal.

By the early 1980s, it was apparent that the dominant terminal in the non-IBM market was the DEC VT-100. Many clone terminals began to appear that understood exactly the same control sequences as VT-100s, so they would work in all the places that VT-100s did. ANSI, the organization in charge of technical standards in the United States, adopted control sequences almost identical to the VT-100 sequences as an official standard.

So now you can assume that every terminal is a VT-100, right? Well, no. For one thing, many of those old terminals refuse to die. (We recently stumbled across an old Volker-Craig, a modestly popular Canadian model from the 1970s, for sale at the Salvation Army.) For another, terminal manufacturers progressed far beyond the VT-100, adding such features as color and graphics that the VT-100 didn't have. So most terminals made today are more or less ANSI-compatible, but with their own grotey warts. The world is stuck with multiple terminal types for the foreseeable future. At this point, if you don't know which kind of terminal you have, either VT-100 or ANSI is your best guess.

For another failed attempt at terminal standardization, see the sidebar "Disregard this discussion about network virtual terminals," later in this chapter.

Depending on how well implemented your local version of telnet is, it may automatically advise the remote system about which kind of terminal you're using. With luck, you won't actually have to set your terminal type, or perhaps you'll just have to reply **y** when it says something like `Terminal type VT100 OK?`

Escaping from Telnet

The normal way to leave telnet is to log out from the remote host. When you log out, the remote host closes its end of the telnet connection, which tells your local telnet program that it's finished. Easy enough — normally. Sometimes, though, the other end gets stuck and pays no attention to what you type. Or it doesn't get permanently stuck, but the host responds so slowly that you have no interest in waiting for it anymore. (This sometimes happens when network congestion occurs between you and the other host.)

Some versions of host software, which we won't name, for looking-gift-horses-in-the-mouth-type reasons, get hopelessly slowed down by congestion, much more than the congestion itself causes. So you have to know how to escape from telnet. Here's where the magic escape character comes in handy:

- First, you have to get telnet's attention by pressing the escape character, usually Ctrl-]. (If nothing happens after a few seconds, try pressing Enter as well.) Telnet should come back with a prompt telling you that it's there.

- Then type **quit** to tell it that you're finished. You should see something like the following:

```
^]
telnet> quit
Connection closed.
```

You can give telnet a dozen other commands (press **?** to see them), but none of them is anywhere near as useful as `quit`.

Terminals Served Here

One specialized host increasingly found on the Internet is a terminal server. The *terminal server* is basically a little computer with a number of modems or hard-wired terminal ports, and all it does with its life is telnet to other hosts. This makes sense if you have a number of regular terminals around the office or many people who dial in over the phone, because it enables many terminals to get on the net at low cost. (Terminal servers are so carefully tuned to their task that, even though a typical one has the computing power of a 1985 PC, it can handle upward of 30 modem connections at 14,000 bps *each.*)

Using a terminal server is similar to logging in to a single-minded computer (indeed, that's just what it is). You dial in and usually have to enter a site password that keeps 12-year-old hackers from calling in at random. (Or hackers of any age, for that matter.) Then you type the name of the host you want to connect to, and you're telnetted in. Here's a session on a typical Cisco terminal server:

```
User Access Verification Password: *****
TS>xuxa.iecc.com
Translating "XUXA.IECC.COM"...domain server (155.178.247.101)
        [OK]
Trying XUXA.IECC.COM (140.186.81.42)... Open
System V UNIX (xuxa)
login:
 . . . regular telnet session deleted here ...
[Connection to XUXA.IECC.COM closed by foreign host]
TS>
```

Terminal servers have escape characters just like regular telnet programs do, although they tend to be more difficult to guess. The usual escape for the popular Cisco servers is two characters, Ctrl-^ (which you usually enter as Ctrl-Shift-6), followed by a lowercase *x*. Other brands of terminal servers have different escape sequences; inquire locally to find out which ones to use.

Most terminal servers also have a small set of commands that they understand to customize your terminal session. Press **?** rather than a host name and see what it says.

Whipping Telnet into Shape

You can tell telnet to change its behavior in a few ways. The two most notable are to turn on and off local echo and line mode. *Local echo* means that the characters you type are sent to your screen by the local host (the one running telnet) rather than the one you have telnetted to. If your remote host echoes slowly or doesn't echo at all (some IBM hosts and game servers are like that), you can try to turn on local echo. Usually, pressing Ctrl-E turns local echo on and off.

Nearly all hosts on the Internet want to process the characters you type one at a time, as soon as you type them. A few ancient ones prefer a line at a time. You usually can recognize them because they don't handle any backspacing over errors. To work around that problem, type the telnet escape character and then **mode line**.

This line tells your local host to save up the characters and send them along a line at a time, handling the backspaces before passing them on. The number of hosts using line mode is small and shrinking. If you think that you've found a host that needs it, ask around to see whether you've overlooked something. If the host sends text a screen at a time and uses acronyms such as VM or MVS (the two most common IBM operating systems), you've probably run into an IBM host and should use `tn3270` instead. See the section "Attack of the IBM Terminals," later in this chapter.

Disregard this discussion about network virtual terminals

Back in 1983 when telnet was defined, the folks working on it were acutely aware of the various kinds of terminals in use. Their solution to the incompatible terminal explosion was to define a *Network Virtual Terminal (NVT)*. The plan was that the telnet *client* (the program you run) would turn the local control glop into standard NVT codes; the telnet *server* (the program at the other end that makes your network connection act like a terminal on that host) would turn NVT codes into whatever the local convention was. As long as each system was configured correctly for the terminals physically attached to it, NVTs would take care of everything.

This plan didn't work, though. What happened? The problem was that telnet came along slightly too early and the kinds of terminals they were worried about were line-at-a-time printing terminals, particularly some IBM terminals known by four-digit numbers such as 2741 and 1050. The 2741 was a slightly beefed-up Selectric type-

writer with a computer interface, but it wasn't beefed up quite enough to handle the wear and tear of being run at full speed by a computer rather than at 30 words per minute by a typist. One of the authors of this book used a terminal room for several years that contained about a dozen 2741s, and he cannot remember all of them ever being in working order at the same time.

NVTs magnificently solve incompatibilities among 2741s, Teletypes, Flexowriters, and many other printing terminals. Unfortunately, video terminals were just coming into fashion, and NVTs didn't address them at all. So Internet users are stuck with multiple terminal types on all the hosts.

(That's not quite true. Major manufacturers such as Digital Equipment Corporation (DEC) tend to support only their own terminals, so if you telnet into a DEC VMS system with anything other than a DEC terminal or clone thereof, you lose. Fortunately, the ubiquitous VT-100 was made by DEC.)

Port, Anyone?

When you telnet into a remote host, you have to select not just the host but also a *port* on the host. The port is a small number that identifies which service you want. The usual port for telnet is (for obscure historical reasons) the number 23, which is taken to mean that you want to log in to the host. You pick another port by putting the port name after the host name as follows:

```
telnet ntw.org 13
```

Port 13 is the *daytime* port. It tells you that host's idea of the time of day and then disconnects. This exercise is not a terribly useful one, although occasionally you may have to see which time zone another host is in.

Some hosts are set up so that the regular telnet to port 23 gets a login prompt for regular users of the system, whereas telnetting to some other port gets you into a special, publicly usable subsystem.

Attack of the IBM Terminals

All the terminals discussed earlier that are handled by telnet are basically souped-up Teletypes, with data passed character by character between the terminal and the host. This kind of terminal interaction can be called *Teletype-ish*.

IBM developed an entirely different model for its 3270-series display terminals. The principle is that the computer's in charge. The model works more like filling in paper forms. The computer draws what it wants on the screen, marks which parts of the screen users can type on, and then unlocks the keyboard so that users can fill in whichever blanks they want. When a user presses Enter, the terminal locks the keyboard, transmits the changed parts of the screen to the computer, and awaits additional instructions from headquarters.

To be fair, this is a perfectly reasonable way to build terminals intended for dedicated data-entry and -retrieval applications. The terminal on the desks at your bank or the electric company are probably 3270s — or more likely these days, cheap PCs *emulating* 3270s. The 3270 terminal protocol squeezes a great deal more on a phone line than Teletype-ish, so it's quite common to have all the 3270s in an office sharing the same single phone line, with reasonable performance.

The Internet is a big place, and plenty of IBM mainframes run applications on the net. Some of them are quite useful. Most large library catalogs, for example, speak 3270-ish. Usually, if you telnet to a system that wants a 3270, it converts from the Teletype-ish that telnet speaks to 3270-ish so that you can use it anyway. But some 3270 systems speak only 3270-ish, and if you telnet to them, they connect and disconnect without saying anything in between.

A variant of telnet that speaks 3270-ish is called *tn3270*. If you find that a system keeps disconnecting, try typing the command **tn3270** instead. (Large amounts of UPPERCASE LETTERS and references to the IBM operating systems VM or MVS are also tipoffs that you're talking to a 3270.) Even if a 3270 system allows regular telnet, you get a snappier response if you use tn3270 instead.

Come On By, Anytime

The Internet is a remarkably friendly place. Many systems let you telnet in with little or no prearrangement. Most just let you telnet in without restriction. Others require that you register the first time you log in but still don't ask you to pay anything. They just want to have some idea who their users are.

The rest of this chapter lists a bunch of computers on the Internet that you can telnet to without having your own account there. The list doesn't include any of the many places where you can telnet to Gopher, Archie, or WWW servers — these servers are covered in chapters 21, 23, and 24.

Some important libraries

Nearly every large library in the country (indeed, in the developed world) now has a computerized catalog, and most of those catalogs are on the Internet. Most of the on-line catalogs also have other research info that is certainly more interesting than the catalogs themselves. This section lists some of the more prominent library systems and how to access them.

Library: Library of Congress
Address: locis.loc.gov
Access code: Telnet, 3270

Your secret decoder ring

In the list of services in this chapter, the codes have the following meaning:

Code Letter	Meaning	Code Letter	Meaning
Telnet	Connect by way of regular telnet.	3270	Connect by way of tn3270. Most tn3270 systems listed in this chapter also allow regular telnet for people without tn3270.
Port Number	Specify a port number after the host name in your telnet command		
Register	Registration required. The first time you log in, you have to say who you are.	Account	Account required. You have to sign up and arrange to pay money. (Not many of these are listed.)

The Library of Congress is the largest library in the world, and it certainly has the biggest catalog system, called LOCIS. (It's your tax dollars at work — or maybe at play.) Along with the regular card catalog, in which you can look up pretty much any book ever published in the United States, the Library of Congress has an extensive and useful congressional legislation system you can use to look up the bills that are in Congress. You can find out which bills have been introduced; what has happened to them (getting a bill through Congress is somewhat more complicated than getting someone canonized as a saint); who sponsored them; and what they say (in summary).

LOCIS is available only during the hours when the Library is open, generally 9 a.m. to 9 p.m. (Eastern time) on weekdays, shorter hours on weekends. Other times it may be unavailable, in which case it disconnects immediately.

Library: Dartmouth College Library
Address: library.dartmouth.edu
Access code: Telnet

Along with the card catalog, this service includes the full text of William Shakespeare's plays and sonnets and the works of other great authors. To search the plays, type **select file s plays**; for sonnets, type **select file s sonnets**.

Library: Harvard Library
Address: hollis.harvard.edu
Access code: Telnet, 3270

Harvard has another huge library, and the service also provides campus info.

Library: Victoria University of Wellington
Address: library.vuw.ac.nz
Access code: Telnet

This library catalog is in New Zealand, if you're planning to head down that way. After you connect, press Enter a few times until it asks you to log in, and then type **OPAC**.

Other libraries

A service called *hytelnet* is a database of and gateway to many other libraries. If you log in to any one of them, it helps you find catalog information for dozens or hundreds of libraries. Current hytelnet servers include the following:

- laguna.epcc.edu   login: library
- info.anu.edu.au   login: info (located in Australia)

Large lists of on-line libraries also are available by FTP (see Chapter 21, "Grabbing Files over the Net," for more information).

Geography databases

Database: Geographic Server

Address: martini.eecs.umich.edu

Access code: Telnet, Port 3000

This database has the name, location, and other facts on every place in the United States. If you've ever wondered where Surf City, U.S.A. really is, this database is for you. (It's in New Jersey, by the way — eat your heart out, California. It doesn't tell you, however, not to miss the world-famous Surf City Fire Breakfast, held the second and fourth Sundays in August, but one of the authors just did.)

Database: GLIS

Address: glis.cr.usgs.gov

Access code: Telnet, Register

The government's *Global Land Use Info System (GLIS)* is an enormous amount of map data available in computer form. GLIS enables you to locate and order it. Impress your friends by whipping out a computerized map of your town, state, or planet.

Outer-space databases

Care to roam the far reaches of the universe (or talk to people who do)? Then the outer space databases are for you.

Database: Spacelink

Address: spacelink.msfc.nasa.gov

Access code: Telnet

This database contains NASA news, including the shuttle launch schedule.

Database: European Space Agency

Address: esrin.esa.it

Access code: Telnet

This database tells you what's new in the European part of outer space.

Book databases

Looking for books, tapes, and CDs? Here are some starting points.

Database: CARL

Address: pac.carl.org

Access code: Telnet, Account

This database of book reviews, magazines, and articles include fax article delivery. For many of the services, you need a library card (or at least the number of a library card) from a participating library in Colorado or Wyoming, such as the Denver Public Library.

Database: Wordsworth Bookstore

Address: wordsworth.com

Access code: Telnet, Register

Wordsworth is a huge bookstore in Cambridge, Massachusetts. It keeps up-to-date inventory information on-line, and you can even place orders.

Ham-radio databases

If you're a ham, you'll be interested in this system:

callsign.cs.buffalo.edu Port: 2000

Gateway systems

The following system acts as a gateway to other systems, like hytelnet does for libraries.

Gateway: Washington University WorldWindow

Address: library.wustl.edu

Access code: Telnet

This gateway to hundreds of other services around the net is the best place to start browsing. When you find an interesting service, make a note of its name (and port and login, if necessary) so that you can telnet in directly next time.

Commercial services

Several commercial on-line services are available too. This section lists a few.

Service: DELPHI

Address: delphi.com

Access code: Telnet, Account

Log in as `joindelphi`, and use the password `info` to find out about Delphi terms and services. If you want to sign up for a five-hour test drive, log in as `joindelphi` and use the password `dummies`.

Service: The World

Address: world.std.com

Access code: Telnet, Account

Log in as `new` both for information and to sign up.

Fun and sheer goofiness

Here are a few services you can access if you're in a frolicsome mood — or if you're just plain bored.

Service: Thought for the day

Address: astro.temple.edu

Access code: Telnet, Port: 12345

Every time you telnet to this service, you get a pithy saying. Here's one:

```
telnet astro.temple.edu 12345
Trying ASTRO.OCIS.TEMPLE.EDU (129.32.1.100, 12345)... Open
Nihilism should commence with oneself.
```

The pithy message flashes by quickly. You may have to "log" your telnet sessions so that you can read them later.

Service: Internet Relay Chat

Address: various

Access code: Telnet

You can telnet to various systems to join the running on-line IRC discussion (see Chapter 25, "Internet Relay Chat: The Ultimate Solution to Free Time," for more details). In each case, log in as `irc`. Here are a few servers that currently work, but be warned that they come and go frequently:

`wbrt.wb.psu.edu` (Pennsylvania)

`irc.demon.co.uk` (England)

`prof.jpl.nasa.gov` (California)

Consult the Usenet group `alt.irc` for more recent information.

Service: Network Go
Address: igs.nuri.net
Access code: Telnet, Register, Port: 6969

Play the Oriental strategy game of Go against other people. This is the only server we know about at this time, but there are probably lots of others.

Service: Sports Info
Address: culine.colorado.edu
Access code: Telnet, Port number below

You should telnet to port 859 for NBA schedules, 860 for the NHL, 862 for Major League Baseball, or 863 for the NFL.

Chapter 21
Grabbing Files over the Net

• •

In This Chapter

▶ Getting files from all over the net
▶ Stashing files all over the net
▶ Lotsa swell stuff for FTP
▶ Navigating in anonymous land
▶ Finding files by name
▶ Log in to Archie
▶ Send Archie a letter

• •

In Chapter 20 of *UNIX For Dummies,* we described how to use the FTP system to transfer files from one computer to another on a network. Let's look at the topic again, from the point of view of the Internet.

You can use FTP to transfer files to or from computers on which you have accounts. You can also use FTP to download (transfer to your computer) files from any of a bunch of publicly available FTP servers out there on the Internet. Thousands of public FTP servers are on the Internet, each with hundreds of files that might be of use, including text, pictures, and programs. It's just a matter of locating them and downloading them!

After we tell you about how to use FTP, we list some of the big FTP servers you might want to use, as well as telling you how to use Archie, a system that helps you find files in the world of FTP.

You're a Copying Machine

It's pretty simple to copy a file from one place to another (but don't forget — computers are involved). Here's how it works: Log in to the other computer for FTP, and tell it what you want to copy and where you want it copied.

Getting connected

To run the `ftp` program, you type **ftp** and the name of the host computer where the FTP server you want is, like this:

```
ftp iecc.com
```

(That's John's computer.) Substitute the FTP server's name for `iecc.com`.

Assuming that it's not too busy to let you connect, the FTP server greets you with a message like this:

```
Connected to iecc.com.
220 iecc FTP server (Version 4.1 8/1/91) ready.
```

The computer asks for your username and password on the host computer. If you don't have an account on the computer, don't panic. See the section "Getting Files Anonymously," later in this chapter. (On this particular computer, unless you happen to be one of the authors of this book, it's extremely unlikely that you have an account. We're using it as an example.)

If the FTP server likes you, it says something like this:

```
230 User john1 logged in.
ftp>
```

The `ftp>` is FTP's prompt, telling you that it's ready for you to type a command.

Getting your file

To copy a file from the FTP server (the host computer) to your own computer, use the `get` command, like this:

```
get README
```

Substitute the name of the file in place of `README` in this command. FTP says something like this:

```
150 Opening ASCII mode data connection for README (12686
          bytes).
226 Transfer complete.
local: README remote: README
12979 bytes received in 28 seconds (0.44 Kbytes/s)
```

FTP always tells you far more than you want to know about the transfer. When it says that the transfer is complete, you've got the file.

You have to type the filename by using the syntax the server uses. In particular, if the server is a UNIX system (as most are), upper- and lowercase are different, so *README, Readme,* and *readme* are different filenames.

Getting out

When you finish transferring files, type the command `quit`. FTP responds with this:

```
221 Goodbye.
```

That's basically how FTP works, but of course you need to know about 400 other odds and ends to use FTP effectively.

When is a file not a file?

When it's a text file. The FTP definition specifies six different kinds of files, of which only two types are useful: ASCII and binary. An *ASCII file* is a text file. A *binary file* is anything else. FTP has two modes, ASCII and binary (also called *image* mode), to transfer the two kinds of files. When you transfer an ASCII file between different kinds of computers that store files differently, ASCII mode automatically adjusts the file during the transfer so that the file is a valid text file when it is stored on the receiving end. A binary file is left alone and transferred verbatim.

You tell FTP which mode to use with the `binary` and `ascii` commands:

```
ftp> binary
200 Type set to I.
ftp> ascii
200 Type set to A.
```

In the preceding example, the *I* is for binary or image mode (after 20 years, the Internet protocol czars still can't make up their minds what to call it), and the *A* is for ASCII mode. Like most FTP commands, `binary` and `ascii` can be abbreviated by lazy typists to the first three letters — so `bin` and `asc` will suffice.

How to foul up your files in FTP

The most common FTP error made by inexperienced Internet users (and by experienced users, for that matter) is transferring a file in the wrong mode. If you transfer a text file in binary mode from a UNIX system to an MS-DOS or Macintosh system, the file looks something like this (on a DOS machine):

```
This file
         should have been
                          copied in
                                   ASCII mode.
```

On a Mac, the entire file looks like it's on one line. When you look at the file with a text editor on a UNIX system, you see strange ^M symbols at the end of each line. You don't necessarily have to retransfer the file. Many networking packages come with programs that do ex post facto conversion from one format to the other.

If, on the other hand, you copy something that isn't a text file in ASCII mode, it gets scrambled. Compressed files don't decompress; executable files don't execute (or they crash or hang the machine); images look unimaginably bad. When a file is corrupted, the first thing you should suspect is the wrong mode in FTP.

If you are FTP-ing (Is that a verb? It is now) files between two computers of the same type, such as from one UNIX system to another, you can and should do all your transfers in binary mode. Whether you're transferring a text file or a nontext file, it doesn't require any conversion, so binary mode does the right thing.

Patience is a virtue

The Internet is pretty fast but not infinitely so. When you are copying stuff between two computers on the same local network, information can move at about 200,000 characters per second. When the two machines are separated by a great deal of intervening Internet, the speed drops — often to 1,000 characters per second or less. So if you're copying a file that's 500,000 characters long, it takes only a few seconds over a local network, but it can take several minutes over a long-haul connection.

It's often comforting to get a directory listing before issuing a `get` or `put` command so that you can have an idea of how long the copy will take.

The directory thicket

Every machine you can contact for FTP stores its files in many different directories, which means that to find what you want you have to learn the rudiments of directory navigation. Fortunately, you wander around directories in FTP in pretty much the same way as you do on your own system. The command you use to list the files in the current directory is `dir`, and to change to another directory you use the command `cd`, as in the following example:

```
ftp> dir
200 PORT command successful.
150 Opening ASCII mode data connection for /bin/ls.
total 23
drwxrwxr-x   19 root      archive        512 Jun 24 12:09 doc
drwxrwxr-x    5 root      archive        512 May 18 08:14 edu
drwxr-xr-x   31 root      wheel          512 Jul 12 10:37 sys-
              tems
drwxr-xr-x    3 root      archive        512 Jun 25  1992
              vendorware
   ... lots of other stuff ...
226 Transfer complete.
1341 bytes received in 0.77 seconds (1.7 Kbytes/s)
ftp> cd edu
250 CWD command successful.
ftp> dir
200 PORT command successful.
150 Opening ASCII mode data connection for /bin/ls.
total 3
 -rw-rw-r—    1 root      archive      87019 Dec 13  1990 R
 -rw-rw-r—    1 root      archive      41062 Dec 13  1990 RS
 -rw-rw-r—    1 root      archive     554833 Dec 13  1990 Rings
drwxr-xr-x    2 root      archive        512 May 18 09:31 admin-
              istrative
drwxr-xr-x    3 root      archive        512 May 11 06:44 ee
drwxrwxr-x    8 root      234            512 Jun 28 06:00 math
226 Transfer complete.
200 bytes received in 63 seconds (0.0031 Kbytes/s)
ftp> quit
221 Goodbye.
```

In a standard UNIX directory listing, the first letter on the line tells you whether something is a file or a directory. d means that it's a directory — anything else is a file. In the directory edu in the preceding example, the first three entries are files, and the last three are other directories. Generally, you FTP to a host, get a directory listing, change to another directory, get a listing there, and so on until you find the files you want; then you use the get command to retrieve them.

You often find that the directory on your machine in which you start the FTP program is not the one in which you want to store the files you retrieve. In that case, use the lcd command to change the directory on the local machine.

To review: cd changes directories on the other host; lcd changes directories on your own machine. (You might expect cd to change directories correspondingly on both machines, but it doesn't.)

What's that name again?

Sometimes on your machine you have to give a file a name that's different from the name it has on a remote machine. (This is particularly true on DOS machines, on which many UNIX names are just plain illegal, and when you're retrieving Macintosh files, which can contain spaces and special characters.) Also, if you need to get a bunch of files, it can be tedious to type all the get commands. Fortunately, FTP has work-arounds for both those problems. Suppose that you've found a file named rose and you want to download it as rose.gif because it contains a GIF-format image. First, make sure that you're in binary mode, and then retrieve the file with the get command. This time, however, you give two names to get — the name of the file on the remote host and the local name — so that it renames the file as the file arrives:

```
ftp> bin
200 Type set to I.
ftp> get rose2 rose2.gif
200 PORT command successful.
150 Opening BINARY mode data connection for rose2 (47935
         bytes).
226 Transfer complete.
local: rose2.gif remote: rose2
47935 bytes received in 39 seconds (1.2 Kbytes/s)
```

Next, suppose that you want to get a bunch of the files that begin with ru. In that case, you use the mget (which stands for *m*ultiple *GET*) command to retrieve them. The names you type after mget can be either plain filenames or wildcard patterns that match a bunch of filenames. For each matching name, FTP asks whether you want to retrieve that file, as in the following:

```
ftp> mget ru*
mget ruby? n
mget ruby2? n
mget ruger_pistol? n
mget rugfur01? n
mget rush? y
200 PORT command successful.
150 Opening BINARY mode data connection for rush (18257
          bytes).
226 Transfer complete.
local: rush remote: rush
18257 bytes received in 16 seconds (1.1 Kbytes/s)
mget rush01? y
200 PORT command successful.
150 Opening BINARY mode data connection for rush01 (205738
          bytes).
local: rush01 remote: rush01
205738 bytes received in 200.7 seconds (1.2 Kbytes/s)
mget rush02?
```

If you find that `mget` matches more files than you expected, you can stop it with the usual interrupt character for your system — typically Ctrl-C or Del:

```
^C
Continue with mget? n
ftp> quit
221 Goodbye.
```

You can even interrupt in the middle of a transfer if a file takes longer to transfer than you want to wait.

You also can do an *express* `mget`, which doesn't ask any questions and enables you to find exactly the files you want. To tell FTP not to ask you about each file, use the `prompt` command before you give the `mget` command, like this:

```
ftp> prompt
Interactive mode off.
ftp> mget 92-1*
200 PORT command successful.
150 Opening BINARY mode data connection for 92-10.gz (123728
          bytes).
226 Transfer complete.
```

(continued)

(continued)

```
local: 92-10.gz remote: 92-10.gz 123728 bytes received in 2.8
        seconds (43 Kbytes/s)
200 PORT command successful.
150 Opening BINARY mode data connection for 92-11.gz (113523
        bytes).
226 Transfer complete.
local: 92-11.gz remote: 92-11.gz 113523 bytes received in 3.3
        seconds (34 Kbytes/s)
200 PORT command successful.
150 Opening BINARY mode data connection for 92-12.gz (106290
        bytes).
226 Transfer complete.
local: 92-12.gz remote: 92-12.gz 106290 bytes received in 2.2
        seconds (47 Kbytes/s)
```

Here's a file in your eye

OK, now you know how to retrieve files from other computers. How about copying the other way? It's just about the same procedure, except that you use put rather than get. The following example shows how to copy a local file called rnr to a remote file called rnr.new:

```
ftp> put rnr rnr.new
200 PORT command successful.
150 Opening ASCII mode data connection for rnr.new.
226 Transfer complete.
local: rnr remote: rnr.new
168 bytes sent in 0.014 seconds (12 Kbytes/s)
```

(As with get, if you want to use the same name when you make the copy, leave out the second name.)

The mput command works just like the mget command does, only in the other direction. If you have a bunch of files whose names begin with uu and you want to copy most of them, issue the mput command, as in the following:

```
ftp> mput uu*
mput uupick? y
200 PORT command successful.
150 Opening ASCII mode data connection for uupick.
226 Transfer complete.
```

```
local: uupick remote: uupick
156 bytes sent in 0.023 seconds (6.6 Kbytes/s)
mput uupoll? y
200 PORT command successful.
150 Opening ASCII mode data connection for uupoll.
226 Transfer complete.
local: uupoll remote: uupoll
200 bytes sent in 0.013 seconds (15 Kbytes/s)
mput uurn? n
```

(As with mget, you can use the prompt command to tell it to go ahead and not to ask any questions.)

 Most systems have protections on their files and directories that limit where you can copy files. Generally, you can use FTP only to put a file anywhere that you could create a file if you were logged in directly. If you're using anonymous FTP (see the section "Getting Files Anonymously," later in this chapter), you usually can't put any files to the other host.

A bunch of other file-manipulation commands are sometimes useful, as in the following example of the delete command:

```
delete somefile
```

This command deletes the file on the remote computer, assuming that the file permissions enable you to do so. The mdelete command deletes multiple files and works like mget and mput do. The mkdir command makes a new directory on the remote system (again assuming that you have permissions to do so), as in the following:

```
mkdir newdir
```

After you create a directory, you still have to use cd to change to that directory before you use put or mput to store files in it.

 If you plan to do much file deleting, directory creation, and the like, it's usually much quicker to log in to the other system by using telnet to do your work and using the usual local commands.

What's with all these three-digit numbers?

You may notice that whenever you give a command to FTP, the response from the remote host begins with a three-digit number. (Or you may not notice, in which case, never mind.)

The three-digit number is there so that the FTP program, which doesn't know any English, can figure out what's going on. Each digit means something to the program.

Here's what the first digit means:

1: It has begun to process your request but hasn't finished it.

2: It has finished.

3: It needs more input from you, such as when it needs a password after you enter your username, or it's an informational message.

4: It didn't work but may if you try again.

5: *You lose.*

Here's what the second digit means: The second digit is a *message subtype.*

The third digit distinguishes messages that otherwise would have the same number (something that in the computer world would be unspeakably awful).

If a message goes on for multiple lines, all the lines except the last one have a dash rather than a space after the number.

Note: Most FTP users have no idea what the numbers mean, by the way, so now that you're one of the few who does know, you're an expert.

Getting Files Anonymously

So far, you have seen how to FTP to systems where you already have an account. What about the other 99.9 percent of the hosts on the net, where no one has ever heard of you?

You're in luck. On thousands of systems, you can log in with the username `anonymous`. For the password, enter your e-mail address. (This is strictly on the honor system — if you lie, they still let you log in.) When you log in for *anonymous FTP,* most hosts restrict your access to only certain directories that are allowed to anonymous users. But you can hardly complain because anonymous FTP is provided free, out of sheer generosity.

Hello, anonymous!

When you log in, you frequently get a friendly message, like this one:

```
230-   If your FTP client crashes or hangs shortly after login
         please try
230-   using a dash (-) as the first character of your pass-
         word.  This will
230-   turn off the informational messages that may be confus-
         ing your FTP
230-   client.
230-
230-   This system may be used 24 hours a day, 7 days a week.
         The local
230-   time is Thu Aug 12 12:15:10 1995.
230-
230-   You are user number 204 out of a possible total of 250.
230-
230-   All transfers to and from wuarchive are logged.  If you
         don't like
230-   this then disconnect now!
230-
230-   Wuarchive is currently a DEC Alpha AXP 3000, Model 400.
         Thanks to
230-   Digital Equipment Corporation for their generous sup-
         port of wuarchive.
230-
230-Please read the file README
230-   it was last modified on Mon May 17 15:02:13 1995 - 87
         days ago
230 Guest login ok, access restrictions apply.
```

When you're logged in, you use the same commands to move around and
retrieve files as you always do.

A few anonymous FTP tips

Here are a few items to remember when you're FTP-ing:

✔ Some hosts limit the number of anonymous users or the times of day that
anonymous FTP is allowed. Please respect these limits because no law
says that the owner of the system can't turn off anonymous access.

✔ Don't store files in the other computer unless the owner invites you to do
so. Usually a directory called incoming or something similar is available
where you can put stuff.

✔ Some hosts allow anonymous FTP only from hosts that have names. That is, if you try to FTP anonymously from a host that has a number but no name, these hosts don't let you in. This problem occurs most often with personal computers, which, because they generally offer no services that are useful to other people, don't always have names assigned. If you have that problem, check with your local administrator to see whether it's possible to assign a name to your PC and to set up the reverse lookup database the remote host uses to figure out what your name is.

An FTP cheat sheet

Command	Description	Command	Description
get *old new*	Copies remote file *old* to local file *new;* can omit *new* if same name as *old*	bin	Transfers files in binary or image mode (all other files)
		quit	Leaves FTP
put *old new*	Copies local file *old* to remote file *new;* can omit *new* if same name as *old*	dir *pat*	Lists files whose names match pattern *pat;* if no *pat,* lists all files
del *xxx*	Deletes file *xxx* on remote system	mget *pat*	Gets files whose names match pattern *pat*
cd *newdir*	Changes to directory *newdir* on the remote machine	mput *pat*	Puts files whose names match pattern *pat*
cdup	Changes to next higher directory	mdel *pat*	Deletes remote files whose names match pattern *pat*
lcd *newdir*	Changes to directory *newdir* on the local machine	prompt	Turn name prompting on or off in mget and mput
asc	Transfers files in ASCII mode (use for text files)		

Great Stuff on FTP

Hundreds of gigabytes of stuff are available for FTP, if you know where to find them. But before you start cruising FTP sites, a few words about strategy.

A word from those etiquette ladies again

Please recall that all *anonymous FTP* servers (hosts that allow you to log in for FTP without having to have an account there) exist purely because someone feels generous. Any or all can go away if the provider feels taken advantage of, so remember these rules:

- ✔ Pay attention to restrictions on access times noted in the welcome message. Remember that servers are in time zones all over the world. If the server says to use it only between 6 p.m. and 8 a.m., but it's in Germany and you're in Seattle, you can use it between 9 a.m. and 11 p.m. your time.

- ✔ Do not upload material unless you're invited to. (And don't upload material inappropriate to a particular archive — we hope that this advice would be obvious, but experience suggests otherwise.)

Mirror, mirror, on the net, where are the files I want to get?

Many archives are *mirrored,* which means that the contents of an archive are copied mechanically from the home server to other servers. Usually, the mirroring systems are larger and faster than the home server, so it's easier to get material from the mirror than from the home system. Mirrors are usually updated daily, so everything on the home system is also at the mirrors.

When you have a choice of mirrors, use the one that's closest to you. You want the one that's closest in terms of the number of network links between you and it. But because the number of hops is practically impossible to figure out, use the mirror that's physically closest. In particular, use one in your own country if at all possible because international network links are relatively slow and congested.

A few words about navigation

All the FTP servers discussed in this chapter require you to log in using the username anonymous. For the password, use your e-mail address.

Many servers have a small file called README that you should retrieve the first time you use the server. This file usually contains a description of the material that's available and the rules for using the server.

If you log in to an FTP server and don't see any interesting files, look for a directory called pub (for public). For reasons lost in the mists of history, it's a tradition on UNIX systems to put all the good stuff there.

The FTP Hit Parade

This section lists some available FTP systems, including the following information:

- ✔ Name and location of the system
- ✔ Particular rules for use
- ✔ What's there

UUNET

ftp.uu.net
UUNET Communications, Virginia
Accepts FTP only from hosts with registered names

UUNET is probably the largest archive available on the net. It has masses of software (mostly for UNIX in source form), archives of material posted on Usenet, files and documents from many publishers and vendors, and mirrors of many other archives around the net.

SIMTEL

Mirrored at wuarchive.wustl.edu, oak.oakland.edu, ftp.uu.net, nic.funet.fi, src.doc.ic.ac.uk, archie.au, and nic.switch.ch

SIMTEL, the premier archive for MS-DOS material, also has a great deal of stuff for Macs, CP/M (remember that?), and UNIX. SIMTEL itself was an ancient

DEC-20 computer at an Army base in New Mexico. It has long since shut down, but the mirror systems are still available, and someone is still updating and maintaining the archive.

WUARCHIVE

wuarchive.wustl.edu

Washington University, Missouri

This large program and file archive includes mirrors of many other programming archives, with megabytes of stuff for DOS, Windows, Macintosh, and other popular computer systems. WUARCHIVE also contains the largest collection of GIF and JPEG pictures (all suitable for family viewing, by the way) on the net.

RTFM

rtfm.mit.edu

Massachusetts Institute of Technology, Massachusetts

RTFM is the definitive archive of all the *FAQs (frequently asked questions)* messages on Usenet. Hence, RTFM is a treasure trove of information for everything from the state of the art in data compression to how to apply for a mortgage to sources of patterns for Civil War uniforms. Look in the directories `pub/usenet-by-group` and `pub/usenet-by-hierarchy`.

RTFM also has an experimental Usenet address database, containing the e-mail address of every person who has posted a message to Usenet in the past several years. That database is in `pub/usenet-addresses`.

Because RTFM is an extremely popular site and limits itself to 50 simultaneous non-MIT connections, it can be extremely difficult to get into. Sometimes it has taken us several days.

InterNIC

ftp.internic.net

Internet Network Information Center, California

This central repository for information about the Internet includes copies of all the standards and RFC documents that define the network. Also, InterNIC has information about many other FTP archives available on the net.

The list of lists

A list of e-mail mailing lists is at `rtfm.mit.edu` (described earlier) in the directory `/pub/usenet-by-group/news.lists` in the files `Publicly_Accessible_Mailing_Lists,_Part_01_14` through `Publicly_Accessible_Mailing_Lists,_Part_14_14`. (By the time you read this, it will probably have more than 14 parts, so the names will change appropriately.)

Ask Archie

Somewhere on the Internet is probably everything you really want and much more you might want if you knew that it existed. "But how do I *find* it?" you ask. Good question.

If it's software you're looking for, ask Archie.

If you know the name of what you're looking for — or kind of know the name, enough so that you can come up with a reasonable guess — Archie goes running around the world, checking database after database, looking for files that match your description.

Archie servers exist all over the world, but you should choose one close to home to help minimize traffic on the net. Different Archie servers get different amounts of use, so you may have to try a few before you find one with a reasonable response time. If everything you try seems painfully slow, try early in the morning or late at night, or try sending your Archie request by e-mail (see the section "E-mail Archie," later in this chapter).

Table 21-1 lists several Archie servers you can try. If you try one and it doesn't let you on because it's too full, chances are that it provides you with another list of Archie servers you can try. Eventually, you get on.

Table 21-1	Archie Servers
Server Name	*Location*
archie.rutgers.edu	New Jersey
archie.sura.net	Maryland
archie.unl.edu	Nebraska
archie.ans.net	New York
ds.internic.net	U.S.A. (run by AT&T)
archie.mcgill.ca	Canada
archie.au	Australia
archie.th-darmstadt.de	Europe (Germany)
archie.funet.fi	Europe (Finland)
archie.luth.	Europe (Sweden)
archie.univie.ac.at	Europe (Austria)
archie.doc.ic.ac.uk	U.K. and Europe
archie.cs.huji.ac.il	Israel
archie.ad.jp	Japan
archie.kuis.kyoto-u.ac.jp	Japan
archie.sogang.ac.kr	Korea
archie.nz	New Zealand
archie.ncu.edu.tw	Taiwan

You can access Archie servers in several ways:

- ✔ If you have *Archie client software* (archie or xarchie), you can run it directly from your machine (see the sections "Plain ol' Archie" and "Xarchie," later in this chapter).

- ✔ You can telnet to an Archie server (see the following section, "Telnet Archie").

- ✔ You can e-mail your request to an Archie server (see the section "E-mail Archie," later in this chapter).

If you have Archie client software on your computer (archie or xarchie, which we describe later in this chapter, in the section "Plain ol' Archie"), that's the fastest way to get to Archie. Telnet is considerably slower; enough slower that it's usually just as easy to send your request by e-mail so that you don't have to wait around while it's processed.

Telnet Archie

Unless you have Archie client software available to you locally (try using the command `archie` or, on a machine with X Windows or one of its variants, such as Motif, `xarchie`), you probably want to telnet to an Archie server. Before you do, however, if you can, you probably want to start a *log file* (a file in which all the text displayed in your window is captured) because Archie's output may come fast and furiously, gushing filenames, host names, and Internet addresses that you really don't want to have to copy by hand if you can avoid it. If you're running on a machine with X Windows or one of its variants, such as Motif, in your xterm window hold down Ctrl, press the left mouse button, and choose Log to File from the Main Options window. If you're not running X, it's worth asking around to see whether some locally available program can capture the text on the screen to a file.

Now choose a server, use telnet, and log in as `archie`, as in the following:

```
% telnet archie.ans.net
Trying...
Connected to forum.ans.net.
Escape character is '^]'.Archie
AIX telnet (forum.ans.net) IBM AIX Version 3 for RISC System/
        6000
(C) Copyrights by IBM and by others 1982, 1991.
login: archie
```

Archie returns with an Archie prompt (it doesn't ask you for a password):

```
archie>
```

Telling Archie how to behave: The set and show commands

Every Archie server is set up with features you can tune to suit your needs. You may have to change them to make Archie do what you want. Not all Archie servers are alike, and you have to pay attention to how things are set up on the server you land on.

To see how the server you're on is set up, use the `show` command:

```
archie> show
# 'autologout' (type numeric) has the value '15'.
# 'mailto (type string) is not set.
# 'maxhits' (type numeric) has the value '100'.
# 'pager' (type boolean) is not set.
# 'search' (type string) has the value 'sub'.
# 'sortby' (type string) has the value 'none'.
# 'status' (type boolean) is set.
# 'term' (type string) has the value 'dumb 24 80'.
```

You can also use show to see specific values one at a time (try typing **show term**, **show search**, and so on). Although all these values are explained next, the variables you have to pay careful attention to are search and maxhits. It's also a good idea to set the pager, which tells Archie to stop after every screen full of text and wait for you to press the spacebar, to help control Archie's output.

Searching for something interesting

Normally Archie searches for a name that contains the string you type, disregarding uppercase and lowercase. So if you search for *pine*, it matches *PINE*, *Pineapple*, and *spineless*, among other things. If you use Archie much, you will want more control over the searching process, so you probably will want to use one of the other search methods for matching what you type. How much you know about the name of the file you're looking for should determine the search method you use.

To set the search method, use the set command:

```
archie> set search sub
```

The search methods Archie supports are called *sub, subcase, exact,* and *regex.* The following sections discuss how they work.

Sub method

The sub method searches to match the substring anywhere in the filename. This search is case insensitive, which means that case doesn't matter. If you have an idea of a character string that likely is contained in the filename, choose sub.

Subcase method

The subcase method searches to match the substring exactly as given anywhere in the filename. This search is case sensitive. Use this method only if you are sure about the case of the characters in the filename.

Exact method

The exact method searches for the exact filename you enter. This search is the fastest, and you should use it if you know exactly which file you're looking for.

Regex method

Use UNIX regular expressions to define the pattern for Archie's search. This is a particular kind of substring search, and Archie tries to match the expression to a string anywhere in the file's name. In *regular expressions,* certain characters take on special meaning, and regular expressions can get absurdly complicated, if you want.

- ✔ If you know that the string begins the filename, start your string with the caret (^) to tie the string to the first position of the filename.

- ✔ If you know that the file ends with a particular string, end your string with the dollar sign ($) to tie the string to the end of the filename.

- ✔ The period (.) is used to specify any single character.

- ✔ The asterisk (*) means zero or more occurrences of the preceding regular expression.

- ✔ Use square brackets ([and]) to list a set of characters to match or a range of characters to match. Combined with a caret (^) in the first position, square brackets list a set of characters to exclude or a range not to include.

- ✔ You can specify more than one range in the same search. If you have to use a special character as part of your string, put a backslash (\) in front of it.

To find any files containing the string birdie and ending with txt, for example, type this line:

```
prog ^birdie.*txt$
```

To find filenames containing numeric digits, type this line:

```
prog [0-9]
```

To exclude filenames containing lowercase letters, type this line:

```
prog [^a-z]
```

How long do you want to look?

The *maxhits* variable determines how many matches Archie tries to find. On many servers, the default for this number is 1,000 — but for most searches that's ridiculous. If you know the name of the file you want, how many copies do you want to choose from? Ten or 20 should give you sufficient choice. But if you don't reset *maxhits,* Archie continues traveling around the net and looking for as many as 1,000 matches.

Remember too that Archie's output goes to your screen and maybe to your log file — so think about how much data you can handle. After you decide just how much you want to know, set *maxhits* equal to that number (suppose that it's 100):

```
archie> set maxhits 100
```

Table 21-2 lists more set settings.

Table 21-2	Other Nifty Features to Set from Set
Variable	*What It Does*
autologout	Sets how long Archie waits around for you to do something before kicking you off.
mailto	Sets the e-mail address used by the mail command.
pager	When set, sends Archie's output through the pager program less, which stops after each screenful of output and waits for you to press the spacebar. Using the command set pager switches the pager from off to on or from on to off, so do a show before you change the pager setting so that you don't do the opposite of what you intend.
sortby	Sorts Archie's output in one of the following orders: by *hostname* in alphabetical order or reversed (*rhostname*); by most recently modified (*time*) or oldest (*rtime*); by *size,* largest first, or smallest first (*rsize*); by *filename* in lexical order, or reverse (*rfilename*); *unsorted* (usually the default). You type something like **set sortby time**.

(continued)

Table 21-2 *(continued)*

Variable	What It Does
status	If set, Archie shows the progress of the search. Can be reassuring when Archie is very slow.
term	Sets the type of terminal you're using so that Archie can tailor your output (try `vt100` if you're not sure).

Find it!

Archie's basic command, the `prog` command, takes this form:

```
prog searchstring
```

And that's it. That command launches the whole search. The nature and scope of the search are determined by the variables you set or didn't set.

Suppose that you want to find what kind of font software is around:

```
archie>  prog font

Host csuvax1.murdoch.edu.au    (134.115.4.1)
Last updated 00:23 31 Jul 1993

    Location: /pub/mups
        FILE        rw-r-r-      4107  Nov 16  1992    font.f
        FILE        rw-r-r-      9464  Nov 16  1992
            fontmups.lib

Host sifon.cc.mcgill.ca    (132.206.27.10)
Last updated 04:22 11 Aug 1993

    Location: /pub/packages/gnu
        FILE        rw-r-r-    628949  Mar  9 19:16    fontutils-
            0.6.tar.z

Host ftp.germany.eu.net    (192.76.144.75)
Last updated 05:24  7 May 1993
```

```
        Location: /pub/packages/gnu
           FILE      rw-r—r—    633005  Oct 28  1992    fontutils-
               0.6.tar.z
        Location: /pub/gnu
           FILE      rw-r—r—   1527018  Nov 13 16:11
               ghostscript-fonts-2.5.1.tar.z

Host ftp.uu.net    (192.48.96.9)
Last updated 08:17 31 Jul 1993

        Location: /systems/att7300/csvax
           FILE      rw-r—r—   1763981  Mar  5 23:30    groff-
               font.tar.z

Host reseq.regent.e-technik.tu-muenchen.de
           (129.187.230.225)
Last updated 06:26 10 Aug 1993

        Location: /informatik.public/comp/typesetting/tex/
              tex3.14/DVIware/laser-sett ers/umd-dvi/dev
           FILE      rw-r—r—        51  Sep 24  1991    fontdesc

Host nic.switch.ch    (130.59.1.40)
Last updated 04:48  7 Aug 1993

Host nic.switch.ch    (130.59.1.40)
Last updated 04:48  7 Aug 1993

        Location: /software/unix/TeX/dviware/umddvi/misc
           FILE      rw-rw-r—       607  Oct  2  1990    fontdesc
```

As you quickly find out, a great deal of duplication is out there. If you're looking for variety, you can make a series of inquiries that eliminate the stuff you've already found and make subsequent queries more fruitful.

After you've found it, or some of it, what is it?

There sure is a great deal of *stuff* out there. But what the heck is it? Sometimes Archie can help you to figure that out. We say "sometimes" because Archie's information is only as good as that provided by the folks who hung the stuff out there in the first place. But for those packages that have been supplied with a description, the whatis command might provide you with useful information. The whatis command is another kind of search — it searches a database of software descriptions provided by the individual archive managers and looks for the string you provide rather than search directories for filenames. If you're looking for software of a specific nature, regardless of what it's called, you can use the whatis command to augment your search.

If you use whatis rather than prog in your search for font software, for example, you get the following:

```
afm2tfm          Translate from Adobe to TeX page support)
gftodvi          Converts from metafont to DVI format
gftopk           Converts from metafont to PK format
gftopxl          Converts from metafont to PXL format
her2vfont        Hershey fonts to 'vfont' rasterizer
hershey          Hershey Fonts
hershey.f77      Hershey Fonts in Fortran 77
hershtools       Hershey font-manipulation tools and data
hp2pk            Hewlett-Packard font-conversion tool
jetroff/bfont    Jetroff Basic Fonts
jis.pk           The JTeX .300pk fonts (Japanese language sup-
                 port)
k2ps             Print text files with Kanji; uses JTeX fonts
                 (Japanese language support)
mkfont           Convert ASCII font descriptions to or from
                 device-independent troff (ditroff) format
ocra-metafont    METAFONT sources for the OCR-A "Alphanumeric
                 Character Sets for Optical Recognition"
```

Note: The string font appears in some of these filenames, but only in the description of others.

You can't get there from here

Archie is great for *finding* stuff but no help at all in *retrieving* stuff for you. (Xarchie is a big help, however, so if you have it, you probably want to use it.) To actually get stuff off the net, you have to do what Archie did to find it in the first place: Use FTP to copy it from the archive in which it lives back to your computer.

If you're on a quest for related software, after you have FTP'd to a host that has relevant stuff, you might want to look around in the directory containing the file you know about (use the FTP dir command to list the contents of a remote directory) and in any subdirectories near it.

Plain ol' Archie

If you try to type the archie command directly and it returns a comment telling you how to use it, you're in luck. You can use the Archie client software directly without telnetting to an Archie server. One big advantage of using Archie from a command line is that you can easily redirect its output to a file, as in the following:

```
$ archie -ld font > fontfiles
```

(This line stores the result of the search in a file called fontfiles, which you can later peruse at your leisure by using any text editor or file viewer.) Be aware, however, that the client software is limited and that you may want to telnet to an Archie server to take advantage of more of Archie's capabilities. For one, you can't set all the tuning variables described in the section "Telnet Archie," earlier in this chapter. Also, you cannot use the whatis command.

Using Archie directly means using a command line that may get complex. You can specify the kind of search and the Archie server you want to use and format the output to a limited extent. If you supply the search string and no modifiers, Archie defaults to an exact search with a maximum of 95 matches. For details about choosing a search method, and other available options, see the section "Telnet Archie," earlier in this chapter.

Table 21-3 lists the modifiers you can supply.

Table 21-3	**Search String Modifiers**	
Archie Modifier	*Telnet Equivalent*	*Archie Meaning*
-c	subcase	Sets search mode for a case-sensitive substring
-e	exact	Sets search mode for an exact string match (default)
-r	regex	Sets search mode for a regular expression search
-s	sub	Sets search mode for a substring search
-l		Lists one match per line
-t	sortby	Sorts Archie's output by date, newest first
-m#	maxhits	Sets the maximum number of matches to return (default 95)
-h		Specifies the Archie server to use
-L		Lists the known Archie servers and the current default

For example, to use the server `archie.ans.net` to do a regular expression search for no more than 50 files that contain digits in their names:

```
$ archie -r -m50 -h archie.ans.net "[0-9]"
```

(The pattern [0-9] is enclosed in double quotes to avoid having it misinterpreted as the name of a file to match locally. In general, put your patterns in quotes if they contain anything other than letters and digits.)

Xarchie

If you're lucky enough to be running X Windows or a near relative of X Windows (such as Motif) and xarchie is available to you, use it. It enables you to set most Archie settings from the main menu and the settings menu. Furthermore, after completing the search, xarchie enables you to scroll through the hosts and filenames and click the selections that interest you (see Figure 21-1).

| Quit | Query | Abort | Save | Ftp | Search Type | Sort Type | Nice Level | Settings... |

Status: Found 94 matches -- Ready

```
amiga.physik.unizh.ch      /local              font/
athene.uni-paderborn.de
bongo.cc.utexas.edu
cac.washington.edu
colonsay.dcs.ed.ac.uk
cs.tut.fi
csc2.anu.edu.au
emx.cc.utexas.edu
export.lcs.mit.edu
ftp.germany.eu.net
```

Figure 21-1:
Using
xarchie to
search for
files.

Search Term:	font	
Host:	cac.washington.edu	
Location:	/local	
File:	font/	
Size:	512	Mode:	drwxr-xr-x	Date:	Aug 25 1992

After you find something you want, you can choose Ftp from the main menu; xarchie turns itself into a junior version of the FTP program, retrieves the remote file for you, and puts the file in your current directory or in the direc- tory you specify from the settings menu (see Figure 21-2).

Figure 21-2:
Xarchie's
option
menu.

| Done | Apply | Default |

Search Mode:	exact
Sort Mode:	default
Host:	archie.sura.net
Max Hits: 99
Initial Timeout: 4
Retries: 3
Nice Level:	0
Local Ftp Directory: .
Ftp Transfer Type: binary

E-mail Archie

If you're unable to telnet to an Archie server either because of the limitations of your network connection or because you have been unsuccessful in logging on to an Archie server, you can send your request to Archie by using e-mail. If you're planning to launch a major search and don't want to wait for the re- sponse, using Archie from e-mail is a good way to go.

Not all of telnet Archie's capabilities are available to you through e-mail, but you can still carry out a substantial search. To send a request to Archie, send mail to `archie@servername`, where `servername` is any of the Archie servers mentioned earlier in this chapter.

The body of the e-mail message you send contains the commands you want to issue to Archie. Enter as many commands as you want, each beginning in the first column of a line. Choose from the commands shown in Table 21-4.

Table 21-4	E-Mail Archie Commands
Command	*What It Does*
prog	Searches for matching names; assumes a regular expression search (regex)
whatis	Supplies the keyword for the software-description database search
compress	Sends the reply in a compressed and encoded format
servers	Returns a list of Archie servers
path	Gives the e-mail address you want Archie to use to respond to your mail request, if the automatically generated return address on your e-mail isn't correct
help	Returns the help text for e-mail Archie
quit	Ends the request to Archie

The most common commands are `prog` and `whatis`, which take exactly the same form you use in telnet Archie. For example:

```
prog font.*txt
whatis font
```

Archie has become extremely popular, so popular that it's common for each server to be handling several dozen requests at a time, all the time, all day. That means that telnet or command-line Archie can be sl-l-l-o-o-o-w-w-w. If it's going to be *that* slow, you may as well send in your request by e-mail and go do something else. As soon as Archie finishes your request, it drops its answer in your mailbox, where you can peruse it at your leisure. An added advantage of e-mail is that if the response turns out to be 400 lines long, it's easier to deal with a 400-line e-mail message than with 400 lines of stuff flying off your screen.

Chapter 22
What's in That File?

Great. Now you can retrieve zillions of files by using FTP (well, maybe three or four). But when you look at them with your text editor, you may notice that they're garbage. In this chapter, we consider the various kinds of files on the net, how to tell what they are, and what to do with them. We also tell you how to deal with files that are archived or compressed.

A Feast of Fancy Files

How many kinds of files are there?

Hundreds. Luckily, they fall into a few categories, which we tell you about.

Text files

Text files contain readable text (what did you expect?). Sometimes the text is human-readable text (such as the manuscript for this book, which we typed into text files). Sometimes the text is source code to computer programs in languages such as *C* or *Pascal*. And occasionally the text is data for programs.

There isn't much to say about text files — you know them when you see them. The way text is stored varies, however, from one system to another, so you should FTP text files in ASCII mode to convert them to your local format automatically.

If you encounter a text file that starts out something like the following, you have a PostScript document:

```
%!PS-Adobe-3.0
%%Title: Some Random Document
%%CreationDate: Thu Jul 5 1990
/pl transform 0.1 sub round 0.1 add exch
 0.1 sub round 0.1 add exch itransform bind def
```

A PostScript document is actually a program in the PostScript computer language that describes a document. Unless you are a world-class PostScript weenie, the only sensible thing to do with this type of document is to run the program and see the document. And the normal way to do that is to send it to a PostScript printer. Lacking a PostScript printer, PostScript interpreters, such as *GNU Ghostscript,* are also available that can turn PostScript into other screen and printer formats.

A few text documents are really archives or nontext files in drag. See the discussions of shar and uuencoded files in Chapter 19, in the section "When Is an Article Not Really an Article?"

Archives and compressed files

Often a particular package requires a bunch of related files. To make it easier to send the package around, the files can be glommed together into a single file known as an *archive.* (Yes, the term "archive" also refers to a host from which you can FTP stuff. Sorry. So sue us. We didn't make up these terms. In this section of the chapter, at least, an "archive" refers to *a multifile file.*) After you retrieve an archive, you use an *unarchiving program* to extract the original files.

Some files are also *compressed,* which means that they're encoded in a special way that takes up less space but that can be decoded only by the corresponding *uncompressor.* Most files you retrieve by anonymous FTP are compressed because compressed files use less disk space and take less time to transfer over the net. In the PC world, archiving and compression usually happen together by using utilities such as PKZIP. In the UNIX world, however, the two procedures are usually done separately — the programs tar or cpio do the archiving, and the programs compress, pack, or gzip do the compressing.

Data files

Some files are not text, executable, archived, or compressed. For lack of a better term, we refer to these as *data files*. Programs often arrive with some data files for use by the program. Microsoft Windows programs usually come with a data file that contains the help text.

The most common kinds of data files you find on the net are pictures, most often digitized photographs in *JPEG* format. An increasing number of digitized movies in *GL* and *MPEG* format also can be found on the net (see the section "For the Artistically Inclined," later in this chapter, for details about pictures).

You also occasionally find formatted word-processor files to be used with programs such as WordPerfect and Microsoft Word. If you encounter one of these files and don't have access to the matching word-processor program, you can usually load them into a text editor, where you see the text in the file intermingled with nonprinting junk that represents formatting information. In a pinch, you can edit out the junk to recover the text.

The most commonly used text-processing programs on the net remain the elderly but serviceable TeX and troff. Both of them take as their inputs plain text files with formatting commands in text form, something like this:

```
\begin{quote}
Your mother wears army boots.
\end{quote}
```

If you want to know more about TeX, see the Usenet newsgroup `comp.text.tex`. Free versions are available for most computers, described in a monthly posting on the newsgroup. Versions of troff, either the older AT&T Documenter's Workbench troff or GNU groff, are commonly distributed with UNIX systems; see the newsgroup `comp.text.troff`.

Executable files

Executable files are actual programs you can run on a computer. Executable programs are particularly common in archives of stuff for PCs and Macs. Some executable programs are also available on the net for other kinds of computers, such as various workstations.

The most commonly found executable programs are for DOS and Windows. These files have filenames like FOOG.EXE, FOOG.COM, or (sometimes for Windows) FOOG.DLL. There's not much to do with them on a UNIX machine.

Executable programs for UNIX don't have easily recognizable filenames, although any file whose filename contains a dot is unlikely to be an executable. Even though nearly every kind of workstation runs UNIX, the executables are not interchangeable. Code for a SPARC, for example, doesn't work on an IBM RS/6000 or vice versa. Several different versions of UNIX run on 386 PCs, with different executable formats. Newer versions of PC UNIX generally run executables from older versions, but not vice versa.

Packing It in

If you retrieve many files from the net, you have to learn how to uncompress stuff. The three main compression schemes are

- ✔ compress
- ✔ gzip
- ✔ ZIP

Compression classic

Back in 1975, a guy named Terry Welch published a paper on a swell, new compression scheme he had just invented. A couple of UNIX programmers implemented it as the program compress, and it quickly became the standard compression program. Better compressors are available now, but compress is still the standard.

You can easily recognize a compressed program because its name ends with .Z. You recover the original file with uncompress (which is actually the same program as compress running in a different mode), as shown in this example:

```
uncompress blurfle.Z
```

This line gets rid of blurfle.Z and replaces it with the original blurfle. Sometimes uncompress is unavailable, in which case you can do the equivalent by using compress:

```
compress -d blurfle.Z
```

Frequently, UNIX files are archived and compressed and have names such as blurfle.tar.Z. In that case, you first uncompress to get blurfle.tar and then unarchive.

If you want to see what's in a compressed file without uncompressing the whole thing, you can use `zcat`, a command that sends an uncompressed copy of its input to the screen. Any file big enough to be worth compressing is longer than one screenful, so you should run it through a paging program such as `more`:

```
zcat blurfle.Z | more
```

It's patently obvious: gzip

Something that the people who wrote `compress` didn't realize is that Welch not only published the scheme that compress uses, but he also patented it. (Two guys at IBM named Miller and Wegman independently invented the same scheme at the same time and also got a patent on it, something that's not supposed to happen because only the first person to invent something is allowed to patent it. But the patents are definitely there.) UNISYS, which employs Welch, has said from time to time that it might someday begin to collect royalties on `compress`, and it has recently begun to demand royalties from people who use the GIF-image format, which uses the same compression scheme.

So the Free Software Foundation, which runs the GNU free software project, wrote gzip, which uses 100 percent nonpatented algorithms. Files that are gzipped end with `.gz` and are uncompressed with the command `gunzip`:

```
gunzip blurfle.gz
```

Patent owners seem to feel less strongly about decompression than about compression, so `gunzip` can also decompress .Z files from `compress` as well as from some other earlier and less widely used schemes. It can even uncompress a ZIP archive as long as only one file is in it. If you have a mystery compressed file, try feeding it to `gunzip` and see what happens. There is also `gcat`, which, like `zcat`, sends its output to the screen. So a good way to peek inside a mystery file is to enter this command:

```
gcat mysteryfile | more
```

UNIX versions of gzip and gunzip are available in the GNU files at `ftp.uu.net` and elsewhere.

ZIP-ing it up

The most widely used compression and archiving program for DOS is the
shareware program PKZIP. Zipped files all end with .ZIP. Compatible UNIX zip
and unzip programs called `zip` and `unzip` (the authors are creative programmers but not creative namers) are available at `ftp.uu.net` and elsewhere.

In the Archives

Two different UNIX archive programs are `tar` and `cpio`. They were written at
about the same time by people at two different branches of Bell Laboratories in
different parts of New Jersey. They both do about the same thing; they're just
different.

An important difference between UNIX-type archives and ZIP files is that UNIX
archives usually contain subdirectories; ZIP files almost never do. You should
always look at a UNIX archive's *table of contents* (the list of files it contains)
before extracting the files so that you know where the files will end up.

The tar pit

The name *tar* stands for *t*ape *ar*chive (it was originally designed to put archives
of files on old reel-to-reel tapes). Files archived by tar usually have filenames
ending with `.tar`. To see what's inside a tar archive, enter the following
command:

```
tar tvf blurfle.tar
```

(The `tvf` stands for *t*able of contents *v*erbosely from *f*ile.) To extract the
individual files, use this command:

```
tar xvf blurfle.tar
```

Copy here, copy there

The name cpio stands for *copy in* and *out*. The program was also intended to
copy archives of files to and from old reel-to-reel tapes. (It was a pressing issue
back then because at the time the disks on UNIX systems failed about once a
week — tape was the only hope for restoring work.) Files archived by cpio
usually have filenames ending with `.cp` or `.cpio`. To see what's in a cpio
archive, type the following:

```
cpio -itcv <blurfle.cpio
```

Notice the left bracket (<) before the name of the input file. (If you wonder why it's necessary, see *UNIX For Dummies*. The answer is pretty technoid.) The -itcv means *i*nput, *t*able of contents, *c*haracter headers (as opposed to obsolete *octal* headers), *v*erbosely.

To extract the files, enter this line:

```
cpio -icdv <blurfle.cpio
```

The letters in this line stand for *i*nput, *c*haracter headers, *v*erbosely, and create *d*irectories as needed.

PAX vobiscum

Modern versions of UNIX (versions since around 1988) have a swell, new program called pax, for *p*ortable *a*rchive e*x*change. It speaks both tar and cpio, so it should be capable of unpacking *any* UNIX archive. (Pretty advanced, huh? Only took them 20 years to think of it.) If your system has pax, you'll find it easier to use than either tar or cpio. To see what's inside an archive, enter this command:

```
pax -v <tar-or-cpio-file
```

(The v is for *v*erbose listing).

And to extract its contents, enter this line:

```
pax -rv <tar-or-cpio-file
```

(That's *r*ead, *v*erbose output).

For the Artistically Inclined

A large and growing fraction of all the bits flying around the Internet is made up of increasingly high-quality digitized pictures. About 99.44 percent of the pictures are purely for fun, games, and worse. But we're sure that you're in the 0.56 percent of users who need them for work, so here's a roundup of picture formats.

You almost never find GIF or JPEG image files compressed or archived. The reason is that these formats already do a pretty fair job of compression internally, so `compress`, `zip`, and the like don't help any.

I could GIF a . . . .

The most widely used format on the Internet is CompuServe's *GIF* (*Graphics Interchange Format*). The GIF format is well-matched to the capabilities of the typical PC computer screen — no more than 256 different colors in a picture and usually 640×480, 1024×768, or some other familiar PC screen resolution. Two versions of GIF exist: *GIF87* and *GIF89*. The differences are small enough that nearly every program that can read GIF can read either version equally well. GIF is well standardized, so you never have problems with files written by one program being unreadable by another.

Under the X Window system, quite a few free and shareware programs are available, probably the most widely used of which are ImageMagick and XV. You can find them in the Usenet `comp.sources.x` archives, such as the one at wuarchive in `/usenet/comp.sources.x`. (All these programs are in source form, so you have to be able to compile C programs to install them. Grab some chocolate-chip cookies and sweet-talk a local nerd into doing it for you.)

The eyes have it

A few years back, a bunch of digital photography experts got together and decided that it was time to have an official standard format for digitized photographs and that none of the existing formats was good enough. So they formed the *Joint Photographic Experts Group (JPEG),* and after extended negotiation, JPEG format was born. JPEG is specifically designed to store digitized, full-color or black-and-white photographs, not computer-generated cartoons or anything else. As a result, JPEG does a fantastic job of storing photos and a lousy job of storing anything else.

A JPEG version of a photo is about one-fourth the size of the corresponding GIF file. (JPEG files can be *any* size because the format allows a trade-off between size versus quality when the file is created.) The main disadvantage of JPEG is that it's considerably slower to decode than GIF, but the files are so much smaller that it's worth it. Most programs that can display GIF files also now handle JPEG. JPEG files usually have filenames ending in `.jpeg` or `.jpg`.

The claim has occasionally been made that JPEG pictures don't look anywhere near as good as GIF pictures do. What is true is that if you take a full-color picture and make a 256-color GIF file and then translate that GIF file into a JPEG file, it doesn't look good. For the finest in photographic quality, however, demand full-color JPEGs.

The same programs that display GIF files, notably xv, display JPEG files. There are also widely available programs called cjpeg and djpeg that create and decode JPEG files.

A trip to the movies

As networks get faster and disks get bigger, people are starting to store entire digitized movies (still rather *short* ones at this point). The standard movie format is called *Moving Photographic Experts Group (MPEG)*. MPEG was designed by a committee down the hall from the JPEG committee and — practically unprecedented in the history of standards efforts — was designed using the earlier JPEG work.

MPEG viewers are found in the same places as JPEG viewers. You need a reasonably fast workstation to display MPEG movies in anything resembling real time. Both commercial and free MPEG players are available for UNIX, the best known of which are called MPLAY and XMPEG.

Let a hundred formats blossom

Many other graphics-file formats are in use, although GIF and JPEG are by far the most popular ones on the Internet. Other formats you run into include the following:

- ✔ **PCX:** A DOS format used by many paint programs — also OK for low-resolution photos

- ✔ **TIFF:** An enormously complicated format with hundreds of options — so many that a TIFF file written by one program often cannot be read by another

- ✔ **TARGA (called TGA on PCs):** The most common format for scanned, full-color photos. In Internet archives, TARGA is now supplanted by the much more compact JPEG

- ✔ **PICT:** A format common on Macintoshes because the Mac has built-in support for it

UNIX systems usually have a package known as PBMPLUS (Poskanzer Bit Map, after Jef Poskanzer, who originally put it together) or its successor NETPBM, which can convert pretty much any graphic format to any other. Check with a local expert to see whether one of the PBM packages is available and which of the umpteen PBM programs to use to decode whatever particular files you're interested in.

One of the authors can't help noting that he wrote a book called *Programming for Graphics Files in C and C++* (Wiley, 1993), also available in Chinese, which describes the PBM package in extreme detail for the benefit of programmers who are interested in it.

A few words from the vice squad

You're probably wondering whether any on-line archives contain, er, *exotic* photography, but you're too embarrassed to ask. Well, they don't. Nothing in any public FTP archive is any raunchier than fashion photos from *Redbook* or *Sports Illustrated*.

That's for two reasons. One is political. The companies and universities that fund most of the sites on the Internet are not interested in being accused of being pornographers nor in filling up their expensive disks with pictures that have nothing to do with any legitimate work. (At one university archive, when the *Playboy* pictures went away, they were replaced by a note which said that if you could explain why you needed them for your academic research, they would put them back.)

The other reason is practical. From time to time someone makes his (almost always *his,* by the way) private collection of R-rated pictures available for anonymous FTP. Within five minutes, a thousand sweaty-palmed undergraduates try to FTP in, and that corner of the Internet grinds to a halt. After another five minutes, out of sheer self-preservation, the pictures go away.

Sweaty-palmed users of the World Wide Web might want to take a look at `http://www.penthousemag.com/` which, astonishingly, is exactly what you might think it is. With pictures, even.

Chapter 23
Gopher the Gusto

• •

In This Chapter

▶ What is Gopher?

▶ Looking for documents and files with Gopher

▶ Remembering interesting Gopher menus

▶ Gopher under X Windows

• •

Exploring Gopherspace

As the Internet has grown, users have run into two related problems. One is that so much information is available that nobody can find it all. (This is the same problem that Archie addresses.) The other is that umpteen different ways exist to get to different resources (telnet, FTP, finger, Archie, and so on), and it's getting hard to remember what you say to which program in order to make it do its tricks.

Gopher solves this problem quite well by reducing nearly everything to menus. You start up Gopher, and it shows you a menu. You choose an item, and it shows you another menu. After a certain amount of wandering from menu to menu, you get to menus with actual, useful stuff. Some menu items are files that Gopher can display, mail to you, or (usually) copy to your computer. Some are telnet items that start a telnet session for you to a host that provides a particular kind of service. And some are search items that ask you to enter a *search string,* the name or partial name of what you're looking for, and then use the search string to decide what to get next — more menus, files, or whatever.

You can also think of Gopher menus as directories like the ones on your disk, in which some of the entries are files of various sorts and other entries are other directories. Whether you think of it as menus or directories, Gopher gets much of its power from the fact that any item in any menu can reside on any host in Gopherspace. It's common to have a menu on which every item refers to a different host. Gopher automatically takes care of finding whatever data you want, no matter where it is. You may use a dozen or more different Gopher servers in a single session, but you hardly know it.

This extremely simple model turns out to be very powerful, and Gopher is usually the fastest, easiest, and most fun way to wander around the net looking for and frequently finding the information you need.

TIP

Why did they name it Gopher?

They named it Gopher for two reasons: One is that the gopher is an industrious little animal, always busy scurrying about on behalf of its family. The other is an obvious pun on "go fer" because Gopher "goes fer" your files.

The fact that the mascot of the University of Minnesota (where Gopher was written) is a gopher is, of course, *completely* irrelevant.

Gopher has been so successful that an improved version has appeared, called *Gopher+*. Fortunately, the main difference between the two is that Gopher+ can handle more and different kinds of information than plain Gopher can. Other than that, they're so similar that you can think of them as interchangeable, and plain Gopher and Gopher+ items can intermix in the same menu.

The Good, the Bad, and the Ugly

All the services we've discussed to this point have had a bunch of different client programs that run on different systems (the *client* is the program you run on your computer, and the *server* is the one on the other end). But by and large, although the clients look different, anything you can do with one client, you can do with another.

Gopher is different. You can do much more with a good client than with a bad one. In particular, Gopher is moving into the multimedia era with a vengeance, but the classic UNIX client (the original Gopher program you get at all the telnet sites) handles only text. For anything else, it goes into what one may call *cruel joke mode,* in which it tells you that it has a swell picture you would just love to look at, but you can't. A good client, on the other hand, wastes no time in finding the picture, copying it to your computer, and popping it up in a window on your screen.

This chapter looks at the original, ugly, UNIX terminal Gopher, and the new, snazzy, graphical xgopher.

Where Do I Find a Gopher?

In your vegetable garden of course (yuk, yuk) — oh, sorry, you mean the other kind of Gopher. The number of systems that have Gopher servers grows almost daily. Most of the servers talk to only Gopher clients, not to mere mortals using telnet. If you have a Gopher client available, use it, because it's faster and more flexible than the telnet version. The exact name of the program varies from system to system. Ask around locally if you don't see any obvious Gophers available.

If you don't have your own client, telnet to Gopher is much better than no Gopher at all. Fortunately, several Gopher systems offer telnet access. Table 23-1 lists hosts that offer telnet to Gopher. Because nearly all Gopher servers have references to each other (or at least to the master Every Gopher in the World list in Minnesota), you can get to any Gopher information from any Gopher system. So choose one close to you.

Unless otherwise instructed, if the Gopher server asks you to log in, log in as gopher.

Table 23-1	Gopher Servers	
Country	*Server Address*	*Special Instructions*
Australia	info.anu.edu.au	Log in as info
Austria	finfo.tu-graz.ac.at	Log in as info
Britain	info.brad.ac.uk	Log in as info
Chile	tolten.puc.cl	
Ecuador	ecnet.ec	
Germany	gopher.th-darmstadt.de	
Spain	gopher.uv.es	
U. S. A.	gopher.msu.edu	
	cat.ohiolink.edu	
	wsuaix.csc.wsu.edu	Log in as wsuinfo
	infopath.ucsd.edu	Log in as infopath; then choose 9 and then 4
	ux1.cso.uiuc.edu	
	panda.uiowa.edu	Log in as gopher, and press Ctrl-C to quit
	gopher.virginia.edu	Log in as gwis (pronounced "gee whiz")
	ecosys.drdr.virginia.edu	
	internet.com	Log in as enews

Jumping Down a Gopher Hole

Enough of this Theory of Pure Gopherology — let's take Gopher for a test drive. If you have a Gopher client on your system, type **gopher** (if you're not sure, try it). With any luck, you get a copyright screen, and when you press Enter, you get a screen like the following:

```
                Internet Gopher Information Client v1.1
                Root gopher server: gopher.micro.umn.edu  —
> 1.  Information About Gopher/
  2.  Computer Information/
  3.  Discussion Groups/
  4.  Fun & Games/
  5.  Internet file server (ftp) sites/
  6.  Libraries/
  7.  News/
  8.  Other Gopher and Information Servers/
  9.  Phone Books/
 10.  Search Gopher Titles at the University of Minnesota <?>
 11.  Search lots of places at the University of Minnesota
          <?>
 12.  University of Minnesota Campus Information/
Press ? for Help, q to Quit, u to go up a menu
Page: 1/1
```

If you don't have a local Gopher client program, telnet to one of the systems listed earlier in this chapter, in the section "Where Do I Find a Gopher?" The items in the menu differ, but the general appearance of the screen is the same for local client Gopher and telnet Gopher.

This particular menu contains two kinds of items. The ones that end with a slash (/) are other menus, and the ones with <?> are search items, which we describe later in this chapter.

Although Minnesota is a swell place, gophers and all, let's look farther afield in the Gopher tour. Choose number eight, Other Gopher and Information Servers/. That is, either move the cursor down to line 8 or go there directly by pressing 8, and then press Enter. When you press Enter, the next menu appears. (*Note:* We leave out the top and bottom headers to save space):

```
 ->    1.   All the Gopher Servers in the World/
       2.   Search titles in Gopherspace using veronica/
       3.   Africa/
       4.   Asia/
       5.   Europe/
       6.   International Organizations/
```

```
 7.  Middle East/
 8.  North America/
 9.  Pacific/
10.  South America/
11.  Terminal Based Information/
12.  WAIS Based Information/
```

Choosing North America and then USA gives you a menu that lists all the states. The menu is too big to fit on a single screen, which it tells you by putting `Page: 1/3` at the bottom (which means that this is page one of three). You move from page to page in the listing by pressing + and - or to a particular item by pressing its number. If you know the name of the item you want, you can search for it by pressing / (slash) and then part of the name, and then pressing Enter, at which point Gopher finds the next menu item that matches what you typed.

Eventually (in this example), you might end up at the National Bureau of Economic Research because you're looking for a position paper it published. The menu looks like this:

```
-->  1.  NBER Information.
     2.  About this Gopher.
     3.  Search for any NBER publication <?>
     4.  Penn-World Tables v. 5.5/
     5.  Phone books at other institutions/
     6.  NetEc (Universal) Economics Working Paper Server/
```

These indexes are a mess

If you use Gopher much, you quickly notice that there isn't a great deal of consistency from one menu to another. The reason is that Gopher is a totally decentralized system: Anyone who wants to can put up a Gopher server. It's easy to do and requires only that the system manager install a few programs and create some index files containing the text of the local menus. If one site wants to include in its Gopher menu a link to an item or menu somewhere else, it can just do so without requiring any cooperation from the *linkee*.

So the *good* news is that hundreds of Gopher servers are on the net, put up by volunteers who want to make it easier to get to their data. The *bad* news is that, because almost none of these people has any experience in indexing and information retrieval (for that, you would need a degree in library science), the same item may appear on five different menus under five different names, and no two Gopher menus are quite the same.

It can take some experimenting and poking around to figure out where people have hidden stuff, but it's invariably worth the effort.

It Must Be Around Here Somewhere

Now let's take advantage of a search item, indicated by <?>. When you choose it, Gopher pops up a box in which you type words for which to search. In this case, you might type the name of the author of the paper, and it soon returns a menu of papers the author has written:

```
Search for any NBER publication: Krugman  —
>      1.  |TI| Pricing to Market when the Exchange Rate
               Changes
       2.  |TI| Industrial Organization and International
               Trade
       3.  |TI| Is the Japan Problem Over?
    ...
```

Gopher search items are a general feature. In this case, we searched through a local database, but the interpretation of any particular search key is entirely up to the Gopher server that does the search. People can and do write extremely clever servers that do all sorts of searching (see the section "Veronica Saves the Day," later in this chapter).

Finally, Some Files

Now you have a menu of file items, which in this case contains citations of the papers you want. When you choose any of the items, its file begins displaying on-screen, a page at a time. When the entire file has been displayed (or after you press Q to shut it up), Gopher says:

```
Press <RETURN> to continue, <m> to mail, <s> to save, or <p>
            to print:
```

If you decide that you liked that file, you can arrange to get a copy of it for your very own. If you press m, Gopher asks for your e-mail address and mails you a copy. If you press s, it asks for a filename and copies the file (invisibly, using FTP) to your computer. If you press p, it sends a copy to the printer. If you're telnetted in, the only option is m because the disk and the printer may be thousands of miles away from where you are.

Gopher can download any file in its menus, even if it's not text, on the theory that you probably have a program that handles it.

A Gopher Cheat Sheet

Table 23-2 contains all the keys for the basic UNIX Gopher. Except as noted, each key takes effect immediately as you type it.

More your cursor up and down to move up and down in the current menu. Moving the cursor left moves the screen back to the preceding menu. Moving the cursor to the right chooses the current item.

Table 23-2	Basic UNIX Gopher Commands
Command	*What It Does*
Enter	Chooses current item; same as moving cursor to the right
u	Moves up, back to preceding menu; same as moving the cursor to the left
+	Moves to next menu page
−	Moves to preceding menu page
m	Goes to main menu
digits	Goes to particular menu item; terminate with Enter
/	Searches menu for string
n	Searches for next match
q	Quits; leaves Gopher
=	Describes current item
Bookmark commands	
a	Adds current item to list
A	Adds current menu to list
v	Views bookmarks as a menu
d	Deletes current bookmark
File commands	
m	Mails current file to user
s	Saves current file (not for telnet)
p	Prints current file (not for telnet)
D	Downloads current file

Telnetting via Gopher

Some menu items are flagged with <TEL> to indicate telnet items. When you choose one of these items, Gopher automatically runs telnet to connect you with a system that provides a service. More often than not, you have to log in to the remote system — if so, just before it starts the connection, it tells you the login to use.

If your short-term memory isn't great, you may want to write down the login name the telnetted-to system requires, because it can take awhile before it gets around to asking you for the login name.

To get back to Gopher, log out of the new system. If you can't figure out how to do that, press Ctrl-], and then at the `telnet>` prompt, type **quit**. (*Note:* If you've telnetted to Gopher instead of running it directly, read the following sidebar, "How many telnets would a telnet telnet if a telnet . . . ." before trying this maneuver.)

Some telnet items actually invoke *tn3270*, a mutant version of telnet that works with IBM mainframes. The principle is the same, but figuring out the escape keys to use can be difficult.

When Gopher telnets to a system, it's not doing anything magical — if Gopher can telnet somewhere, so can you. If you find one of Gopher's on-line systems to be interesting, make a note of its hostname, which is displayed just before connection. Next time, you can telnet there yourself without Gopher's help.

How many telnets would a telnet telnet if a telnet . . . .

Here's one of those problems that no one had to worry about before computers existed. Suppose that you're working on your UNIX system and you telnet to a Gopher system. You use that Gopher to telnet to a *third* system, and your session on the third system is messed up, so you want to stop it. As Gopher never tires of pointing out, you can interrupt its telnet session by pressing Ctrl-].

But wait a minute. Pressing Ctrl-] also interrupts the telnet session from your computer to the Gopher system. If you press Ctrl-], which one does it interrupt? The first session (you to Gopher) or the second session (Gopher to third system)? Both? Neither?

The answer is that it interrupts the first session.

In that case, though, how do you interrupt the second session? For that, a trick is available: Change your interrupt character:

```
Ctrl-]
telnet> set escape ^X
```

Note: That last line ends with the two keys ^ (caret) and X. They tell the first telnet that henceforth you press Ctrl-X to interrupt it. Now, if you press Ctrl-], you interrupt the second telnet session, which is what you wanted to do in the first place. If Gopher itself messes up, you can press Ctrl-X to get the local telnet's attention.

Incidentally, after you have telnet's attention, the command to tell it to quit is `quit`.

Veronica Saves the Day

Gopher quickly became a victim of its own success. So many Gopher servers are out there that finding the Gopher menu you want has itself become difficult. *Veronica* comes to the rescue. Like Archie, Veronica has a big database of available services. Veronica tracks all the Gopher menus that can be accessed directly or (often very) indirectly from the mother Gopher in Minnesota.

Using Veronica is easy — it's just another search item. You can find Veronica under "Other Gophers" or a similar name in most public Gophers.

For example, one time we wanted to find the on-line computerized *Jargon Dictionary* (which has been around in various forms since the late 1960s). We chose a Veronica Gopher item — there are usually several, one for each of the available Veronica servers — and for the search string we entered `jargon dictionary`. Veronica constructed for us a custom menu that contained only entries that matched our search string:

```
-->  1.   The Jargon Dictionary File/
     2.   The Jargon Dictionary File/
     3.   The Jargon Dictionary File/
     4.   The Jargon Dictionary File/
     5.   The New Hacker's Dictionary (computer jargon) <?>
     6.   jargon: The New Hacker's Dictionary <?>
     7.   jargon: The New Hacker's Dictionary <?>
     8.   Fuzzy search in "The New Hackers Dictionary"
              (jargon.txt) <?>
     9.   The Jargon Dictionary <?>
    10.   Computer Jargon Dictionary <?>
```

Redundant items mean that a resource is available at more than one place. It usually doesn't matter which one you use.

Why did they name it Veronica?

According to its authors, the name Veronica is just a coincidence, unrelated to Archie, because it's an acronym for the true name, which is *very easy rodent-oriented netwide index to computerized archives.*

But we hear that the next index searcher is called *Jughead,* which is supposed to stand for *Jonzy's universal Gopher hierarchy excavation and display.* If the next one is called Betty or Moose, we'll be *really* suspicious.

Leaving a Trail of Bread Crumbs

The final Gopher feature is *bookmarks*. As you move through Gopherspace, you often come to a menu you want to revisit later. One way to do that is to note carefully the sequence of menus that led up to the one you like — but that's exactly the sort of thing computers do better than people do. Gopher bookmarks, then, note your favorite places in Gopherspace.

To remember the current item, press a (lowercase), for *a*dd a bookmark. To remember the entire current menu, press A (uppercase).

To use your bookmarks, press v (for *v*iew), and Gopher constructs a menu that contains all your bookmarks. You can use that menu like any other menu and move ahead from there. You can prune that menu if you want by pressing D to *d*elete the current item.

We find that we come up with a set of bookmarks that are close to most of the items we regularly use. That lets us get to our regular Gopher haunts in only one or two keystrokes, starting from our bookmark menu.

If you're running the Gopher client directly, your bookmarks are saved in a file so that they're available every time you go Gophering. If you telnet in, the bookmarks are discarded (unfortunately) at the end of each session.

High-Class Gopher

Well, enough of that grotey old user interface. Let's try xgopher, the gopher client written for the X Window system. Pretty much every X system on the net has xgopher for one of these reasons:

- ✔ It's an ergonomically superior interface offering a more systemically integrated data universe manipulation environment and enhanced client/server interaction transparency.
- ✔ It's available for free and looks sort of cute, so what the heck.

When you run xgopher, it displays a window like the one shown in Figure 23-1. The exact menu differs, depending on which Gopher server your system administrator has made your default.

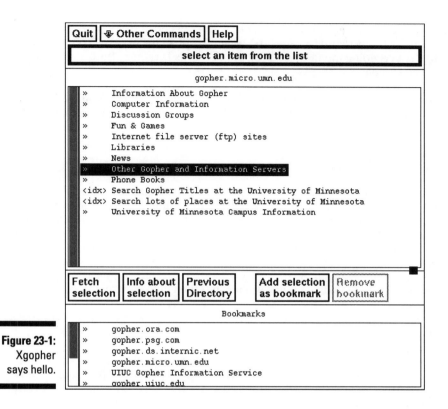

Figure 23-1:
Xgopher
says hello.

That window has buttons at the top, and the upper section is the Gopher menu. in the middle are more buttons, and at the bottom are your bookmarks.

Gopher menus

Mostly what you find are Gopher menus. In a Gopher menu, the type of each entry is indicated by some characters to the left of the entry name. The most common type codes are shown in this list:

Code	Meaning
blank	Text file
>>	Menu
<idx>	A searchable index
<tel>	A telnet session
<tn3>	A tn3270 (IBM mainframe telnet) session
<bin>	A binary file
<img>	A picture

You choose an entry from the menu by double-clicking it. If you choose another menu, the new menu replaces the original one on the screen. You can go back to the preceding menu by clicking the Previous Directory button in the middle of the screen.

If a menu is too big to fit in the window (as most are, unless you have a gigantic screen), you use the scroll bar to the left of the menu to move up and down.

Bookmarks

The bottom part of the screen is a menu of your bookmarks. If you've just fetched a menu, you can add a bookmark for that menu by clicking Add Selection As Bookmark in the middle of the screen. You can add a bookmark for any of the menu entries by clicking the entry once to highlight it and then clicking the button, which will have surreptitiously changed its name to Add Entry As Bookmark.

To get rid of a bookmark, click it once and then click Remove Bookmark.

To go to a bookmark, double-click it, in the same way as you go to an entry in a regular menu.

 Your bookmarks are saved in a text file called `.gopherrc`. If you sometimes use xgopher and sometimes the regular text Gopher program on the same computer, they should (in theory, at least) share the same bookmark file, so any bookmarks you create in one program should work in the other.

Indexes

If you click an index item, xgopher pops up a little window like the one shown in Figure 23-2. Move the cursor into the text rectangle in the window, and type the words to look for. Then press Enter or click Do Index. The gopher server (with luck) sends you a menu of items that match your request.

Figure 23-2:
An xgopher
search.

```
Search of:  Find GOPHER DIRECTORIES by Title word(s) (↖
 Do index   Cancel   Help
recipes▁
```

If you don't move the cursor into the text rectangle, xgopher ignores anything you type. If the term "poor design" didn't already exist, they would have to invent it for this feature.

Fetching files

If you click a text-file entry, xgopher fetches the file for you and displays it as shown in Figure 23-3. You can scroll the text up and down by using the scroll bar on the left side of the window or the Page Up and Page Down buttons. If you like the text and want to keep it, click Save To File; xgopher then displays a window suggesting a filename. Edit the filename if you don't like it, and click Save.

Done	⬆ Page down	⬆ Page up	Print	Save To File

```
Oh!  Bibot had a keen sense of humour, and it was well worth
hanging round that West Barricade, in order to see him catch an aristo
in the very act of trying to flee from the vengeance of the people.

Sometimes Bibot would let his prey actually out by the gates,
allowing him to think for the space of two minutes at least that he
really had escaped out of Paris, and might even manage to reach the
coast of England in safety, but Bibot would let the unfortunate wretch
walk about ten metres towards the open country, then he would send two
men after him and bring him back, stripped of his disguise.

Oh! that was extremely funny, for as often as not the
fugitive would prove to be a woman, some proud marchioness, who looked
terribly comical when she found herself in Bibot's clutches after all,
and knew that a summary trial would await her the next day and after
that, the fond embrace of Madame la Guillotine.

No wonder that on this fine afternoon in September the crowd
round Bibot's gate was eager and excited.  The lust of blood grows
with its satisfaction, there is no satiety: the crowd had seen a
hundred noble heads fall beneath the guillotine to-day, it wanted to
make sure that it would see another hundred fall on the morrow.

Bibot was sitting on an overturned and empty cask close by the
```

Figure 23-3: A text file.

The text window has lots of poorly documented text-manipulation features. The most useful feature is that Ctrl-S lets you search for a particular text string in the text file.

Incidentally, this text file is the classic *Scarlet Pimpernel,* by Baroness Orczy. To find it, start at the Mother Gopher, choose Other Gopher and Information Servers, then North America, then USA, then California, and then Internet Wiretap. (Despite its ominous name, it's one of the best text archives on the net.) At Wiretap, choose Electronic Books at Wiretap; in that menu, you find, among other things, the Scarlet Pimpernel.

Fetching binary files is just like fetching text files except that xgopher makes no attempt to display them. It immediately asks you to specify a filename and then copies the remote file to a local file.

Finding out about Gopher entries

If you're feeling nosy, you can see the details of any Gopher menu entry. Click that entry once and then click Info About Directory. You see a window like the one shown in Figure 23-4. The most interesting part is the Host, the name of the computer on which the file is stored.

```
┌────────────────────────────────────────────────────────────────┐
│ Done │⬇ Page down│ ⬆ Page up │ Print │ Save To File │           │
│ ┌──────────────────────────────────────────────────────────────┐│
│ │          Gopher Item Information                               ││
│ │          -----------------------                               ││
│ │Name:  'Find GOPHER DIRECTORIES by Title word(s) (via PSINet)'  ││
│ │Type:  7 (index search)                                         ││
│ │                                                                ││
│ │Host:  'info.psi.net'                                           ││
│ │       (Computer where information is maintained)               ││
│ │Port:  2347                                                     ││
│ │       (Network connection port)                                ││
│ │                                                                ││
│ │Path:  '-t1 '                                                   ││
│ │       (Tells host where to find the information)               ││
│ │                                                                ││
│ └──────────────────────────────────────────────────────────────┘│
└────────────────────────────────────────────────────────────────┘
```

Figure 23-4:
Inside a
search item.

After your curiosity is sated, click Done to get rid of the info window.

It's a breath mint! No, it's a floor wax! No, it's both!

The astute reader (you, of course) may be wondering why both Archie and Gopher exist. They both let you look for files and retrieve them. Don't they really do the same thing?

Yes and no. Their original goals were quite different: Archie is an index to FTP files, and Gopher is a menuing system.

But they turn out to be complementary. In Chapter 21, "Grabbing Files over the Net," you saw that at least five different ways are available to send a request to Archie (telnet, mail, and so on). The Gopherologists figured that a Gopher search item is as good a way as any to send a request to Archie. They then went beyond that and arranged to intercept the response from Archie so that the directory names Archie returns turn into Gopher menus and the files turn into items. This arrangement enables you to use Gopher to retrieve the files Archie found. A marriage made in heaven, no?

Chapter 24

Stuck to the World Wide Web

● ●

In This Chapter

▶ What is the Web?

▶ Using Lynx

▶ Using Motif Mosaic

▶ Finding great Web pages

● ●

The What?

The World Wide Web (WWW) is the zoomiest, coolest Internet facility around. It contains lots of information, including pictures and other nontext stuff, in the form of *hypertext*. As you read through the information, therefore, you can click (or otherwise select) words, pictures, or buttons to zoom right to related information. These clickable words, pictures, and buttons are called *links*.

The amazing thing about all these linked pages is that a page might be stored on any Internet host computer in the world. If you are looking at a page stored on a computer in Brookline, Massachusetts, a link on that page might jump you to a page stored in Basel, Switzerland. You never even notice, unless you look carefully at the names of the Web pages.

You read the World Wide Web by using a *browser*. If you use plain, old UNIX, you can use a browser named Lynx. If you use Motif or another windowing system, you can use Mosaic, the browser that made the Web famous. Lynx can display the text only in Web pages, and Mosaic can show you the cool graphics that many Web pages contain. This chapter describes both Lynx and Mosaic, in addition to giving you some pointers to some great Web pages.

When you start Mosaic or Lynx, you can begin with the WWW page it suggests and find your way to the information you want by following the hypertext links. (Don't worry — we tell you how.) Alternatively, you can jump directly to a WWW page if you know its name. These names are called *URLs* (for Uniform Resource Locators) — see the nearby sidebar about them.

URL!

The World Wide Web brought us the extremely useful concept of Uniform Resource Locators, or URLs. The point of a URL is to have a simple and consistent way to name Internet resources that tells you both the type of a resource and where to find it. A URL consists of a resource type, a colon, and a location. They look horrendous. In most cases, the location is two slashes, the host name where the resource can be found, a slash, and a filename on that host.

Commonly used resource types are shown in this list:

gopher: A gopher menu

http: A HyperText Transfer Protocol document; that is, something in native WWW format

ftp: A directory or file on an FTP server

news: A Usenet news item (unsupported by many WWW client programs)

Here are some typical URLs:

```
http://www.ncsa.uiuc.edu/demoweb/
    demo.html
```
and
```
gopher://wx.atmos.uiuc.edu:70/1
```

The first is a WWW document, whose URL means that it's accessible by way of HTTP (the standard scheme the Web uses), that the host name is `www.ncsa.uiuc.edu`, and that the filename on that site is `demoweb/demo.html`. The second is a Gopher directory at `wx.atmos.uiuc.edu`, accessible by way of port 70, and its filename is `1`.

Although URLs were originally intended as a way for computers to pass around resource names, they've also become widely used as a way to tell people about Internet resources, and that's how we use them in this section of the book. It's unfortunate that they are so difficult to type!

There's no place like home . . . .

You hear a great deal these days about *home pages.* Everyone who is anyone has a home page. So what are they?

A *home page* is a page on the World Wide Web that serves as a starting point for information about something. If, for example, you want information about *...For Dummies* books, you might want to start at the Dummies Home Page, which is at `http://www.dummies.com` (or will be, if we ever get it set up).

Home pages generally contain introductory information about the entity whose home page it is, along with lots of links to other pages. Many home pages for organizations have URLs such as `http://www.something,` where `something` is the Internet domain name for the organization. Guess whose home page is `http://www.microsoft.com`?

A Day on the Lynx

Lynx is a boring-looking, character-based, graphics-impaired Web browser, but by gosh, it works. For most UNIX users (except those with GUI interfaces), Lynx is the only browser they can use. It and its DOS-based version were created at the University of Kansas. This chapter describes version 2.3.7.

If your UNIX system doesn't have Lynx, you (or your system administrator) can get it for free by anonymous FTP from `ftp2.cc.ukans.edu` in the `pub/lynx` directory. For up-to-date information about Lynx, you can subscribe to the Lynx mailing list by sending the message `subscribe lynx-dev <your-name>` to `listserv@ukanaix.cc.ukans.edu`.

You can try out Lynx by telnet to the University of Kansas. Telnet to `hnsource.cc.ukans.edu`, and log in as `www`. If you like it, arrange to FTP and install it locally, because the extra telnet step slows things down and makes it impossible to use some of Lynx's nicer features.

Coming and going

To run Lynx, just type **lynx**. You see a Web page (for example, the page shown in Figure 24-1). This particular page is the home page of The World, a Boston-based Internet provider.

┌ Brief instruction
┌ A link   Title of page

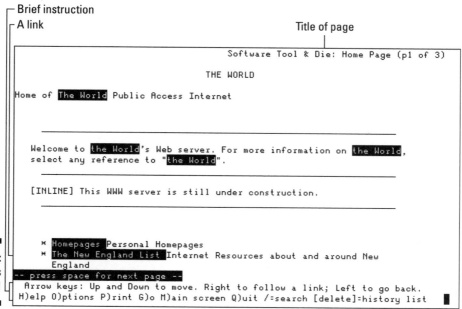

Figure 24-1:
Lynx springs
into action!

When you are in Lynx, you can exit at any time by pressing q. Lynx asks whether you really want to leave — press y.

If you don't want Lynx to ask you whether you really, really, truly want to leave, press Q (capitalized) or Ctrl-D to quit.

Anatomy of a page

Lynx tells you the name of the Web page (in words, not the URL) in the upper right corner of the screen. The bottom two lines of the screen comprise a cryptic little menu that reminds you about which keys do what. The third line from the bottom displays various helpful messages — in Figure 24-1, it tells you that this Web page is too long to fit on the screen as well as how to see the rest of it. And the rest of the screen is the Web page itself.

A Web page can contain text, links, pictures, sounds, and movies. Unfortunately, Lynx can deal with only text and links. Text looks (not surprisingly) like text. Hypertext links (things you can click to view a related Web page) are displayed in reverse video. Graphics, sound, and movies aren't displayed at all — instead, Lynx shows you something like [INLINE] or [IMAGE]. This is Lynx's way of saying, "Nyaah, nyaah! There's a picture here, but I'm not going to show it to you!"

Skating the Web

Each link (highlighted word or phrase) on the Web page connects to another page on a related topic. The links that say The World, for example, connect to a page that describes Software Tool & Die's World Internet service. The Homepages link connects to a list of home pages about individual people.

One of the links appears in a different color on the screen. (This color difference doesn't show up worth a darn on paper, so in Figure 24-1, you can't tell that the first link is displayed in white letters on black and that the others are in yellow on black. Your colors may differ.) This link is the selected link. To select a link:

1. **Press the arrow keys so that the link you want is selected.**

2. **Press the right-arrow key to jump to the linked page.**

The linked page appears (sometimes after a short delay while Lynx retrieves the page over the Internet).

So that's it! To "surf the Web," you just move from page to page until you find something interesting. Here are some surfing pointers:

- ✔ The links you see may be numbered — if they are, you can choose a link by typing its number and pressing Enter.

- ✔ To return to the page you were looking at previously, press the left-arrow key.

- ✔ To return to the first screen you saw when you started Lynx, you can press m at any time. Lynx calls this first screen your *main screen*.

- ✔ To display a good starting point for surfing, press i for index. The Web page that Lynx displays depends on the one your system administrator chose. One popular index page is the Welcome to the World-Wide Web page at CERN, the laboratory near Geneva, Switzerland, where the Web was invented (see Figure 24-2).

- ✔ Sometimes a link doesn't take you to a different Web page. Sometimes it takes you to another part of the same page. It is common (and convenient) for long Web pages to contain a table of contents at the top of the page, with links to the major headings.

Figure 24-2:
One of the
World Wide
Web's own
home
pages.

```
                                      Welcome to the World-Wide Web (p1 of 2)
                      THE WORLD-WIDE WEB

     This is just one of many access points to the web, the universe of
     information available over networks. To follow references, just type
     the number then hit the return (enter) key.

     The features you have by connecting to this telnet server are very
     primitive compared to the features you have when you run a W3 "client"
     program on your own computer. If you possibly can, please pick up a
     client for your platform to reduce the load on this service and
     experience the web in its full splendor.

     For more information, select by number:
       * A list of available W3 client programs
       * Everything about the W3 project
       * Places to start exploring

     Have fun!

  -- press space for next page --
     Arrow keys: Up and Down to move. Right to follow a link; Left to go back.
   H)elp O)ptions P)rint G)o M)ain screen Q)uit /=search [delete]=history list
```

Where do all these pages come from?

Web pages don't all come from any one source. Lots of universities and companies have Web pages — in fact, right now it's the in thing for anyone and everyone to have a Web page about themselves (so much for humility). Most Internet providers run *Web servers,* or programs that store Web pages and make them available to any Web browser that wants to display them. If you get the urge to have your own Web page, contact your Internet provider to find out whether they can help you.

Web pages are stored as ASCII text files. In addition to the text that is displayed by the Web browser, special instructions are written in a language called HTML (hypertext markup language), which is discussed in another sidebar in this chapter. These instructions include marking headings and lists, links to other pages, and information about nontextual stuff such as pictures and sounds. Several books are out about how to write Web pages in HTML, including our *Internet Secrets* (IDG Books, 1995).

But before you rush to create your own Web page, with a picture of your dog and a list of your kids' latest cute utterances, consider this question: How are people going to find your page? Sure, your friends will see your page after they type the URL you proudly give them. But will anyone else ever see it? Remember that the way most people display most pages is by selecting a link to the page. Will any other pages contain links to your page? Probably not.

Handling long pages

Some Web pages just fit on the screen, and others are miles long (or they seem like it). You can press the PgUp and PgDn keys to move around the page one screenful at a time. Pressing the Home and End keys (if your keyboard has them) moves you to the very top and the very bottom of the page (we'll let you guess which does which).

If you are looking for something in particular on a very long page, you might want to try Lynx's search commands. The page shown in Figure 24-2, for example, is 14 screens long and can be tedious to look through for a specific topic.

Instead, press the slash key (/) to begin a search. Lynx says `Enter a search string`. Type a word or phrase and press Enter. Lynx skips to the part of the page that includes the word or phrase, if it occurs in the page.

Getting help

If you want help, you can see hypertext help pages by pressing H (be sure to capitalize it). You see a page like the one shown in Figure 24-3.

The help pages are themselves Web pages, so move around them as you would any Web page. Of course, if you need help navigating the Web, this might not be so easy!

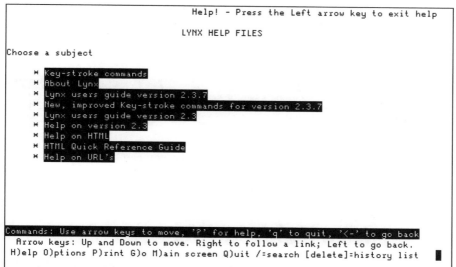

Figure 24-3:
Help! I'm being attacked by a lynx!

Where have I been?

Lynx keeps a list of the pages you have seen, in order. It needs this list to make the left-arrow key back you up through the pages. You can also see the list of pages by pressing the Del key (if it doesn't work, try the Backspace key). You see the Lynx History Page, shown in Figure 24-4.

```
                                                        Lynx History Page

                        YOU HAVE REACHED THE HISTORY PAGE


     5.  -- You selected:  The World-Wide Web Virtual Library: Beer & Brewing

     4.  -- You selected:  The World-Wide Web Virtual Library: Subject Catalogue

     3.  -- You selected:  Data sources classified by access protocol

     2.  -- You selected:  Overview of the Web

     1.  -- You selected:  Welcome to the World-Wide Web

     0.  -- You selected:  Software Tool & Die: Home Page




 Commands: Use arrow keys to move, '?' for help, 'q' to quit, '<-' to go back
   Arrow keys: Up and Down to move. Right to follow a link; Left to go back.
   H)elp O)ptions P)rint G)o M)ain screen Q)uit /=search [delete]=history list
```

Figure 24-4:
The history
of Lynx.

The pages you've seen are listed, and you can jump to any of them by choosing the link and pressing the right-arrow key. (If the links are numbered, you can also type the number and press Enter.)

Going right to a URL

If you know the URL of the Web page you want to see, and if you have the stomach to attempt to type it, press g (for *goto*). Type the URL, and be careful about both the punctuation and the capitalization (yes, capitalization counts). Then press Enter. Lynx gets the page you want.

Printing or saving good stuff

What if you want to print what's on a Web page? If you press p, you see the Lynx Printing Options page, which looks something like Figure 24-5. The exact options on this page depend on your Lynx installation.

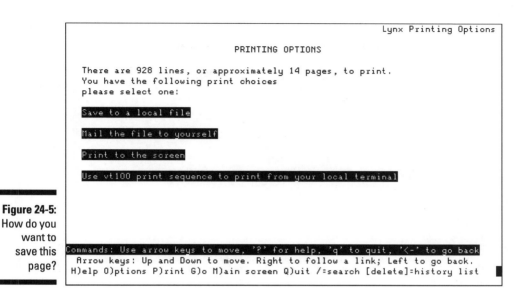

Figure 24-5:
How do you
want to
save this
page?

Some of the options on this page let you save the text of the page in a file rather than print it.

Fake Web pages

As you wander around the Web, you might stumble across a Usenet newsgroup, telnet session, or list of files on an FTP server. How did that stuff sneak onto the Web, you may ask. Lynx, like most Web browsers, can display not only Web pages but also information from other Internet services. Lynx makes the information look like a Web page, but it's not.

This is a wonderfully clever way to make lots of information about a topic accessible by way of a single program (your browser). Lynx can display Usenet newsgroups, FTP sites, Gopher menus, and telnet sessions for you. How convenient!

News of the weird

Figure 24-6 shows you how a Usenet newsgroup looks in Lynx. It lists the latest 30 or so articles, with a link at the top of the page to display earlier articles. (See Chapter 19, "Turbocharge Your Newsreading," for background information about Usenet.)

TECHNICAL STUFF

Here's HTML in your eye!

As you may know, Web pages are written in a language called *HTML,* which includes instructions to tell the browser about text, headings, links, graphics, and anything else a Web page might contain. Each browser reads the HTML information about a page, formats it tastefully, and displays it. Different browsers use different formatting.

If you want to see the actual HTML version of a page, just press the backslash (\). You see something like this:

```
<HTML>

<HEAD>

<TITLE>The World-Wide Web Virtual
   Library: Subject Catalogue</TITLE>

<!— Changed by: Arthur Secret,
  6-Dec-1994 —>

<NEXTID N="z196">

</HEAD>

<BODY>
```

```
<H1><IMG ALT="Virtual Library"
   SRC="http://www.w3.org/
   hypertext/WWW/Icons/WWW/V

See also arrangement   by <A

NAME="52" HREF="../ByAccess.html">
   service

type</A> ., and <A

NAME="z154" HREF="Virtual_libraries/
   Overview.html">other subject
   catalogues

of network information</A> . <P>
```

All those brackets surround HTML markings, which tell Lynx (and other Web browsers) about how to format the text and where to put pictures and links. If you want more information about HTML, the Lynx help system includes an introduction to HTML. There are also links to HTML introductory documents on the CERN home page.

```
                         Newsgroup misc.rural,  Articles 16918-16947 (p1 of 2)

   (Earlier articles...) Articles in misc.rural
    * "Re: How can I make pressure treated wood?" - Geoffrey Leach
    * "Well, I have a nice friend looking for a rural mate." - Dean
      Hughson
    * "Re: How can I make pressure treated wood?" - Tropical Steve
    * "Re: Septic Problem?" - an48068@anon.penet.fi
    * "Re: Septic Helpers" - Joshua_Putnam
    * "Re: Propose new group: alt.living.tightwad" - Neil McLaughlin
    * "Re: Propose new group: alt.living.tightwad" - Cara Vandy
    * "Re: How can I make pressure treated wood?" - Denison Rich, 3-5105
    * "Re: Squirrels in garden" - Denison Rich, 3-5105
    * "Re: Propose new group: alt.living.tightwad" - Walter Vose
      Jeffries
    * "Re: Propose new group: alt.living.tightwad" - B.M. Paquet
    * "Re: moving to the country" - John A. Stanley
    * "Re: Propose new group: alt.living.tightwad" - Richard & Marsha
    * "please snail me yer rosehips" - FLORIBUNDA
    * "Re: Propose new group: alt.living.tightwad" - Paul J. Lucas
    * "Re: STUMPS!!" - Jon Fox
-- press space for next page --
  Arrow keys: Up and Down to move. Right to follow a link; Left to go back.
  H)elp O)ptions P)rint G)o M)ain screen Q)uit /=search [delete]=history list
```

Figure 24-6:
Here's a list
of articles
in the
newsgroup
misc.rural.

To read an article, just select its link and you see something like Figure 24-7. Lynx shows you all the newsgroups to which the article was posted and lets you jump to them.

```
                         Re: Propose new group: alt.living.tightwad (p1 of 2)

      Reply to: Cara Vandy

                   RE: PROPOSE NEW GROUP: ALT.LIVING.TIGHTWAD


      9 Mar 1995 17:52:02 -0500
      Rutgers University
      Newsgroups:
              news.config,
              news.groups,
              misc.consumers,
              misc.rural,
              rec.gardens
      Reply to newsgroup(s)
      References:
              <3jj9vs$91p@isnews.calpoly.edu>
              <3jn385$18c@redstone.interpath.net>
Great idea.  I'd love having a group I could post to like I knew what I
-- press space for next page --
  Arrow keys: Up and Down to move. Right to follow a link; Left to go back.
  H)elp O)ptions P)rint G)o M)ain screen Q)uit /=search [delete]=history list
```

Figure 24-7:
More
Usenet
gossip.

The first link, Reply to: author, lets you send e-mail to the person who wrote the article. If you choose it, Lynx asks for your name, e-mail address, and the subject of the e-mail and then runs an editor to let you type your post. (See the section "Controlling your Lynx," later in this chapter, to learn how to tell Lynx which editor to run.) If you specified an editor, Lynx runs the editor and lets you type the message. Save and exit as you usually do, using that editor. If you didn't specify an editor, Lynx lets you type the lines one line at a time and lets you type a period on a line by itself to signal that you are finished. After you type the message, Lynx asks you whether you really want to mail it. If it's angry, petty, or not funny, think again.

Another link, Reply to newsgroup(s), posts a follow-up article. If you choose it, Lynx asks for your e-mail address, the subject of the post, and whether you want to include the original message, and then it runs an editor to let you type your post. After you type the message, Lynx asks you whether you really want to post it. Think twice — will it really be of interest to lots of people in the newsgroup, not just to you and the person who wrote the post to which you are replying?

Gopher it

If you follow a link that leads to a Gopher menu, Lynx displays it as a Web page, which looks something like Figure 24-8. (In this figure, Lynx displays numbers next to the links — see the section "Controlling your Lynx," later in this chapter, to learn how to set this option.)

```
     Select one of:

(FILE) [1]About Gopher
 (DIR) [2]Gopher News Archive
 (DIR) [3]GopherCON '95
 (DIR) [4]GopherCON '94
 (DIR) [5]Gopher Software Distribution
 (DIR) [6]Commercial Gopher Software
 (DIR) [7]Gopher Protocol Information
(FILE) [8]University of Minnesota Gopher software licensing policy
(FILE) [9]Frequently Asked Questions about Gopher
 (DIR) [10]Gopher+ example server
 (DIR) [11]comp.infosystems.gopher (USENET newsgroup)
(FILE) [12]Adding Information to Gopher Hotel
 (MOV) [13]Gopher T shirt on MTV movie (big)
 (MOV) [14]Gopher T shirt on MTV movie (small)
 (IMG) [15]Gopher T-shirt on MTV #1
 (IMG) [16]Gopher T-shirt on MTV #2
(FILE) [17]How to get your information into Gopher
-- press space for next page --
  Arrow keys: Up and Down to move. Right to follow a link; Left to go back.
 H)elp O)ptions P)rint G)o M)ain screen Q)uit /=search [delete]=history list
```

Figure 24-8: This Gopher menu is displayed as though it were a Web page.

At the left edge of the page, Lynx tells you what kind of thing each menu item is. (See Chapter 23, "Gopher the Gusto!," for information about items on Gopher menus.) To choose an item from a Gopher menu, select it and press the right-arrow key as usual. (If the links are numbered, you can type the number and press Enter instead.) Items marked (DIR) display another Gopher menu. Other item types you might see include the ones in this list:

- ✔ **(FILE):** An ASCII text file
- ✔ **(IMG):** A picture
- ✔ **(MOV):** A movie

Files via Lynx

With Lynx, you don't need a separate FTP program for downloading files. If a Web page contains a link to an FTP server and you choose that link, you see the mess Retrieving FTP directory, and Lynx displays the files on the FTP server as a Web page, like the one shown in Figure 24-9.

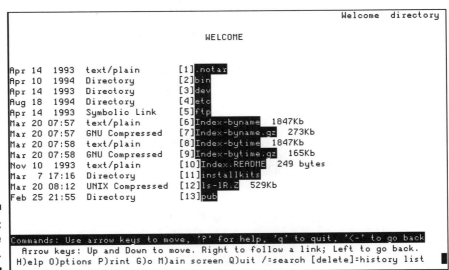

Figure 24-9: Files on the Web.

You see one directory on the FTP server. For each item in the directory, lynx displays its date and time, which type of thing it is (directory or file), its name, and its size. For files, it guesses which type of file it is. Here's what you do:

1. **Move to the directory that contains the file you want.**

If you select a directory, you see the contents of the directory. All directories except the root (/) have a link that lets you move up to the directory's parent directory.

2. When you see the file you want, select it.

If the file is a text file or contains a Web page, Lynx displays it. You are finished.

If the file is anything else (not text), Lynx says that this file can't be displayed on this terminal. True enough — you don't want to display it; in fact, you want to store it in a file on your system. Lynx asks what you what to do with it — download it to a file or cancel.

3. Press d to download the file.

Lynx displays the menu shown in Figure 24-10.

4. Choose one of the options for downloading a binary file.

(We recommend the last option on the menu, downloading by using ZMODEM to download a binary file, because it's the fastest.)

Lynx asks for the name to give the file on your system. It suggests the same name the file now has, but you can change it.

5. Type the filename and press Enter when you are finished.

The download begins! That is, Lynx and FTP begin transferring the file to your disk. You see various messages, depending on which type of transfer you chose in step 4.

```
                                                    Lynx Download Options
                        DOWNLOAD OPTIONS

        You have the following download choices
        please select one:

        [1] Save to disk

        [2] Use Kermit to download a file

        [3] Use Xmodem to download a text file

        [4] Use Xmodem to download a binary file

        [5] Use Ymodem to download a text file

        [6] Use Ymodem to download a binary file

        [7] Use Zmodem to download a text file

        -- press space for next page --
        Arrow keys: Up and Down to move. Right to follow a link; Left to go back.
        H)elp O)ptions P)rint G)o M)ain screen Q)uit /=search [delete]=history list
```

Figure 24-10:
How do you
want to
download
this file?

Here are a few tips for downloading files with Lynx:

✔ It may take some time to connect to the FTP server. Many FTP servers are overburdened and overbooked — you may not be able to connect at all in some cases.

✔ If you start at the root directory of the FTP server, you may have to press PgDn once or twice before you get to the directories you are looking for. (Many FTP servers store their publicly accessible files in a directory called /pub.)

✔ If you want to use lynx to access an FTP site, just press **g** and type **ftp://** **ftpsite/**, replacing ftpsite with the name of the site. To look at the files at gatekeeper.dec.com, for example, type **ftp://gatekeeper.dec.com/**.

✔ If the file transfer doesn't seem to work, try another type of transfer in step 4. You may have to exit from Lynx and use the ls command to see whether the file has in fact arrived. If it still doesn't work, it's time to make a note of the FTP server name and the file you want and then fire up the regular FTP program.

Lynx can act like telnet too

Chapter 20, "Telnetting Around the Net," explains how you can log in to other computers to get information. Some of the computers are mentioned on Web pages, and amazingly enough, you can use Lynx to telnet to them.

When you click a telnet link, Lynx automagically connects by way of telnet. You have to log in, and so on, just as you would if you were using the telnet program. When you are finished, be sure to log out — you can press q to tell Lynx to log you out. When you see the Connection closed by foreign host message, you are logged out.

Remembering the good parts

The World Wide Web has thousands of pages in it, and hundreds are added every day. (Well, almost.) When you find one that looks really interesting and useful (or fun), it would be nice to be able to return to it easily. Otherwise, it can be impossible to find it again!

There is! You can create a *bookmark* for the page — that is, add its address (its URL) to a list of your favorite Web pages.

Before you can begin making your own bookmarks, you have to tell Lynx where to store them. Press O (the letter) to see the Options Menu, which is described in more detail in the next section. The third option is the name of the file in which bookmarks are stored. If you see a filename for this option, fine — just leave it alone. It may already be set to something like lynx_bookmarks.html. If no filename appears, press B, type a filename, and press Enter. To leave the Options Menu, press > (that is, Shift-.) to save your changes and then r to return to your normal Lynx screen.

Now you have a file just waiting to contain some bookmarks. To add a page to your bookmark file, press a. Lynx asks whether you want to make a bookmark for that page you are looking at (if so, press d) or to the page you would see if you chose the selected link (if so, press l, the letter). All that seems to happen is that Lynx displays the friendly, upbeat message Done!

Behind the scenes, however, Lynx has added the URL of the current page or link to your bookmark file. To see your list of bookmarks, press v. You see a page like the one shown in Figure 24-11. To go to a Web page on your list of bookmarks, just select its link. It's like having your own Web page full of your favorite links!

```
                                                            Bookmark file

    You can delete links using the new remove bookmark command. it is
    usually the 'R' key but may have been remapped by you or your system
    administrator.
    This file may also be edited with a standard text editor. Outdated or
    invalid links may be removed by simply deleting the line the link
    appears on in this file. Please refer to the Lynx documentation or
    help files for the HTML link syntax.
      1. [1]Virtual Library by Subject
      2. [2]subject
      3. [3]Lynx Users Guide v2.3.7B
      4. [4]Data sources classified by access protocol
```

Figure 24-11:
Some of our
favorite
places.

```
Commands: Use arrow keys to move, '?' for help, 'q' to quit, '<-' to go back
  Arrow keys: Up and Down to move. Right to follow a link; Left to go back.
  H)elp O)ptions P)rint G)o M)ain screen Q)uit /=search [delete]=history list
```

Controlling your Lynx

Lynx has some options you can set to control some things about how it works. When you press o, you see the Lynx Options Menu, shown in Figure 24-12.

```
                         Options Menu

    E)ditor                   :
    D)ISPLAY variable         : iecc.com:0
    B)ookmark file            : lynx_bookmarks.html
    F)TP sort criteria        : By Filename
    P)ersonal mail address    : moreunix@dummies.com
    S)earching type           : CASE INSENSITIVE
    C)haracter set            : ISO Latin 1
    V)I keys                  : ON
    e(M)acs keys              : ON
    K)eypad as arrows
          or Numbered links   : Links are numbered
    U)ser mode                : Novice




    Select first letter of option line, '>' to save, or 'r' to return to Lynx.
    Command:
```

Figure 24-12:
Controlling
how Lynx
works.

To change an option, press the capitalized letter in the option name. For some options, you then type the setting you want (such as the name of your favorite editor for the Editor option). For other options, there are only a few possibilities, and you can press any key (except Enter) to flip among them. Then press Enter when you see the one you want.

When you finish setting your options, press > to save them. Then press r to return to what you were doing in Lynx.

Here are some options you might want to fool with:

✔ **Editor:** This option controls which editor Lynx runs when you use it for sending mail. We recommend emacs because it's our favorite, but you may prefer vi. Type the full pathname of your editor. You can send e-mail to the owners of most Web pages by using the Lynx c command.

✔ **Personal mail address:** Set this option to your own, complete e-mail address. Lynx uses it when you mail Web pages to yourself or as your return address when you mail things to others.

✔ **Keypad as arrows or numbered links:** If you set this option to numbered links, each link in a page is numbered, and you can choose a link by typing its number. *Note:* After you change this option, exit from Lynx and start it up again.

> ✔ **User mode:** This option is usually set to Novice, so that Lynx displays two lines of helpful menu items at the bottom of the screen. If you already know all the Lynx commands you need and would rather see two more lines of Web page, set this option to Intermediate. If you want to see the URL of each Web pages, set it to Advanced.

Problems

The third line from the bottom of the screen displays various messages to tell you what to do or to let you know what's going on. Here are a few messages you might see:

> ✔ `Making HTTP connection to kufacts.cc.ukans.edu`. This message means that Lynx is asking `kufacts.cc.ukans.edu`, or whatever host computer it mentions, for the Web page you want.

> ✔ `http request sent: waiting for response`. If the Internet is very busy, a message like this one tells you that there's a brief delay. Lynx has spoken (metaphorically) to the host on which the Web page lives and is waiting to get the actual page.

> ✔ `Alert! Unable to connect to remote host` or `Alert! Unable to access document`. If you see one of these messages, the host on which the information is stored is so busy that it doesn't have time for you. Or maybe it's down for repairs. Either way, try again later.

Using Mosaic

Mosaic is a WWW browser that was written by Chris Wilson and Jon Mittlehauser at the University of Illinois, at the National Center for Supercomputing Applications. The NCSA also runs a World Wide Web server that provides lots of information about Mosaic itself as well as other things.

There are versions of Mosaic for UNIX, for Windows, and for the Macintosh. They all work in more or less the same way. Because UNIX Mosaic was developed by university students, they created lots and lots of versions. Your version may be a tad different from the one we describe here. The items on menus may not match the one we used, but you'll get the general idea.

(Don't bother) configuring Mosaic

Because Mosaic is an X and Motif application, it uses dozens and dozens of X resources that you can customize. But here's our advice: Forget it. The standard configuration works fine, and our sad experience is that most changes you make only make it worse.

Starting it up

You start Mosaic by typing `xmosaic` to your shell. (Or with luck, maybe you have a Mosaic entry on your Motif menu (see Chapter 15, "Lite Motif").

Mosaic automatically loads its home page from headquarters in Illinois. You see a window like the one in Figure 24-13.

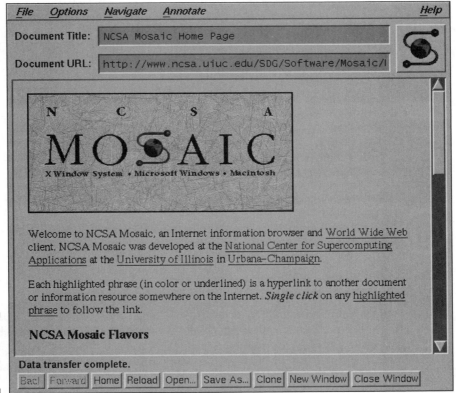

Figure 24-13:
Mosaic
Mission
Control.

If you have a slow Internet connection, it may take quite awhile to load the attractive faux-marble graphic at the top of the window. If you find yourself getting impatient, choose Options⇨Delay Image Loading to tell it not to bother loading the images in pages you retrieve. In that case, it replaces the images with little squashed-bug things. To tell it to load an image, click the squashed bug with the right mouse button. Mosaic is relatively smart about remembering which images it already has, so if a page uses an image it already has, it auto-matically displays the image.

Leaving

When you finish using Mosaic, choose File⇨Exit Program from the menu. You can also use the Close Window at the bottom of the Mosaic window.

Jumping around the Web

When you are looking at a WWW page, some words and phrases are underlined and displayed in a different color. These things, called *links,* refer to another, related WWW page about that topic. For example, if you see *National Center for Supercomputing Applications* underlined, it is a link to a WWW page about (not surprisingly) the National Center for Supercomputing Applications (NCSA), the folks who wrote Mosaic.

A link may not necessarily lead to another WWW page — instead, it may connect to a Gopher menu, a Usenet newsgroup, or an FTP site. In any case, the information is related to the topic you click, and Mosaic can display it just fine.

Occasionally you may get an error message when you try to retrieve a page. If this happens, try it again because it frequently works on the second or third try.

You can also use buttons at the bottom of the screen to move around:

- **Back button:** Takes you to the preceding page you retrieved. If the button is gray, there's no page to back up to.

- **Forward button:** After you have backed up by using the Back button, goes forward to the next page you retrieved. If the button is gray, there *is* no next page yet.

- **Home button:** Returns you to your home page, which is usually a page about Mosaic, unless your system manager has made it something else.

- **Reload button:** Reloads the current WWW page. Click it if Mosaic can't load a page correctly or if you think that the page may have changed since the last time Mosaic loaded it and you want to try again.

- **Open button:** Pops up a window like the one shown in Figure 24-14, in which you can type the URL of a page you want to visit. Type the URL, and click Open to go to the URL.

- **Save As button:** Opens a window that lets you specify a file in which to save the current page. It lets you choose the format in which to save the page: Plain text or Formatted text if you want to use it in a text editor; PostScript if you want to print it to a PostScript printer and have it look nice; or HTML to save it in WWW native form.

✔ **Clone and New Window buttons:** Do roughly the same thing — open a new Mosaic window. The Clone button makes the new window contain the same page as the current window, and New Window creates a new window looking at the Home page.

✔ **Close Window button:** Closes the current window. (Are you surprised?) If it's the last or only Mosaic window, Mosaic exits.

Figure 24-14:
Where to now?

Stop everything!

If Mosaic takes forever to retrieve something, you tell it to forget it. Click the spinning-globe Mosaic logo.

Changing fonts

You can change the fonts Mosaic uses when it displays most WWW pages, Gopher menus, and other stuff. Choose Options⇨Fonts from the menu, and you see a list of the different fonts you can define. Choose one if you want.

Printing, saving, or copying good stuff

To print the displayed page, choose File⇨Print from the menu. It suggests a print command, which you generally should leave alone, and a format for the printed document, which should be PostScript if you have a PostScript printer, HTML if you want to see all the WWW codes in the page, and Plain text or Formatted text otherwise. Then click the Print button in that window to send the page to the printer.

Remembering good places

When you find a particularly interesting page, you can add it to your Hotlist of favorite Web pages. Choose Navigate⇨Add Current To Hotlist to remember the current page.

To go to a page in your Hotlist:

1. **Choose Navigate⇨Hotlist to see a window like the one shown in Figure 24-15.**

2. **Click the entry you want in the Hotlist.**

   If the list is too big for the window, scroll it up or down by using the scroll bar on the right side of the window, and then click.

3. **Click Go To.**

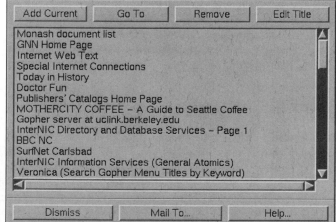

Figure 24-15:
Get them
while
they're hot.

You can also click Remove to get rid of a Hotlist entry, or Edit Title to adjust the title of an entry (often helpful when the original titles make sense only in the context of the pages to which they're linked).

Finding other WWW pages

If you know the URL (the official technical name) of a WWW page you want to see, you can tell Mosaic to go directly to it:

1. **Choose File Open URL from the menu (or click the Open button).**

   Mosaic asks for the URL name, using the dialog box shown in Figure 24-14.

2. **In the URL box, type the URL.**

   With luck, you have the URL in a file on your computer somewhere, so you can copy it by using the Windows Clipboard.

3. Click OK or press Enter.

Mosaic retrieves the URL you requested.

The URL of the page you are looking at is displayed in the Document URL box at the top of the Mosaic window. When you point to a link on a Mosaic page, the URL of the link appears on the status line at the bottom of the Mosaic window.

Often you get e-mail or read a Usenet item that contains a URL. Rather than retype the URL, highlight the URL in the mail or news window, and then switch to Mosaic, click Open, click Clear (if there's already some text in the text window), and then click the *middle* mouse button in the text window to paste in the URL you selected.

Searching for info

"But where's all this great hypertextual stuff I keep hearing about?" we hear you cry. "I want to find out about pigs in space!" Stay calm — it's out there. The problem is finding it.

There are a bunch of Web directories, but one of the best is Yahoo, at `http://www.yahoo.com/`. The Yahoo home page has links to categories and subcategories and, a couple of levels down, to interesting pages all over the net. It's the directory we use most often.

If you think that you'll use Yahoo much, add it to your Hotlist by choosing Navigate Add Current to Hotlist from the menu.

Gophers on the Web

Some of the information you see in Mosaic is actually Gopher menus. If a Gopher menu appears as a link on a page and you click it, Mosaic shows you the menu. In fact, you may not even know that you have entered Gopherspace.

If you know the URL of a Gopher menu, you can tell Mosaic to go right to it. URLs for Gopher menus look a little odd (but all URLs look strange, so what the heck), like this:

```
gopher://gopher.micro.umn.edu:70/11/
          Other%20Gopher%20and%20Information%20Servers
```

All the menus begin with the word *gopher,* though. The part after the double slashes up to the second colon is the name of the host on which the Gopher item lives (in this example, `gopher.micro.umn.edu`):

1. **Choose File Open URL (or press Ctrl-O).**

   Mosaic asks for the URL of the information you want, using the dialog box shown in Figure 24-12.

2. **In the URL box, enter a URL and click OK.**

   Good luck typing it correctly! Mosaic fetches the Gopher item. Items with little folders display other menus. Items with little paper pictures are documents you can view.

3. **Click menu-item links until you see a document you want.**

4. **Click a document you want to see.**

   Mosaic retrieves the document and displays it.

Files on the Web

You can use Mosaic to download files from FTP servers. Here's how:

1. **Choose File Open URL (or press Ctrl-O).**

   Mosaic asks for the URL of the information you want, using the dialog box shown in Figure 24-12.

2. **In the URL box, enter a URL like this:**

```
ftp://hostmachine/
```

   In place of `hostmachine`, type the name of the FTP server. Don't forget the two slashes before it and one slash after it.

3. **Click OK.**

   Mosaic connects to the FTP server, logs in as `anonymous`, and displays the root directory of the system. Items with a little folder icon are directories, and clicking them moves to that directory. Items with little paper icons are text files. Items with a little block of ones and zeroes are binary information.

4. **Move to the directory that contains the file you want.**

5. **Choose Options Load to Local Disk.**

   This command tells Mosaic to store stuff it retrieves to disk rather than display it on-screen.

6. **Click the file to download it.**

   Mosaic retrieves the file and stores it to disk, asking you where to put it.

7. Choose Options Load to Local Disk again.

This command turns off the load-to-disk business so that Mosaic goes back to displaying stuff on-screen.

Telnetting with Mosaic

If you are given a URL that begins with `telnet`, you can use Mosaic to run a telnet program for you and look at particular information on other systems:

1. Choose File Open URL (or press Ctrl-O).

2. In the URL box, enter the URL that begins with `telnet`.

Mosaic starts an xterm window running telnet, which telnets to the Internet host computer, asks you for the username and password to use, and displays whatever the information is that the URL describes.

How to Swing on the Web

This section presents a few useful Web pages you might want to try.

The World Wide Web is a dynamic place. All these URLs worked when we wrote this book, but they may have moved by now!

WWW Virtual Library: Subject Catalog

```
http://info.cern.ch/hypertext/DataSources/bySubject/
            Overview.html
```

A good index to the Web.

Yahoo Index

```
http://www.yahoo.com/
```

A great index to the Web, updated daily.

Clearinghouse for Subject-Oriented Internet Resource Guides

```
http://www.lib.umich.edu/chhome.html
```

Another good index to the Web.

Comprehensive List of Sites, with search boxes

```
http://www.netgen.com/cgi/comprehensive
```

Yet another index to the Web, this one with the capability to search for a particular topic.

The White House

```
http://www.whitehouse.gov/
```

Stop in and see what's doing at the White House!

CIA

```
http://www.ic.gov/
```

Find out what information the CIA is dishing out today. You can read the excellent CIA *Fact Books* about lots of different countries.

IRS

```
http://www.ustreas.gov/treasury/bureaus/irs/irs.html
```

Who knows — maybe this Web page will have tax advice that's a little more reliable than its phone advice (which gives the wrong answer one time in four). It also has a complete set of tax forms you can print.

AIR

```
http://web.mit.edu/afs/athena/org/i/improb/www/home.html
```

The home page for the *Annals of Irreproducible Research.*

Comix

```
http://nearnet.gnn.com/gnn/news/comix/index.html
```

This page usually has several different on-line comic strips.

Declassified LandSat satellite photos

```
http://edcwww.cr.usgs.gov/dclass/dclass.htm
```

What could be cooler! But big pictures take time to transfer over the net.

Chapter 25

Dealing with Excess Free Time: Internet Relay Chat

● ●

In This Chapter
▶ What is IRC?
▶ Getting connected
▶ Using up every shred of your spare time

● ●

What Is IRC?

Chat programs enable you to talk to dozens of people at a time, who may be located all over the globe. The most widely used chat program is called *Internet Relay Chat,* or *IRC.* At any given time of the day or night (especially night), hundreds or thousands of people are hunched over their keyboards, communicating with folks by typing instead of by good old-fashioned human face-to-face contact. Most of these people turn out to be lonely undergraduates, in our experience, but some interesting people are out there, if you can only find them.

In theory, Internet Relay Chat is a way for individuals around the world to have stimulating, fascinating, on-line discussions. In reality, it's more often a way for bored undergraduates to waste time. But IRC, more than any other Internet service, is what you make of it. If you can find interesting people to have interesting discussions with, it's wonderful. If not, well, it's an OK way to waste a great deal of time.

Worldwide Gossipmongering

Like every other Internet service, IRC has client programs and server programs. The *client* is, as usual, the program you run on your local machine (or perhaps on your provider's system) that you type at directly. An IRC *server* is similar to a large switchboard, receiving everything you type and sending it back out to other users, and vice versa. What's more, the different servers are all in constant contact with each other: Stuff you type at one server is relayed to the other servers so that the entire IRC world is one big, chatty family.

To add some small degree of coherence, IRC conversations are organized into *channels,* with each channel dedicated to a single topic, in theory at least. Any user can create a channel, so you get some pretty funky ones (not to say downright *dirty*).

Chatting in Theory and in Practice

You can use lots of different client programs for IRC that run on lots of different kinds of computers. But fortunately, the steps to use them are practically identical:

1. Establish contact with an IRC server.

2. Tell it who you are.

3. Choose a couple of channels.

4. Waste a large amount of time.

Where did IRC come from?

Finland, actually, where it was written by Jarkko Oikarinen in 1988. It has since spread all over the world and is now one of the standard Internet services.

IRC's most notable hours were in the 1991 Persian Gulf War and the 1993 coup in Russia against Boris Yeltsin: IRC users on the spot sent reports to thousands of other users around the world.

Getting Connected

Some UNIX systems have an IRC client program called `irc` or `ircii`. If yours doesn't, you can telnet to a *public IRC server* — see Chapter 20, "Telnetting Around the Net," for information. Public IRC servers come and go all the time because they are widely (and not without justification) viewed as useless resource hogs. The best way to find current IRC servers is by reading the Usenet newsgroup `alt.irc` (see Chapter 19, "Turbocharge Your Newsreading."

When you are connected to IRC, you see a message like this:

```
*** Connecting to port 6667 of server irc.std.com
*** Welcome to the Internet Relay Network jlevine (from
        world.std.com)
*** If you have not already done so, please read the new user
        information with
+/HELP NEWUSER
*** Your host is world.std.com, running version 2.8.20
*** There are 4757 users and 3045 invisible on 104 servers
*** There are 93 operators online
*** 2184 channels have been formed
*** This server has 5 clients and 1 servers connected
*** -
*** -        For additional details on IRC, check 'help irc'
             on World.
*** -        Topics include a guide to basic commands and a
             schedule
*** -        of special IRC discussions for World customers.
```

IRC then waits for a command.

Talking the Talk, Chatting the Chat

The most commonly used client program by IRC users is called *IRCII* (that's "IRC two"). It's the one you're most likely to run into if you type `irc` to a shell provider's system. Because it's so popular, most other IRC client programs use the same commands, so we can slay a multitude of avians with a single projectolith by telling you about IRCII commands here.

Everything you type to IRCII and its relatives is taken as lines of text. There are two kinds of lines: commands to IRC and messages to other people. If a line begins with a slash, it's a command. If not, it's a message. (If only computers were this simple all the time.) The following command, for example:

```
/join #hottub
```

says to join the Hot Tub Channel, a cheerful and usually crowded hangout.

What Channels Are on?

As mentioned, IRC discussions are organized (if we can call it that) into *channels*. Each channel has a name that begins with a sharp sign (#). For example, we occasionally have a channel called #dummies for readers of the ...*For Dummies* Internet books. To find out which channels are available, type **/list**.

Your IRC program gets the list of available channels, which is usually *very* long. The list of channels goes zooming by on your screen, probably faster than you can read it.

You can limit the list of channels to those with an interesting number of people. Type this line:

```
/list -min 5
```

to see just the channels with at least five people. That should limit the list to a useful size.

Why do all IRC channel names begin with # ?

We don't know. Maybe it means something special in Finnish. In principle, there can also be channels which begin with an ampersand (&) that are limited to a single server, but they're not common.

Hey, Aren't We Ever Going to Do Some Chatting?

Oh, all right, we've stalled as long as we can. To join a channel, type the **/join** command followed by the name of the channel (don't forget the #). In the following example:

```
/join #dummies
```

IRCII lets you switch rapidly from one channel to another, and it even lets you join multiple channels. The messages are jumbled together, however, which makes them hard to follow.

After you've joined a channel, everything that people on that channel type appears in the window, and everything you type is sent to them. Whenever someone joins or leaves a channel, a message is sent to all the rest of the participants so that when you join a channel, everyone else immediately knows that you're there.

As is so often the case on the Internet, naïve users can easily make fools of themselves. When you join a channel, lurk for a while. Don't immediately begin typing — wait and see what the tenor of the conversation is. Then type away. If you find that you like IRC, this stage keeps you up all night and well into the next day.

Some other handy commands include the ones in this list:

✔ /names lists the people in a channel. Plain /names lists all the channels, or you can follow it by the name of a particular channel of interest.

✔ /whois followed by someone's nickname tells you something about the person behind the nickname, usually the e-mail address and any other info that's been registered.

Enough, Already!

If you tire of a channel, you can leave it. Just type **/leave**.

Then you can join another channel, or exit, by typing **/quit**.

Starting Your Own Channel

If you have nothing better to do, you can start your own IRC channel. Just make up a name and join it, as shown in this example:

```
/join #cephalopods
```

(Remember that the name has to begin with a #.) That's all you have to do.

You might as well set a topic line to be displayed to other IRCers, by using the /topic command:

```
/topic Squid, cuttlefish, and their cousins
```

Then you wait, perhaps for a long, long time, until someone else joins your channel and begins talking. If you're the first person on a channel, you're considered to be the channel's operator, which gives you the greatly overrated privilege of kicking off people on your channel whom you don't like. See the nearby sidebar, "Operator, is this the party to whom I am connected?"

When you lose interest, you leave your channel in the same way as you leave any other, by typing **/leave** or by closing its window.

Attack of the robots

Most participants on IRC are people. Some aren't — some are robots. It turned out not to be very difficult to hook up an IRC client to a program, usually known as a *bot,* which can participate like a person can (more exactly, like a very, very stupid person). Some bots are inoffensive and do things such as hold a channel open and send a cheery welcome message to anyone who joins it. Some are really obnoxious and send large numbers of annoying messages to people whom the bot's creator doesn't like.

In many parts of IRC Land, bots are considered to be terminally antisocial, and they aren't the least bit welcome. We don't tell you how to create a bot, but you should keep in mind that a particularly cement-headed user may actually have a microchip for a brain.

Operator, is this the party to whom I am connected?

IRC channels and IRC servers both have *operators*, people with particular authority to give some kinds of commands. The first person on a channel is considered the channel's operator, and the operator can anoint other users as operators as well. In the /NAMES listing, an operator's nickname is preceded by an at-sign (@).

The main command you get to use as a channel operator is /kick, which kicks someone off your channel, at least for the three seconds until he rejoins it. It's a thrill, but a rather small one, sort of like finding that you've won 75 cents in the lottery.

Server operators manage entire servers and can kick unruly users entirely off a server, permanently. Don't let that happen to you; be a ruly user, please.

Private Conversations

IRC lets you send messages directly to individuals as well as to channels. To send a message to an individual:

```
/msg nickname your personal message here.
```

For example:

```
/msg johnny Can you believe how dumb that guy is?!!!
```

You can also have a private conversation with someone. Type /query and the nickname, and subsequent lines you type are sent to only that person. Type /query with no nickname, and you're back to normal, sending lines to your current channel.

Your private conversation probably will be routed through a dozen IRC servers. The operators of each server can read your messages if they really want to. So don't say anything that has to be really private.

It's a Jungle Out There

The Internet is pretty anarchic, and IRC is one of the most extreme parts of the anarchy. In particular, all you really know about the people you're chatting with is their nicknames and who they purport to be. Unfortunately, some IRC users with a sick sense of humor delight in offering other chatters "helpful speed-up files" that in fact delete your files or let them crack into your account. Also, many users have a completely different persona in IRC than in real life: They alter details of age, interests, lifestyle, gender — you name it. In some cases, it's fun; in others, it's just strange. So chat all you want, but keep in mind that not all your IRC friends may be who or what they claim to be.

Finally, IRC is a form of virtual reality, and some people find it unbelievably addicting. Students have been known to miss entire semesters of classes because they spent every minute on IRC. Remember that IRC can be fun but that it's no substitute for real life.

Index

(continued)

(continued)

(continued)

(continued)

(continued)

(continued)

The fun & easy way to learn about computers and more!

Title	Author	ISBN	Price
INTERNET / COMMUNICATIONS / NETWORKING			12/20/94
CompuServe For Dummies™	by Wallace Wang	1-56884-181-7	$19.95 USA/$26.95 Canada
Modems For Dummies™, 2nd Edition	by Tina Rathbone	1-56884-223-6	$19.99 USA/$26.99 Canada
Modems For Dummies™	by Tina Rathbone	1-56884-001-2	$19.95 USA/$26.95 Canada
MORE Internet For Dummies™	by John R. Levine & Margaret Levine Young	1-56884-164-7	$19.95 USA/$26.95 Canada
NetWare For Dummies™	by Ed Tittel & Deni Connor	1-56884-003-9	$19.95 USA/$26.95 Canada
Networking For Dummies™	by Doug Lowe	1-56884-079-9	$19.95 USA/$26.95 Canada
ProComm Plus 2 For Windows For Dummies™	by Wallace Wang	1-56884-219-8	$19.99 USA/$26.99 Canada
The Internet For Dummies™, 2nd Edition	by John R. Levine & Carol Baroudi	1-56884-222-8	$19.99 USA/$26.99 Canada
The Internet For Macs For Dummies™	by Charles Seiter	1-56884-184-1	$19.95 USA/$26.95 Canada
MACINTOSH			
Macs For Dummies®	by David Pogue	1-56884-173-6	$19.95 USA/$26.95 Canada
Macintosh System 7.5 For Dummies™	by Bob LeVitus	1-56884-197-3	$19.95 USA/$26.95 Canada
MORE Macs For Dummies™	by David Pogue	1-56884-087-X	$19.95 USA/$26.95 Canada
PageMaker 5 For Macs For Dummies™	by Galen Gruman	1-56884-178-7	$19.95 USA/$26.95 Canada
QuarkXPress 3.3 For Dummies™	by Galen Gruman & Barbara Assadi	1-56884-217-1	$19.99 USA/$26.99 Canada
Upgrading and Fixing Macs For Dummies™	by Kearney Rietmann & Frank Higgins	1-56884-189-2	$19.95 USA/$26.95 Canada
MULTIMEDIA			
Multimedia & CD-ROMs For Dummies™, Interactive Multimedia Value Pack	by Andy Rathbone	1-56884-225-2	$29.95 USA/$39.95 Canada
Multimedia & CD-ROMs For Dummies™	by Andy Rathbone	1-56884-089-6	$19.95 USA/$26.95 Canada
OPERATING SYSTEMS / DOS			
MORE DOS For Dummies™	by Dan Gookin	1-56884-046-2	$19.95 USA/$26.95 Canada
S.O.S. For DOS™	by Katherine Murray	1-56884-043-8	$12.95 USA/$16.95 Canada
OS/2 For Dummies™	by Andy Rathbone	1-878058-76-2	$19.95 USA/$26.95 Canada
UNIX			
UNIX For Dummies™	by John R. Levine & Margaret Levine Young	1-878058-58-4	$19.95 USA/$26.95 Canada
WINDOWS			
S.O.S. For Windows™	by Katherine Murray	1-56884-045-4	$12.95 USA/$16.95 Canada
MORE Windows 3.1 For Dummies™, 3rd Edition	by Andy Rathbone	1-56884-240-6	$19.99 USA/$26.99 Canada
PCs / HARDWARE			
Illustrated Computer Dictionary For Dummies™	by Dan Gookin, Wally Wang, & Chris Van Buren	1-56884-004-7	$12.95 USA/$16.95 Canada
Upgrading and Fixing PCs For Dummies™	by Andy Rathbone	1-56884-002-0	$19.95 USA/$26.95 Canada
PRESENTATION / AUTOCAD			
AutoCAD For Dummies™	by Bud Smith	1-56884-191-4	$19.95 USA/$26.95 Canada
PowerPoint 4 For Windows For Dummies™	by Doug Lowe	1-56884-161-2	$16.95 USA/$22.95 Canada
PROGRAMMING			
Borland C++ For Dummies™	by Michael Hyman	1-56884-162-0	$19.95 USA/$26.95 Canada
"Borland's New Language Product" For Dummies™	by Neil Rubenking	1-56884-200-7	$19.95 USA/$26.95 Canada
C For Dummies™	by Dan Gookin	1-878058-78-9	$19.95 USA/$26.95 Canada
C++ For Dummies™	by Stephen R. Davis	1-56884-163-9	$19.95 USA/$26.95 Canada
Mac Programming For Dummies™	by Dan Parks Sydow	1-56884-173-6	$19.95 USA/$26.95 Canada
QBasic Programming For Dummies™	by Douglas Hergert	1-56884-093-4	$19.95 USA/$26.95 Canada
Visual Basic "X" For Dummies™, 2nd Edition	by Wallace Wang	1-56884-230-9	$19.99 USA/$26.99 Canada
Visual Basic 3 For Dummies™	by Wallace Wang	1-56884-076-4	$19.95 USA/$26.95 Canada
SPREADSHEET			
1-2-3 For Dummies™	by Greg Harvey	1-878058-60-6	$16.95 USA/$21.95 Canada
1-2-3 For Windows 5 For Dummies™, 2nd Edition	by John Walkenbach	1-56884-216-3	$16.95 USA/$21.95 Canada
1-2-3 For Windows For Dummies™	by John Walkenbach	1-56884-052-7	$16.95 USA/$21.95 Canada
Excel 5 For Macs For Dummies™	by Greg Harvey	1-56884-186-8	$19.95 USA/$26.95 Canada
Excel For Dummies™, 2nd Edition	by Greg Harvey	1-56884-050-0	$16.95 USA/$21.95 Canada
MORE Excel 5 For Windows For Dummies™	by Greg Harvey	1-56884-207-4	$19.95 USA/$26.95 Canada
Quattro Pro 6 For Windows For Dummies™	by John Walkenbach	1-56884-174-4	$19.95 USA/$26.95 Canada
Quattro Pro For DOS For Dummies™	by John Walkenbach	1-56884-023-3	$16.95 USA/$21.95 Canada
UTILITIES / VCRs & CAMCORDERS			
Norton Utilities 8 For Dummies™	by Beth Slick	1-56884-166-3	$19.95 USA/$26.95 Canada
VCRs & Camcorders For Dummies™	by Andy Rathbone & Gordon McComb	1-56884-229-5	$14.99 USA/$20.99 Canada
WORD PROCESSING			
Ami Pro For Dummies™	by Jim Meade	1-56884-049-7	$19.95 USA/$26.95 Canada
MORE Word For Windows 6 For Dummies™	by Doug Lowe	1-56884-165-5	$19.95 USA/$26.95 Canada
MORE WordPerfect 6 For Windows For Dummies™	by Margaret Levine Young & David C. Kay	1-56884-206-6	$19.95 USA/$26.95 Canada
MORE WordPerfect 6 For DOS For Dummies™	by Wallace Wang, edited by Dan Gookin	1-56884-047-0	$19.95 USA/$26.95 Canada
S.O.S. For WordPerfect™	by Katherine Murray	1-56884-053-5	$12.95 USA/$16.95 Canada
Word 6 For Macs For Dummies™	by Dan Gookin	1-56884-190-6	$19.95 USA/$26.95 Canada
Word For Windows 6 For Dummies™	by Dan Gookin	1-56884-075-6	$16.95 USA/$21.95 Canada
Word For Windows For Dummies™	by Dan Gookin	1-878058-86-X	$16.95 USA/$21.95 Canada
WordPerfect 6 For Dummies™	by Dan Gookin	1-878058-77-0	$16.95 USA/$21.95 Canada
WordPerfect For Dummies™	by Dan Gookin	1-878058-52-5	$16.95 USA/$21.95 Canada
WordPerfect For Windows For Dummies™	by Margaret Levine Young & David C. Kay	1-56884-032-2	$16.95 USA/$21.95 Canada

FOR MORE INFORMATION OR TO ORDER, PLEASE CALL ▶ 800. 762. 2974

For volume discounts & special orders please call
Tony Real, Special Sales, at 415. 655. 3048

Fun, Fast, & Cheap!

CorelDRAW! 5 For Dummies™ Quick Reference
by Raymond E. Werner

ISBN: 1-56884-952-4
$9.99 USA/$12.99 Canada

Windows "X" For Dummies™ Quick Reference, 3rd Edition
by Greg Harvey

ISBN: 1-56884-964-8
$9.99 USA/$12.99 Canada

Word For Windows 6 For Dummies™ Quick Reference
by George Lynch

ISBN: 1-56884-095-0
$8.95 USA/$12.95 Canada

WordPerfect For DOS For Dummies™ Quick Reference
by Greg Harvey

ISBN: 1-56884-009-8
$8.95 USA/$11.95 Canada

Title	Author	ISBN	Price
DATABASE			
Access 2 For Dummies™ Quick Reference	by Stuart A. Stuple	1-56884-167-1	$8.95 USA/$11.95 Canada
dBASE 5 For DOS For Dummies™ Quick Reference	by Barry Sosinsky	1-56884-954-0	$9.99 USA/$12.99 Canada
dBASE 5 For Windows For Dummies™ Quick Reference	by Stuart J. Stuple	1-56884-953-2	$9.99 USA/$12.99 Canada
Paradox 5 For Windows For Dummies™ Quick Reference	by Scott Palmer	1-56884-960-5	$9.99 USA/$12.99 Canada
DESKTOP PUBLISHING / ILLUSTRATION/GRAPHICS			
Harvard Graphics 3 For Windows For Dummies™ Quick Reference	by Raymond E. Werner	1-56884-962-1	$9.99 USA/$12.99 Canada
FINANCE / PERSONAL FINANCE			
Quicken 4 For Windows For Dummies™ Quick Reference	by Stephen L. Nelson	1-56884-950-8	$9.95 USA/$12.95 Canada
GROUPWARE / INTEGRATED			
Microsoft Office 4 For Windows For Dummies™ Quick Reference	by Doug Lowe	1-56884-958-3	$9.99 USA/$12.99 Canada
Microsoft Works For Windows 3 For Dummies™ Quick Reference	by Michael Partington	1-56884-959-1	$9.99 USA/$12.99 Canada
INTERNET / COMMUNICATIONS / NETWORKING			
The Internet For Dummies™ Quick Reference	by John R. Levine	1-56884-168-X	$8.95 USA/$11.95 Canada
MACINTOSH			
Macintosh System 7.5 For Dummies™ Quick Reference	by Stuart J. Stuple	1-56884-956-7	$9.99 USA/$12.99 Canada
OPERATING SYSTEMS / DOS			
DOS For Dummies® Quick Reference	by Greg Harvey	1-56884-007-1	$8.95 USA/$11.95 Canada
UNIX			
UNIX For Dummies™ Quick Reference	by Margaret Levine Young & John R. Levine	1-56884-094-2	$8.95 USA/$11.95 Canada
WINDOWS			
Windows 3.1 For Dummies™ Quick Reference, 2nd Edition	by Greg Harvey	1-56884-951-6	$8.95 USA/$11.95 Canada
PRESENTATION / AUTOCAD			
AutoCAD For Dummies™ Quick Reference	by Ellen Finkelstein	1-56884-198-1	$9.95 USA/$12.95 Canada
SPREADSHEET			
1-2-3 For Dummies™ Quick Reference	by John Walkenbach	1-56884-027-6	$8.95 USA/$11.95 Canada
1-2-3 For Windows 5 For Dummies™ Quick Reference	by John Walkenbach	1-56884-957-5	$9.95 USA/$12.95 Canada
Excel For Windows For Dummies™ Quick Reference, 2nd Edition	by John Walkenbach	1-56884-096-9	$8.95 USA/$11.95 Canada
Quattro Pro 6 For Windows For Dummies™ Quick Reference	by Stuart A. Stuple	1-56884-172-8	$9.95 USA/$12.95 Canada
WORD PROCESSING			
Word For Windows 6 For Dummies™ Quick Reference	by George Lynch	1-56884-095-0	$8.95 USA/$11.95 Canada
WordPerfect For Windows For Dummies™ Quick Reference	by Greg Harvey	1-56884-039-X	$8.95 USA/$11.95 Canada

FOR MORE INFORMATION OR TO ORDER, PLEASE CALL ▸ **800. 762. 2974**

For volume discounts & special orders please call
Tony Real, Special Sales, at 415. 655. 3048

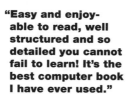

IDG BOOKS

Order Center: **(800) 762-2974** *(8 a.m.–6 p.m., EST, weekdays)*

12/20/94

Quantity	ISBN	Title	Price	Total

Shipping & Handling Charges

	Description	First book	Each additional book	Total
Domestic	Normal	$4.50	$1.50	$
	Two Day Air	$8.50	$2.50	$
	Overnight	$18.00	$3.00	$
International	Surface	$8.00	$8.00	$
	Airmail	$16.00	$16.00	$
	DHL Air	$17.00	$17.00	$

*For large quantities call for shipping & handling charges.
**Prices are subject to change without notice.

Ship to:

Name _____

Company _____

Address _____

City/State/Zip _____

Daytime Phone _____

Payment: ☐ Check to IDG Books (US Funds Only)

☐ VISA   ☐ MasterCard   ☐ American Express

Card # _____ Expires _____

Signature _____

Subtotal _____

CA residents add
applicable sales tax _____

IN, MA, and MD
residents add
5% sales tax _____

IL residents add
6.25% sales tax _____

RI residents add
7% sales tax _____

TX residents add
8.25% sales tax _____

Shipping _____

Total _____

Please send this order form to:

IDG Books Worldwide
7260 Shadeland Station, Suite 100
Indianapolis, IN 46256

Allow up to 3 weeks for delivery.
Thank you!